The Christian Right, the far right and the boundaries of American conservatism

The Christian Right, the far right and the boundaries of American conservatism

MARTIN DURHAM

MANCHESTER UNIVERSITY PRESS

Manchester and New York

distributed exclusively in the USA by St. Martin's Press

Published by Manchester University Press
Oxford Road, Manchester M13 9NR, UK
and Room 400, 175 Fifth Avenue, New York, NY 10010, USA
http://www.manchesteruniversitypress.co.uk

Distributed exclusively in the USA by
St. Martin's Press, Inc., 175 Fifth Avenue, New York, NY 10010, USA

Distributed exclusively in Canada by
UBC Press, University of British Columbia, 2029 West Mall
Vancouver, BC, Canada V6T 1Z2

British Library Cataloguing-in-Publication Data
A catalogue record for this book is available from the British Library

Library of Congress Cataloging-in-Publication Data applied for

ISBN 0 7190 5485 0 *hardback*
    0 7190 5486 9 *paperback*

First published 2000

09 08 07 06 05 04 03 02 01 00   10 9 8 7 6 5 4 3 2 1

Typeset in Palatino with Frutiger
by Servis Filmsetting Ltd, Manchester, UK
Printed in Great Britain
by Bell & Bain Ltd, Glasgow

For Stephanie, Nicholas,
Laura and Alan

Contents

Acknowledgements

I have worked on this area for many years before writing this book, during which time I have been helped by a large number of people. I am especially grateful for the generosity of Eddie Ashbee, Nigel Ashford, Michael Barkun, Chip Berlet, Didi Herman, Jeff Kaplan, Larry Jones, Darren Mulloy, Nick Toczek and Laird Wilcox, but my thanks are also owed to many others, including Edward Artinian, Andy Bell, Bob Clark, Laura Lee Downs, David Edgar, Colin Francome, Gerry Gable, Steve Gill, Alan Grant, Deborah Kaplan, James S. and Ardyce Masters, Carol Maxwell, Fiona Morgan, John O'Reilly, Mark Phythian, Tony Picken, Sunetra Puri, Sue Reinhold, Al Ross, Anna Marie Smith, Alasdair Spark, Wendy Thomas and Nigel Woodcock. I would also like to thank the staff at Birmingham Central Reference Library, the British Library of Political and Economic Science, the British Newspaper Library, the University of Hull Library, the University of Warwick Library and the University of Wolverhampton Learning Centre. Finally, I would like to thank the staff at the Wilcox Collection of Contemporary Political Movements at the University of Kansas and at Political Research Associates, Somerville, Massachussetts for all the help they gave me during my all too brief visit to two of the finest archives any researcher could want.

Introduction

The American right has attracted a remarkable amount of attention in recent years. The Christian Right, having survived the premature obituaries of the late 1980s, has revived to become a significant part of the Republican Party and a leading force in the struggles over abortion, homosexuality and other social issues in post-Reagan America. Before his defection to the Reform Party, the conservative journalist and former White House functionary, Pat Buchanan, had launched three bids for the Republican presidential nomination and surprised many by his denunciation of multinational big business just as he has appalled others with his opposition to immigration and multiracialism. If the right has been highly visible within the Republican Party, it has been active outside it too, above all through the militias, tax resisters and other components of what is best described as the Patriot movement. Much else has happened, from the Republican Congressional landslide in 1994 to the failure of the attempt to impeach President Clinton four years later, and this book will attempt to give a sense of the modern American right as a whole. It is most concerned, however, with the Christian Right, with the forces that have gathered around Pat Buchanan and with the Patriot movement, and its contention is both simple to make and difficult to demonstrate. To put it at its most controversial, while Buchanan has yet to prick the interest of many scholars, we have been fortunate in the appearance of a number of excellent studies of the Christian Right and the beginnings of a comparable body of work on the Patriot movement. Too often, however, it has been eclipsed by a considerable amount of other material, in book form, in the press, and on television, that, rather than bringing an understanding of the American right within reach, has instead made it more elusive. It is, no doubt, very tempting to collapse together the Christian Right and the anti-abortion movement and credit both of them with responsibility for terrorism at abortion clinics, just as it may seem obvious to see the militias as a modern manifestation of racist vigilantism. It is certainly witty to suggest, as one journalist did, that Pat Buchanan's most (in)famous speech sounded better in the original German. Unfortunately, what none of this does is enable us to understand what different strands of the American right believe, what they do, and, particularly importantly, in what ways they are divided.

This book takes issue with some of these movements' own understandings. It rejects, for instance, the claim of some in the Patriot movement that allegations of racism have been simply manufactured by their opponents just as it is unpersuaded by attempts by leading figures in the Christian Right to present their movement as solely concerned with saving America from the excesses of modern liberalism. The Patriot movement, it will be argued, has proved distinctly amenable to anti-Semitism, while the Christian Right, despite the concerns it shares with American conservatism as a whole, is profoundly affected by an elaborate and far-reaching conspiracy theory of history. But while we will be disputing the arguments of movement participants, it is the interpretations that have been taken up by the media that most need addressing and, all too often, rebutting.

In such a contentious field, it would be wise to be particularly careful in the way we describe movements. Such terms as mainstream and extreme, moderate and radical, all bring with them implications and assumptions, and we will return to some of these in the concluding chapter. For now, it will be suggested that while those on the right who are committed to white supremacism and/or anti-Semitism are best defined by the term 'extreme right', those that hold a conspiracy theory of history, without attributing an ethnic identity to the conspirators, are better described by some other term. To render the situation more difficult, there are strands of the right who seem at the same time to be attracted to a racial framing of politics and resistant to it, an indeterminate battleground between other more settled forms of rightism. Elements within both the Patriot movement and the Buchanan movement, it will be argued, are just such strands, just as the Christian Right occupies the ground that stretches from mainstream conservatism to non-racist conspiracism. Rather than stretching the term 'extreme right' beyond breaking point, non-racist conspiracists will instead be described as the radical right, while in discussing the two groupings together, along with those still unresolved between them, another category, that of the far right, will be used. We will see as the book progresses whether such definitions and distinctions prove valuable or not. This, no doubt, will be a matter of dispute, as will the account it informs. For both, however, the test should be not whether they support our presuppositions, but whether they are successful in challenging them.

The rise of the right

As a complex set of groupings, the American right is not to be understood as having a single point of origin. In its modern form, however, we are discussing a political constellation that predominantly came into existence during the 1950s. As we shall see, there is some dispute about its relationship to a number of earlier developments. In what sense, for instance, was it prefigured by the opposition to the New Deal in the 1930s or by the isolationists who gathered around the America First Committee in its attempt to avert entry into the Second World War? We shall be touching on the question of the continuities and discontinuities between the modern right and its predecessors during our discussion. Nevertheless, we are primarily concerned with the American right since the late 1970s, and within that, will be focusing on three particular groupings – the Christian Right, the Patriot movement and the forces that have gathered around Pat Buchanan. In order best to understand them, however, we must start somewhat earlier.

At first sight, it would appear obvious that the eight years of Republican Presidential administration that began in 1953 would precisely constitute conservatism in power, a moment to be savoured in contrast to the Roosevelt–Truman years that preceded it or the Kennedy–Johnson years that followed it. But both mainstream conservatism and its radical right sibling emerged in precisely those years in reaction not only to the liberalism of the Democrats but to what was seen as the compromise – or even capitulation – of the Republicans. For conservatism, the key moment was the launching, in 1955, of what would turn out to be its flagship journal, *National Review*. The creation of a diverse group, whose leading member was the Catholic writer William Buckley, the journal sought to bring together three strands, each of which was opposed to the direction in which liberalism had taken America. The first was a defence of the free market, associated with the economist Friedrich von Hayek and others, whose emphasis on the individual and the threat to freedom posed by an over-mighty state often led them to contend that they were the true heirs of liberalism, and that the doctrine that now took that name had abandoned liberty in pursuit of other, incompatible, goals. If the first strand has been described as libertarianism or economic conservatism, the second has been termed traditionalism or social conservatism. Associated with the writer Russell Kirk and others, traditionalism maintained that America had lost its roots in Western Christendom, and instead of retaining its faith in a divine moral order was now pursuing instead the chimeras of equality and unlimited rights. These two strands, as can readily be appreciated, were not obviously in accord, and one of the most important contributions of *National Review*, particularly in the person of an ex-Communist, Frank Meyer, was to attempt to bring them together in what was described as fusionism, an approach that claimed that the free market concern with freedom and the traditionalist focus on authority were perfectly compatible and, indeed, had been proved to be so in the very creation of the republic. If one strength of this attempt at synthesis was in its claim that conservatism was not alien to American experience, another derived from the third strand within the *National Review* camp, anti-Communism. In addition to drawing to the magazine a number of writers who had once been Communists, or Trotskyists, themselves, anti-Communism also gave American conservatism a sense of global conflict in which those who prioritised rights and those who emphasised duties could put aside their differences and join together against what was both a statist and an irreligious foe, international Communism. (For libertarianism, traditionalism and the early years of *National Review*, see Nash 1976; Judis 1988: 113–80.)

The argument that it was impossible to be a conservative in a country that had been brought into existence through a liberal revolution or that the task of a conservative was to conserve the liberal institutions that were now in place was to be a recurring irritation to conservatives. In declaring that conservatism defended rights, not least property rights, against a collectivist onslaught, figures such as Meyer showed the impossibility of avoiding the use of liberal language against a liberal enemy. But this was not unique to American conservatism, and its adherents (or, at least, most of them) believed that such a stance was squarely in the American tradition that their enemies sought to deny could (and, indeed, should) be read in a conservative way. Conservatism did not have to champion monarchy or a fixed class system, it was argued, and to defend a particular way of life in a particular national community against encroachments by government domestically or threats by Communism globally was precisely what conservatism was called upon to do. In the American context, this involved a peculiarly American movement but, it was argued, one that could forge links with conservatives elsewhere (Nash 1976: 136–8, 161–2; Meyer 1964a: 7–8, 19, 1964b: 231).

If the right, in America as elsewhere, saw itself as defending nationhood and private property, conservatism represented the most important component of it. Rival strands disagree as to the relationship between one conservative concern, liberty, and another, order. Other disputes have ranged beyond the conservative movement. Conservatives have frequently talked in terms of a liberal establishment. For some on the right, however, the forces that control America are far more sinister, and the methods that will be needed to remove them correspondingly more drastic. If the right is defined partly as a reaction to the left, different segments of the right can partly be defined in relationship to each other. At certain points, what can be usefully called mainstream conservatism has included tendencies that at other points have been defined as outside the movement. Conversely, on occasion, the boundaries have been redrawn to allow particular strands back in. Both of these developments have made both the right and conservatism highly contested concepts in the American context, and it makes two other terms that have been introduced into the discussion, the radical right and the extreme right, similarly contentious. But if we have to remain somewhat tentative in how we use each term, it is still worth doing so, as an examination of how the incipient conservatism of the 1950s became the powerful force of the late twentieth century makes clear (Eatwell 1989a: 49–50, 60, 1989b: 63).

In the early years of the conservative movement, as traditionalists, libertarians and anti-Communists came together and began to coalesce, this involved a process of self-definition that was to leave some sections of the right outside. One strand was never brought in, that of the overtly anti-Semitic extreme right. The 1950s saw the emergence of several such groups, notably the American Nazi Party and the National States Rights Party. The tradition that they represented, traceable back to both indigenous groups of the 1930s and to the

fascist movements and states of Europe, was distinct from that championed by *National Review*, and while in the years that followed the
two tendencies would periodically come into contact around particular issues or even particular candidacies, the extreme right and the
mainstream right were sharply opposed. The situation would be complicated, however, by three factors. The first, a recurring problem on
the right, was the issue of race. In addition to being a central concern
of the overtly anti-Semitic groups, race had also been the driving force
of America's own distinctive contribution to right-wing extremism,
the Ku Klux Klan. The 1954 Supreme Court decision against school
segregation and the subsequent rise of the civil rights movement
fuelled both an upsurge of Klan violence and a more genteel although
often little less virulent response on the part of (white) Citizens'
Councils. *National Review*, in its early years, defended what it saw as
the traditional way of life of the American South and, while conservatism would come to terms with the end of segregation, this has not
been without considerable dispute about what stance it should take
towards African Americans. Secondly, while contemporary American
conservatism shows considerable enthusiasm for Israel, this has not
always been the case. In its early years, *National Review* was sometimes highly critical of the new state, and the occasional appearance
since then of such tendencies within the conservative camp has
brought not only condemnation by other conservatives but praise
from the extreme right. One final factor must also be taken into
account. The conservative movement's views on race and on the state
both distinguish it from those who openly champion National
Socialism. There have been greater problems, however, in avoiding
entanglement with groupings that are somewhat less blatant in their
rhetoric. This has particularly been the case with an organisation that
came into existence two years after *National Review*, the Liberty
Lobby. Through its publications, particularly a newspaper launched
in the mid-1970s, the *Spotlight*, Liberty Lobby has built up a substantial following for a form of politics that accuses America's leaders of
serving 'Zionist' interests but avoids some of the more inflammatory
rhetoric of such figures as the American Nazi leader, George Lincoln
Rockwell. In 1971, *National Review* was to publish a sharp attack on
Liberty Lobby's founder, Willis Carto, arguing that rather than representing a particularly uncompromising form of conservatism, he was
actually pursuing a long-term racist and anti-Semitic agenda. Despite
such attacks, however, Carto's movement was to continue to exert an

attraction on some within the conservative camp. (For *National Review*, anti-Semitism and race, see Judis 1988: 137–9, 173–4; Mintz 1985: 112–13, 218–19; for a succinct discussion of the Ku Klux Klan and the Citizens' Councils, see Diamond 1995: 66–82; for Carto, and others on the extreme right, see Mintz 1985; George and Wilcox 1992: 251–65, 354–8, 382–9.)

If the Liberty Lobby was to present problems for the conservative movement, another, and more important, grouping also emerged in the late 1950s. *National Review* had argued that the expansion of the state presided over by Roosevelt and Truman had not been reversed by the Eisenhower Administration, while overseas it had refused to confront the Soviet Union and had allowed the Hungarian Rising of 1956 to be crushed. But where *National Review* had chastised what it saw as weakness, others went considerably further. Conservatives had long argued that Democratic administrations had been infested by Communist agents and Buckley had distinguished himself before the inception of *National Review* by co-authoring a defence of Senator Joe McCarthy. Numerous anti-Communist organisations were already in existence when, in 1958, yet another body was established. What distinguished the John Birch Society, however, was the claim by its founder, Robert Welch, that Eisenhower could only to be understood as a tool of the Communist conspiracy. During the 1960s, as we discuss later, the Society was to become convinced of an even more wide-ranging plot against the republic. *National Review* was to become so disturbed both by the Society's belief that America was predominantly under Communist control and by its consequent refusal to support intervention in Vietnam that it found it necessary to redraw the boundaries of conservatism to exclude Birchism from its confines. But, as we shall see, just as the radical right was part of the conservative movement in the 1950s, its exclusion in the following decade was to be far from total. (For the John Birch Society, see Lipset and Raab 1971: 248–87; George and Wilcox 1992: 214–24; Mintz 1985: 141–62; for its excommunication from the mainstream right, see *National Review* 19 October 1965.)

If conservatives were highly critical of Eisenhower Republicanism, they did not write off the Republican Party as a whole. While some were drawn to third-party efforts, most believed that the GOP was the appropriate vehicle for the right. Fiercely opposed to party moderates, notably the governor of New York, Nelson Rockefeller, they also distrusted Eisenhower's Vice-President, Richard Nixon, whom they saw as more of a Republican centrist than a conservative. In the late 1950s, however, the emergence of Barry Goldwater as a critic of the administration's domestic and foreign policies offered hope of a politics that could move from criticising events to shaping them. The Arizona Senator, whose best-selling book, *The Conscience of a Conservative*, was ghost-written by Buckley's brother-in-law, Brent Bozell, quickly came to be seen as the movement's political standard-bearer, and, while he had been unwilling to challenge Nixon for the ill-fated 1960 presidential nomination, conservatives subsequently worked all-out to outmanoevre their moderate opponents and make him the candidate for 1964. They were stunningly successful in doing so, creating a formidable political machine that won party caucuses and even primaries in great enough numbers to beat any alternative candidate decisively. In less than ten years, conservatives had moved from being a scattered guerilla band to dominating the Republican Party. But while they could gain the party's presidential nomination, they were unable to win the presidency. Instead of the anticipated contest with Kennedy, an assassin's bullet had put the Southern Democrat, Lyndon Johnson, in the White House, and while Goldwater, a critic of the 1964 Civil Rights Act, was able to win five states in the hitherto Democratic South, he was only able to win one other state, his own. Where Johnson had gained 43 million votes (61 per cent), Goldwater had attained 27 million (39 per cent). It was a landslide for the Democrats and, at first sight, appeared to have stopped the long march of conservatism dead in its tracks (Overstreet and Overstreet 1964: 228, 231–2; Rusher 1984: 66–7, 87–178; White with Gill 1967).

But it had not. Goldwater had proved an inept campaigner, frightening voters with proposals to privatise the Social Security system and end farming subsidies and offering a perfect target to the Democrats with a foreign policy that appeared more than willing to be dangerously confrontational. But conservatives had gained vital experience both in capturing a party and in building a national movement, and in the figure of Ronald Reagan, whose televised speech in support of Goldwater made the case for conservatism more attractively than the candidate had, the Republican right had a potential successor for their defeated champion (Goldberg 1995: 224; Edwards 1995: 296–302; Rusher 1984: 172–4).

The 1964 campaign had brought together most sections of the right. The Young Americans for Freedom, a key group of the period, were enthusiastic Goldwater supporters and *National Review* too backed the candidate, while doubting if he could win. The Liberty Lobby was also involved, while unsurprisingly calling for the Republican Party to put a greater emphasis on race, and the John Birch Society, which had been very visible in Goldwater's support, recruited a wave of new members after his defeat under the slogan '*Now* Will You Join The John Birch Society?' Even the Minutemen, a paramilitary group that had emerged in the early 1960s in anticipation of an imminent Communist invasion of America, was active in the campaign. By the time of the next presidential contest, however, the right would find itself torn between two candidacies. For many, including Goldwater, Nixon deserved support, both for reasons of party loyalty and because conservatives could expect to gain influence if they had been crucial to his election. But the efforts of Democrat presidents to enforce civil rights legislation had not only disrupted the historic hold of the party on white voters in the South, but were having repercussions on its support elsewhere, and the short-lived attempt by the segregationist Alabama governor George Wallace to win the Democratic candidacy in 1964 was now followed by his full-blown third-party candidacy in the name of the newly-created American Independent Party (Andrew 1997: 171–204; Judis 1988: 225–31; Mintz 1985: 86, 94–5; Gilder and Chapman 1966: 186–9; Epstein and Forster 1966: 5, 70; *On Target* 4 November 1964; George and Wilcox 1992: 274–5; Edsall with Edsall 1992: 33–81; Diamond 1995: 88–90, 112–13).

For many conservatives, Wallace was unacceptable. *National Review*, for instance, accused him of both dividing the conservative vote and favouring high state spending for whites. For the John Birch Society, the Liberty Lobby and other groupings, however, Wallace represented an opportunity to take an uncompromisingly right-wing stance into mass politics. His campaign, conducted against the background of student protest and an increasingly militant black power movement, sounded firmly populist tones against an establishment he accused of coddling criminals and despising ordinary Americans, and while Nixon was to be the victor, Wallace won nearly ten million votes, 13.5 per cent of the total. With so many voting to his right, Nixon reacted to Wallace's electoral support by emphasising some of the same themes, most notably in his condemnation of the busing of (white) children in pursuit of racially integrated education, while the conservative journalist, Pat Buchanan, now one of his speech-writers, was to urge the President to emphasise his opposition to abortion. In

1964, the Goldwater campaign had prepared a film portraying America as in the grip of black rioters and rising immorality. Goldwater, 'sensitive to charges of racism', had refused to use it. But he had raised such themes during the campaign and, by 1968, conservatives were increasingly at home with them (Diamond 1995: 114, 112; Carter 1995: 295–7, 343; Lipset and Raab 1971: 345, 348–50, 356–7; Edsall with Edsall 1992: 79, 81–2, 88–9; O'Connor 1996: 71; Edwards 1995: 329–30; Goldberg 1995: 218–19, 229–31).

This development would not be without its critics, however. Anti-Communism, as we have noted, had been crucial in holding libertarians and traditionalists together; but the strains could not always be held at bay. Meyer's fusionism had critics in both camps, and where in the early 1960s one journal, the *New Individualist Review*, had argued that a professed anti-statism was incompatible with support for a massive military establishment, in the late 1960s this critique was both turned against the burgeoning Vietnam war and wedded to a defence of the very changes in morality that traditionalists deplored. In 1969 the Young Americans for Freedom convention was riven by a bitter row, and conservatism was henceforth often to find itself at loggerheads with a full-fledged libertarianism that argued for *laissez-faire* not only in the economy but in society too. Taking both a party form (the Libertarian Party was created in 1972) and other manifestations (journals, think-tanks, etc.), libertarians would eventually come to exert a considerable influence on the broader conservative movement. But they also harried it from the outside, and some, notably its intellectual gadfly, Murray Rothbard, would even find allies on the New Left. As we shall see, however, he would prove equally capable of forging alliances elsewhere (Nash 1976: 174–8; *New Individualist Review* November 1961; Tuccille 1970: 96–109; Diamond 1995: 123–7; Hardisty 1998b: 123–6).

There were other developments too. The Wallace campaign had left behind it a number of splinter groupings. While many of Wallace's supporters on the radical right remained in the American Independent Party or its rival American Party, the Liberty Lobby was instrumental in creating a Youth for Wallace organisation that, after the election, was first relaunched as the National Youth Alliance and then exploded amidst bitter recrimination. Wallace himself was to run again in 1972, this time once more in pursuit of the Democrat nomination, before an assassination attempt resulted in grave injury and his withdrawal from the race. Nixon, with the support of most, if not all, conservatives, was re-elected in 1972. But his subsequent disgrace and resignation over Watergate, and the nomination of Nelson Rockefeller as vice-president by Nixon's successor, Gerald Ford, was to throw the conservative movement into disarray and bring into existence a new strand within it (Diamond 1995: 144–6; Mintz 1985: 129–31; Carter 1995: 445–6; Judis 1988: 328–42, 354–61, 367).

Nixon had already been condemned by some on the right for both declaring his support for a Keynesian economic policy and recognising Communist China. His successor was no more popular among conservatives, and, still angry at Rockefeller's opposition to Goldwater ten years earlier, in 1974 a section of the conservative movement drew the conclusion that new methods were called for in the fight against liberal Democrats and moderate Republicans. Some new organisations had already come into existence, most importantly what would prove to be a highly influential policy organisation, the Heritage Foundation. But for what became known as the New Right, a whole new approach was needed. A series of organisations was established, ranging from the Conservative Caucus to the National Conservative Political Action Committee, and techniques, which had been pioneered in the Goldwater campaign, of targeting particular people to receive direct mail appeals for electoral and financial support were brought into play to build a more effective and more intransigent conservative force than before. Although it was later to play an important role in the Republican Party, the New Right was initially unconvinced that the party was capable of becoming a force for conservatism, and in 1976 it made an unsuccessful attempt to take over the American Independent Party. But the New Right was distinguished from many of its predecessors not only by organisation or combativeness but by the issues it emphasised. In part, it was concerned with emotive foreign policy questions, in which, just as they had been accused of betraying Vietnam, liberals were now charged with weakening America's military strength and seeking to surrender American control of the Panama Canal. But what was particularly distinctive about the New Right was that it sought to emphasise social issues, defending gun-owners against restrictions on firearm ownership and parents against the busing of their children, and championing 'the traditional family' against the threats of abortion, feminism and homosexuality (Rusher 1984: 226, 239–50; Viguerie 1981: 50–53, 100, 58, 56, 45–6, 91–6, 65–71; Diamond 1995: 130; *Conservative Digest* June 1979).

While launched under a Republican Presidency, the New Right

was to soon find itself facing a return to power of the Democrats, and much of its campaigning happened during the ill-fated Carter administration. It was then, too, that the most lasting of its achievements occurred. While it was Catholics whose support the New Right was seeking in its opposition to abortion, it soon became aware of another religious grouping with marked potential for conservative mobilisation. In the early part of the century, disputes as to whether the Bible was to be read literally or liberally had divided much of American Protestantism into fundamentalists and modernists. Where the latter retained control of the so-called mainline churches, fundamentalists had set about creating their own institutions, and while some emphasised separation from a fallen world, a larger section held that effective Christian witness necessitated both greater involvement in society and the forging of links with other conservative Protestants. In particular, this regrouping was to involve a willingness to co-operate with charismatics, distinguished by their belief in divine healing and 'speaking in tongues', and the broad evangelical coalition that resulted was to remain an incompletely united force. But a force it had become, and already by the early 1970s, it commanded vast numbers. Evangelicals often voted Democrat or even avoided involvement with politics altogether. A conservative attempt to mobilise them in the mid-1970s had proved unsuccessful and Jimmy Carter, himself an evangelical, had gained many of their votes in 1976. Soon, however, the situation was to change, and in 1979, the New Right journal, *Conservative Digest*, devoted much of an issue to greeting the emergence of what would come to be known as the Christian Right (Oldfield 1996: 15–31, 103–8; Wilcox 1996: 102–3; Diamond 1989: 49–51).

One of its central arguments, that Christian schools and other evangelical institutions were under attack by a hostile state, was to become crucial to the Christian Right; but it would be issues such as abortion and homosexuality that would become its most central concerns, and an accompanying article by a leading New Rightist was particularly revealing in setting out what was hoped for from the incipient movement. The family, Paul Weyrich suggested, would be to the 1980s what the Vietnam war had been to the 1960s. After decades of being on the defensive, fundamentalists, as he continued to call them, now understood the link between religion and politics and were finding new allies within the Catholic Church. They had already come together with Mormons and others against abortion and, he declared, 'this new alliance' had the potential power to defeat those who threatened the family (*Conservative Digest* August 1979).

A number of organisations had come into existence. Weyrich, indeed, had been instrumental in the formation of the best-known group, the Moral Majority, while in California another organisation, Christian Voice, had been established. There were other groups too, and as the 1980 election approached, the Christian Right would become a major component of a conservative onslaught against President Carter and in support of the Republican nominee, Ronald Reagan (Martin 1997: 199–200; Oldfield 1996: 117–18).

As W. B. Hixson and others have emphasised, Carter's failure to win re-election owed far more to disappointment with the country's economic situation than to his alienation of social conservatives. But, as his appearance before a Christian Right rally during the 1980 campaign demonstrated, Reagan was as aware as the New Right of the potential benefits of seeking evangelical support, and his administration was to be marked by a number of initiatives aimed at the newly mobilised constituency. Religious groups were allowed to meet on school premises, government money was spent to encourage school pupils to be sexually abstinent and there was a systematic effort to invite evangelical leaders to the White House. But economic considerations came first, a downgrading of social issues that was worsened still further by the Democrats' control of the House of Representatives and scepticism among the President's advisers as to how important it was to take up the issues that motivated evangelicals. Attempts to pass a comprehensive 'pro-family' law proved unsuccessful, as did efforts to pass either a bill or a constitutional amendment that could end legal abortion. The administration did succeed in stopping family planning facilities in receipt of federal funds from providing abortion counselling, and also removed funding from organisations that provided abortions abroad. But despite its extensive mobilisation for Reagan's re-election in 1984, by the end of his administration the Christian Right appeared to be in terminal crisis. The evangelical subculture as a whole was damaged by a series of financial and sexual scandals affecting leading figures and, amidst reports that sections of the Christian Right were being financed by the controversial religious leader, Sun Myung Moon, Christian Voice declined into obscurity, while the Moral Majority dissolved altogether (Hixson 1992: 255–60; Oldfield 1996: 118–19, 253; Martin 1997: 214–18, 222–6; Moen 1992: 93–4, 20–22; Diamond 1995: 172, 232, 235–6, 244–5; McKeegan 1992: 117–19, 86, 90; Diamond 1989: 69–70, 78–9).

Other developments were more encouraging. For many on the right, the Reagan administration deserved full support, and they were grateful that conservatives were at last in power. And while *National Review* was to continue to be an important force, a number of intellectuals who had moved into the conservative orbit during the 1970s were to become increasingly influential. Often Marxists in their youth, then liberal anti-Communists, neoconservatives, as they were dubbed, held that the modern state had encouraged unreal expectations. America was in the throes of a cultural crisis, they argued, and a revival of social responsibility was crucial if the fires of egalitarianism were to be dowsed. Their continued sympathy for liberal achievements before the late 1960s, their leftist political background and their rapid rise to prominence was to ensure that their arrival in the conservative camp was not universally welcomed by older conservatives. Its predominant effect at the time, however, was to strengthen conservatism as an intellectual force and encourage conservatives in the belief that they, not liberals, were the force of the future (Moen 1992: 78; Judis 1988: 429–30, 445; Steinfels 1979: 29, 55, 58–65; Diamond 1995: 279–83; Nash 1976: 320–34).

But if, during the 1980s, some tensions were by and large kept in check, others were not. The New Right had been critical both of the fate of such issues as abortion and of Reagan's willingness to negotiate with Gorbachev and would effectively disappear, although Weyrich himself would remain highly visible and another of its veterans, the Conservative Caucus's Howard Phillips, would emerge as the leader of a new party in the 1990s. The John Birch Society, which had been highly critical of Reagan, was to decline during the 1980s to a membership of 24,000, a figure that may have been as low as a quarter of its peak during the 1960s. (In the 1990s, it was to enjoy some improvement in its fortunes, its membership rising to over 55,000.) But if its conspiratorialism had proved too extreme for some on the right, for others it was not radical enough (Diamond 1995: 214, 225; Martin 1997: 331, 358; *Boston Phoenix* 14–20 July 1989; Public Eye, n.d.).

Where mainstream conservatives were to find an attractive popular issue in tax cuts, a number of groups had emerged during the 1970s that rejected the legitimacy of the Internal Revenue Service altogether. Tax resistance, often allied to a bitter hostility to the banking system, spread still further in the 1980s, fuelled in part by the agricultural crisis in the early part of the decade. Often describing themselves as Patriots, many within this burgeoning movement were influenced by Birchism, but were often drawn to more radical arguments still. Taxation and farm foreclosures, it was claimed, robbed workers and small owners to serve a Jewish financial system, and, whereas the Christian Right championed America's alliance with Israel, a very different interpretation of the relationship between religion and nation was espoused by a doctrine known as Christian Identity, which held that whites were the lost tribes of Israel and God's true chosen people. (In its most virulent form, espoused by such groups as Aryan Nations, Jews were actually Satan's children, created by his seduction of Eve in the Garden of Eden.) Patriots organised a wide array of different groups. Some, notably the Christian-Patriots Defense League and the Covenant, the Sword and the Arm of the Lord, engaged in paramilitary manoeuvres. One group, the Committee of the States, even declared that it was the rightful government of America and sought to indict officials who did not recognise its authority. Another, Posse Comitatus, claimed that 'the TRUE seat' of government was the county. While never a centralised movement, Patriots often found the politics espoused by the *Spotlight* to their liking and Liberty Lobby's ability to appeal simultaneously to some mainstream conservatives and to those outside the respectable right gave the paper a circulation of over 300,000 during the early 1980s. But its growing criticism of Reagan (and Willis Carto's involvement in Holocaust revisionism) was to ensure that its supporters diminished in number, and when, in 1988, George Bush was to run as the Republican presidential candidate, the Lobby's new political vehicle, the Populist Party, supported instead the former Ku Klux Klan leader David Duke (Aho 1990; Kaplan 1993a; Barkun 1997; Bushart, Craig and Barnes 1998: 40–41; Dobratz and Shanks-Meile 1997: 81; Seymour 1991: 3–6; Ridgeway 1990: 109–29; McLemee 1994: 31–2).

Duke was not the only candidate running to Bush's right. In the 1988 election the Libertarian Party candidate, Ron Paul, was a recent defector from the Republicans who campaigned as 'The Conservative – Libertarian Alternative'. Most importantly, a leading Christian religious broadcaster, Pat Robertson, challenged Bush in the Republican primaries, mobilising an army of supporters that was incapable of winning him the nomination but would turn out to be the basis for a revival of the Christian Right. Little noticed at first, his new organisation, the Christian Coalition, was formed in 1989. By the time of the 1992 Republican convention it would already be a major force (*Monitor* November 1988; Oldfield 1996: 125–82, 188–9).

In 1984 and again in 1988, evangelical voters had been important for Republican victory; but while Bush was to continue with the anti-abortion policy of his predecessor, he was to prove far less successful in retaining Christian Right support. Suspicion that Republican strategists wanted to play down the issue led to considerable distrust, and there was similar concern over what was seen as an attempt to gain support from gay pressure groups. But it was Bush's decision to raise taxes despite promising not to do so that would prove fatal to his administration. Challenged in the Republican primaries by Pat Buchanan, the President was attacked on both social conservative and economic conservative grounds. Furthermore, while the Gulf War was opposed by a relatively small number of conservatives, Bush's enthusiasm for a more multilateral foreign policy set off alarm bells more widely. As we discuss further later, his call for 'a new world order' was to be seen by a number of sections of the right as a threat to American sovereignty. Nor was the issue simply one of how American troops were deployed, important as that was. As the 1990s proceeded, arguments about foreign trade and globalisation would also generate divisions (Oldfield 1996: 121, 180, 193–6; Diamond 1995: 277–8, 293, 286–8).

Conservative unity was strained in other areas too. What had been a long-standing conservative consensus around the crucial importance of the alliance between America and Israel came under attack from Buchanan. (In a smaller version of the argument, a conservative journalist, Joseph Sobran, was sacked from *National Review* after clashes with Buckley over anti-Semitism.) Where Jewish neoconservatives denounced the appearance of anti-Semitism within the conservative movement, a concern with which Buckley and other prominent figures agreed, Buchanan supporters claimed what was actually occurring was an attempt to silence those who placed the national interest first. With the ending of the Cold War, what had once been strong on the right, an isolationist belief in 'America First', was experiencing a resurgence. The creation of modern American conservatism was premised on the belief that defeating the Soviet Union necessitated a world-wide struggle. Now, with the disappearance of the adversary, an argument that foreign alliances were no longer so crucial was coming into conflict with the view that the duty of the world's greatest power was to ensure that the benefits of democratic capitalism were extended to others. In the preceding decade the resolutely fusionist *National Review* had already expressed concern about the arguments made by neoconservatism's critics, particularly those around the enthusiastically traditionalist monthly, *Chronicles*; but now the conflict between neoconservatism and what had come to be dubbed 'paleoconservatism' flared up more virulently than ever. Simultaneously, the libertarian movement was also undergoing its own disputes, and those conservatives who were arguing for a nationalist foreign policy were to find themselves in alliance with a new political variant. Paleoconservatism aligned with paleo-libertarianism, in which Murray Rothbard and others called for the restoration of an older libertarianism that stood for the rolling back of the state and the minimisation of overseas commitments and rejected what it saw as mainstream libertarianism's confusion of personal liberty with libertinism (Diamond 1995: 282–6; Buckley 1992; *Wanderer* 21 October 1993; *National Review* 16 June 1989; Raimondo 1993: 217–33; *Conservative Review* May 1990).

Amidst this ferment, Buchanan and Robertson were to emerge as two of the most important critics of the direction the Republican Party had taken after Reagan. But they were not united on what was needed in its place. Buchanan, a Catholic, fervently opposed abortion, and his argument strongly emphasised this and other issues championed by the Christian Right. But on other issues there was no such agreement. More importantly, differences would also come to the fore within the Christian Right itself (Buchanan 1990: 58, 79, 339, 356).

The 1992 Republican Convention adopted a platform reflecting Christian Right concerns, and in the aftermath of Clinton's victory, critics were to argue that its growing influence had cost the party the election. Without evangelical support, the Christian Coalition's executive director, Ralph Reed, had replied, Bush's defeat would have been even worse. But, as his figures also indicated, nearly half of those evangelicals who had voted in 1992 had not supported Bush, and in the aftermath of his defeat the organisation began to revise its policy priorities and redefine what it meant by 'pro-family'. Where before abortion and homosexuality had been particularly prominent in its agenda, it began to argue that other issues that affected the family were even more important in winning popular support. The level of taxation, crime and economic policy were all now presented in this light, in a repositioning that was intended not only to increase the potential conservative vote among evangelicals but to make the Coalition more central to American politics and to the political calculations of the Republican leadership. For one Christian Right group, the Christian Action Network, Reed's strategy was 'short-sighted' and 'unprincipled'. Later, other forces on the Christian Right would criticise the Coalition's direction. Initially, however, it appeared to offer the opportunity of a major breakthrough (*Christian American* November–December 1992; *Policy Review* Summer 1993; *Human Events* 6 November 1993).

In the summer of 1993, Reed was to claim that the new administration had resulted in the Coalition's growing at 10,000 members a week. (Soon after, it was reported as 450,000 strong.) Other sections of the right were also experiencing an upsurge in support, and within the Republican party, the House Republican Leader, Newt Gingrich, and the chairman of the House Republican Conference, Dick Armey, developed a series of policies, the *Contract with America*, around which Republican candidates could campaign in the 1994 congressional elections. The Coalition's new approach, which it had already carried into practice by campaigning against tax increases and Clinton's health proposals, fitted into this strategy perfectly, and having secured a commitment to press for 'a deep tax cut for families', Reed agreed to postpone demanding action on such contentious issues as abortion (*New Republic* 5 July 1993; *Wall Street Journal* 7 September 1993; Owens 1998: 3; Reed 1996a: 230, 1996b: 184–5).

The Republicans' new strategy, with its call for lowering taxes, curbing the growth of the federal government and reforming welfare, was initially highly successful, with the party winning both houses of Congress. It was a result that could be read in a number of different ways. One conservative strategist, Grover Norquist, argued that reasons ranged from the running of 'an explicitly conservative campaign' to the number of Democrats retiring from office. But among the factors, he argued, was the support of a broad alliance of organisations, stretching from taxpayer and small business groups to the National Rifle Association and the Christian Coalition. (He had, indeed, been instrumental in their coming together.) Broken down into different bills, the *Contract*'s provisions passed the House, with the Coalition putting much of its resources into a campaign in their support. Gingrich, now the House Speaker, promised that Christian Right concerns would receive attention and, when the Coalition issued its own list of proposals, the *Contract with the American Family*, expressed his support. The Republican offensive, however, soon began to hit problems. In part, they derived from Clinton's ability to present himself as the moderate alternative to partisan extremes. But it was connected too both to crucial missteps on the part of Gingrich and resistance to some of the *Contract's* proposals on the part of Republican moderates. Just as a number of conservatives began to turn against Gingrich, who eventually would not survive the party's setbacks in the 1998 elections, so too sections of the Christian Right attacked the Christian Coalition's leadership (Ashford 1998: 96–116; Norquist 1995: 11, 23, 16–17; Balz and Brownstein 1996: 180–82; Reed 1996b: 197–8; *New York Times* 18 May 1995; *Time* 16 November 1998; *National Review* 23 November, 7 December 1998).

Next to the Coalition, which by 1996 was claiming 1.7 million members, the most important group had initially been formed in 1977 in order to support Christian families. Focus on the Family became increasingly involved with political issues, and at the end of the 1980s its leading figure, James Dobson, invited a former White House official, Gary Bauer, to become President of an allied group, the Family Research Council, and set about the creation of a network of state family councils. With a mailing list of over two million, a popular radio programme and an extensive range of publications, Focus on the Family was to emerge to the fore of the Christian Right. A critic of both what he saw as the Christian Coalition's zeal for compromise and the *Contract with America's* neglect of moral issues, Dobson became increasingly strident in his criticisms. Thus, writing to Republican legislators in 1998, he declared that he recognised 'the realities of the political process, and that controversial legislation can be difficult to pass'. He acknowledged too, he went on, that the President was 'not reluctant' to use his veto. 'Our great frustration with Republican leadership, then, is not the failure to pass pro-family legislation . . . It is with the failure to try' (Watson 1997: 54; *Progressive* December 1996; Martin 1997: 341–3; *Christianity Today* 6 March 1995; *Washington Post National Weekly Edition* 30 October – 5 November 1995; *American Enterprise* November–December 1995; Dobson 1998).

Where Dobson was increasingly estranged from the Republican right, the Christian Coalition remained committed to its victory. But, while the Christian Right was strong in the party's grass roots (with one estimate claiming that it dominated 18 state parties and had substantial influence in 13 others), as the 1996 presidential election approached, no candidate emerged who both shared its concerns and was capable of winning. The Coalition concluded that Bob Dole would gain the nomination, but had to join with Bauer and others to stop him from diluting the party's anti-abortion stance. His lacklustre campaign came under fire for its lack of attention to social issues (indeed, Dobson himself was to vote for a rival candidate, former New Right leader Howard Phillips) (Persinos 1994: 20–24; *New Yorker* 25 March 1996; *Focus on the Family Citizen* 23 September 1996; Xanthopoulou 1996; *New York Times* 20 May 1998).

In the aftermath of defeat, Reed was to give up his position in order to set up a political consultancy, and a new leadership, conscious of the discontent within its ranks, took Christian Coalition in a less conciliatory direction. In order to prove more attractive to voters, the Coalition had sought to broaden its agenda, downgrading the very issues that most concerned its activists. When allied with a willingness to compromise with the very Republican leadership that Dobson had found so wanting, Reed's strategy had both built the organisation and risked plunging it into crisis. With a falling financial base, it was forced to cut back on its activities, and the new leadership's unsuccessful demand that the Republican National Committee cease supporting Republican candidates who were unsound on abortion was an important indicator of more difficult relations. (Indeed, the situation worsened still further with the appearance of claims by former officials that the organisation had grossly overstated its membership figures.) By the end of the decade, Gary Bauer, who had built up his own independent standing in the movement, was to briefly emerge as a candidate for the Republican presidential nomination before losing much of his base by his support for a candidate rejected by most of the Christian Right, John McCain. There were problems too for the Coalition. Its preferred option, the Missouri Senator John Ashcroft, was to withdraw from the race, and while some could envisage supporting George W. Bush, others were impressed by Steve Forbes's decision to take a strong anti-abortion stance. It was Bush, however, who was in the best position not only to win the nomination but to secure considerable Christian Right support in doing so (*Washington Times* 7 January 1998; *Washington Post* 20 December 1997, 18 February 1998, 31 January 1999; *New Republic* 27 April 1998; *New York Times* 2 August 1998, 7 March 1999; *Washington Post National Weekly Edition* 3 April 2000, *Houston Chronicle* 7 February 1999; *National Review* 25 October 1999).

Indeed, one indication of the problems of the movement was a series of announcements in early 1999 by the veteran social conservative Paul Weyrich that he no longer believed that a moral majority existed in the country and that the only answer was to cease relying on electoral politics and seek instead, as those who were involved in schooling their children at home were already doing, to create institutions outside 'contemporary culture'. While much of the furore that resulted rested on the mistaken belief that Weyrich was calling for Christians to abandon politics altogether, it was an important sign of the confusion following the 1996 and 1998 results, a confusion that was to worsen with the resignation of the Christian Coalition's new president, and the subsequent demotion of Ralph Reed's successor as executive director. Problems with its tax-exempt status too led to a fundamental restructuring, with one body, Christian Coalition of America, concentrating on voter education, while the other, Christian Coalition International, would offer support to particular candidates. In what direction Robertson would take the Coalition, and with what success, remained unclear (Weyrich 1999; *Washington Post National Weekly Edition* 8 March 1999; *Washington Post* 7 March 1999; *Focus on the Family Citizen* April 1999; *New York Times* 11 June 1999; *International Herald Tribune* 11 June 1999; *Freedom Writer* March–April 1999).

Neither Gingrich nor the Christian Coalition had been able to find a convincing way forward for the post-Reagan conservative movement. Pat Buchanan's challenges for the Republican presidential nomination were to suggest one possible direction. Reviving the term 'America First', Buchanan's initial challenge ranged widely, from denunciation of Bush's increase in taxes and his government's funding of 'pornographic and blasphemous art' to attacks on his commitment to free trade and a New World Order foreign policy. Supported by *Human Events*, a particularly combative conservative publication with its origins in the isolationism of the 1940s, and initially supported by *National Review*, which believed that a strong Buchanan vote would push Bush back to the right, he gained around a fifth of the vote in the Republican primaries, and his campaign manager was to claim that the 1992 party platform had adopted his policies. Buchanan's challenge for the 1996 nomination again emphasised his America First beliefs, as it did his social conservatism; but this time his criticisms of economic policy were more far-reaching. His calls for protection were increasingly accompanied by denunciations of multinational companies, which, he claimed, preferred to move to low-wage economies rather than employ American workers. With just over 3 million votes, he had achieved 21 per cent of the primary vote; but where in 1992 he had been given a prominent place at the Convention, delivering a much-publicised speech on the 'war . . . for the soul of America', this time the Dole campaign was only willing for him to make a token appearance, an offer he declined. 'Our rivals may be the ones waving from the podium', he was to claim in a speech to his supporters the day before the 1996 Convention began, 'but it is our ideas that now reflect the grass roots of this party.' But, just as he had antagonised many within the mainstream of the Republican Party, so his argument that 'America does not need a third party' but a truly conservative second one disappointed many of his supporters, who believed that the GOP would never embrace either their cause or their candidate. That in 1999, rather than continue in his third attempt to gain the Republican nomination, he should decide instead to break away in pursuit of a third-party nomination was a somewhat surprising development. That it should not be for a clearly right-wing party, but for Ross Perot's more difficult to define Reform Party, was more surprising still (Diamond 1995: 292–4, 24; *International Herald Tribune* 28 February 1992, 2 January, 13 August 1996; *New Republic* 6–13 January 1992; Buckley 1992: xvi, 168–71; *Congressional Quarterly Weekly Report* 3 August 1996; Wills 1992: 9; *Washington Post* 26 October 1999).

Such a change represented a number of risks, not least the need to find a way of espousing his social conservatism in a party whose voters and activists often inclined towards libertarianism. If part of his attraction to such a route lay in its ample election funding, another element was the economic nationalism that had made Buchanan and Perot allies in the past. Yet another, intriguingly, was the political fluidity of the Perot movement's appeal. As his intervention in the 1992 presidential contest particularly demonstrated, Perot was a populist, a figure who claimed that the people were denied their rights by a pernicious elite. Buchanan too took such an approach, and as shall see when we discuss his appeal, he was already arguing in the early 1990s that the rise of globalisation was dissolving older disputes between conservatives and liberals and replacing them with a new conflict between nationalists and internationalists. His focus here was particularly on economics, but in announcing his defection to the Reform Party he emphasised too the Perot movement's concern with elite distortions of the political system (*USA Today* 23 September, 19 August 1999; *Washington Post* 26 October 1999; *National Review* 13 September 1999; *Conservative Chronicle* 1 December 1993; *New Yorker* 22 April 1996; *Nation* 1 November 1999; *Free American* December 1999).

But in choosing to defect to the Reform Party, Buchanan was not only rejecting the Republican Party but another political option. As with the 1988 elections, 1992 had again seen candidates to the Republican Party's right. The prominent Patriot and former Green Beret colonel Bo Gritz had run as a candidate for his own America First Coalition (the Populist Party, with which he had initially been involved, was in the process of disintegrating, with the *Spotlight* actually supporting Perot's candidacy). But where Gritz's grouping did not long survive, a more lasting grouping emerged in the shape of New Rightist Howard Phillips's U.S. Taxpayers Party. Phillips's party, for which he would run in 1992, 1996 and 2000, was a particularly interesting development, which we will return to in a later chapter. It deserves attention, in part, because of its relationship to Buchanan, whom it has tried unsuccessfully to persuade to run as its candidate in all three contests. It is noteworthy too in giving a prominent place to Reconstructionism, a doctrine that looks to the Old Testament as its political model and criticises the Christian Right as both theologically mistaken and politically compromising. Finally, the Taxpayers Party (which in 1999 became the Constitution Party) is worth further attention for its ability to gain support from within the Patriot movement. But it was only one of the developments to the right of Republicanism that warrant further discussion. If Phillips's Party has been little commented on, this is certainly not true of another development – the emergence of another, and this time more formidable, generation of armed right-wing groups (Novick 1995: 250, 255, 260; *Nation* 10 June 1996; Diamond 1996: 188; *New Yorker* 22 April 1996; *Free American* October 1996; Clarkson 1997: 104–6; *Front Lines Research* November 1994; *Politics 1 Report* 7 September 1999; Mulloy 1999).

Where, during the mid-1980s, the Covenant, the Sword and the Arm of the Lord had been the object of a government siege and another group, The Order, had robbed armoured cars and murdered a Jewish radio talk show host, similar groups, notably the Aryan Republican Army, emerged in the 1990s. But the most important of what was a considerable number of new groupings was the militia movement. Emerging in response to the death of 76 people during the FBI's siege of a religious sect accused of arms offences in Waco, Texas, militias claimed that only the revival of the armed citizenry of the American Revolution could stop a government that had run amok. Nor was this the only incident that led to such claims. An earlier confrontation in August 1992, when an attempt to arrest an Idaho Christian Identity believer, Randy Weaver, resulted in the death of his son and wife, was also seen as an argument for resisting authority.

Even more, many militia activists claimed, the new movement was needed to stop the destruction of American freedom and the imposition of a New World Order. As we shall explore in greater detail later, this was a phenomenon that has been tended to be interpreted in particular ways. It is seen as part of a backlash against the changes since the 1960s that have fuelled the rise of the right in general. Above all, it is argued, these changes concern race relations in America, and the reaction they have engendered is encapsulated in the figure of the 'angry white male'. But it has also been argued that the influence of such figures as the former Ku Klux Klan leader Louis Beam demonstrates that they are a new manifestation of the extreme right. This latter reading of events was to receive considerable attention in the aftermath of the killing of 168 people in the bombing of a federal building in Oklahoma City on the second anniversary of the deaths at Waco. The attack, it was quickly observed, bore a marked resemblance to one portrayed in *The Turner Diaries*, a racist novel admired by the man later convicted of the attack that was written by William Pierce, a former officer in the American Nazi Party and the leader of the extreme right National Alliance (a remnant of the National Youth Alliance of the 1960s). As with the Patriot movement, of which they are a part, the militias cannot be understood in isolation from either the right as a whole or the extreme right in particular. It will be one of the central tasks of this study, however, to challenge the ways in which they have hitherto been seen (Flynn and Gerhardt 1989: 464; Ridgeway 1990: 91–5; *Intelligence Report* Spring 1998; Barkun 1997: 255–90; *Focus on the Family Citizen* September 1999; Stern 1996: 23, 188, 192; Abanes 1996: 180–81; *New York Times* 26 April 1995; Mintz 1985: 131; George and Wilcox 1992: 357–8).

The rise of the right, as this necessarily brief overview has shown, has been a complex development. What we have described as mainstream conservatism has clearly made considerable headway since its emergence in the 1950s. It has come to wield a major influence in the Republican Party during both the Reagan and, to a lesser extent, the Bush years, and, despite the election of Clinton to the White House, in the House of Representatives subsequently. With its largest single group of activists in the Christian Coalition, conservatism has continued to be represented in a number of other organisations, and the movement overall has proved far more successful than either its radical right or its extreme right rivals. The *Spotlight*, in contrast to its high circulation in the early 1980s, by the early 1990s had fallen to about a 75,000 circulation, while the militias in one account number as few as 15,000 (although other versions suggest a much higher figure). As for the overtly racist extreme right, one estimate at the beginning of the 1990s suggested ten to twenty thousand members and a further 30,000 Identity adherents (Identity believers were thought to number only a little more in the mid-1990s, but by the end of the decade one estimate suggested that there were over 50,000) (McLemee 1994: 23; Mulloy 1999: 28; *Nation* 16–23 July 1990; Dobratz and Shanks-Meile 1997: 81; *Intelligence Report* Winter 1998).

Figures, of course, do not tell the full story. Not only, as we have seen with the Christian Coalition, is there dispute about the accuracy of membership claims, but there is no simple link between numbers and influence. Small organisations can make good use of their activists and pursue strategies that make effective links with those outside the organisation. This can be true of electoral appeals, with the substantial vote for Wallace in 1968 or, to a lesser degree, the support in the Republican primaries for Buchanan in 1992 and 1996. Other approaches too, such as attempts to influence single-issue movements, can also offer opportunities of mass influence. In the chapters that follow, we shall be exploring many of the issues we have sought to bring into view. In the next chapter we shall begin to raise some questions about both the issues that the right has taken up and the social categories to which it appeals. Both towards the end of this chapter and in the earlier discussion of *National Review* we have emphasised the significance of race. As we have seen, however, and as the 'angry white male' term is already half-suggesting, race is not the only factor that needs exploring in understanding the rise of the right.

Angry white males?

From the creation of the white Citizens' Councils in the 1950s to the arguments about affirmative action in the 1990s, race has not only been crucial for much of the far right but has continued to play a significant part in the concerns of the mainstream right. Most importantly, it has been undeniably important in influencing the voting decisions of many who have put Republican candidates into office. As early as the late 1960s, the conservative strategist Kevin Phillips was arguing that the New Deal coalition had run aground on the inability of the Democrats to cope with 'the Negro socioeconomic revolution'. The voters of the South, the West and 'the Catholic sidewalks of New York', he claimed, were in revolt against a liberalism that had once taxed 'the few for the benefit of the many' but now taxed 'the many on behalf of the few'. Where he had looked forward to the rise of a conservative majority, later accounts have taken issue with the methods used to bring about its construction. In both this chapter and later, we shall discuss the role of race in the movements with which we are particularly concerned. But how central has it been to the right in general (Phillips 1970: 37)?

The 1964 election campaign, Thomas and Mary Edsall declare, 'marked the beginning of a fundamentally new partisan configuration, based in large part on the politics of race'. In this argument, Nixon's landslide victory eight years later was particularly due to his ability to win over former Wallace voters by his positioning on such issues as busing. Similarly, when, at the end of the 1970s, a tax revolt was to sweep to victory in California, and then elsewhere, its mobilising force was given much of its power by the contrast between white taxpayers and black welfare recipients. Increasingly, Democrat appeals to fairness were seen through 'a racial filter', as a commitment to redistribution away from whites. Affirmative action was seen as denying jobs or promotion on grounds of colour, while arguments about welfare dependency, drug abuse and births outside marriage are similarly racially freighted, bearing meanings that have proved crucial to right-wing success. It is an argument that we find too when we examine Dan Carter's more recent discussion of the role of 'Race In The Conservative Counterrevolution 1963–1994'. Fears of blackness and of disorder, he holds, were 'the warp and woof of the new social agenda', brought together by the links many whites made between race and criminality, poverty and cultural degradation (Edsall with Edsall 1992: 35, 74–6, 79–90, 131, 184, 125–6, 236, 183, 213–14; Carter 1996: 42).

Race, both accounts argue, suffuses Republican electoral strategy. In 1988, the Republican presidential campaign unremittingly attacked the Democratic candidate, governor Michael Dukakis of Massachussetts, for the rape that occurred in his state following the release of a convicted black murderer on a weekend furlough. Where the Edsalls' discussion only alludes to the importance of race in the re-election of Senator Jesse Helms in 1990, Carter describes his campaign's use of a television advertisement showing a white worker rejected for a job because of affirmative action. And both refer, although surprisingly briefly, to the 1989 election to the Louisiana state House of Representatives of former Ku Klux Klan leader David Duke. His subsequent pursuit of the 1992 Republican presidential nomination was to gain little support, but his election as a Republican in 1989 and his high vote in races first for the Senate in 1990, and then for the governorship in 1991, were, as Sara Diamond has shown, to suggest to more than one conservative commentator the electoral potential for a campaign stance that eschewed open supremacism while denouncing 'the illegitimate welfare birthrate' and calling for the ending of affirmative action. It is in the light of the Republican Party's use of race, Carter argues, that we should see the *Contract with America*, its focus on welfare reform appealing to voters who believed not only that the poor were often undeserving, but that the undeserving were often black (Edsall with Edsall 1992: 222–4, 275, 114; Carter 1996: 72–80, 82–3, 110–11; Moore 1992: 43–5, 47–9; Powell 1992: 13, 32; Rose 1992: 156; Rose with Esolen 1992: 231–2; Diamond 1995: 271–3).

As both accounts make clear, any study of the rise of the right needs to give special attention to the racial views of white voters. However, that does not constitute a sufficient explanation. Carter, in particular, stretches his argument too far when he notes the importance for the Republican Party of such issues as abortion and school prayer only to describe them as 'not directly connected to questions of race', or when he claims that Pat Buchanan's 1972 description of the Democrats as favouring 'weakness abroad, permissiveness at home' had the effect of identifying them 'with the interests of black Americans'. In both cases evidence of the diversity of a conservative appeal is forced to succumb to the temptations of a monocausal explanation. Nor, as we shall see, is this the only problem with such an argument (Carter 1996: 80, 54).

Firstly, while the Republican Party has developed a substantial electoral base among whites, this should not lead us to assume that conservatives are indifferent to their woeful level of support among blacks. In 1956, almost 40 per cent of the black vote went to Eisenhower, and almost a third voted for Nixon against Kennedy. In just four years, however, black GOP support collapsed, with only 6 per cent voting for a presidential candidate whose appeal to many whites was that he had voted against the 1964 Civil Rights Act. In the years that followed, there was a partial recovery, but only to a peak of 15 (or, according to another poll, 18) per cent, and that before the 1980 contest. The Reagan years saw a renewed decline, and when we examine recent elections we see that in 1996 black support stood at 12 per cent as against 10 per cent for Bush four years earlier (Ashbee 1997a: appendix, n.p.; Ladd 1995: 22).

In recent congressional elections too, black support for the Republican Party has been weak. In 1994, 8 (or in another poll 11) per cent of blacks supported Republican candidates; in 1998 11 per cent. Such calamitous results have understandably led analysts to focus on the Republican pursuit of white voters, and it is tempting to take Goldwater's famous observation that rather than pursuing the black vote, Republicans 'ought to go hunting where the ducks are' as applying not only to the 1964 election, but to the situation thereafter. This, however, would be to ignore Republican efforts to increase their proportion of the black vote. As Edward Ashbee has noted, after the 1988 elections, for instance, the party chairman, Lee Atwater (a figure often associated with a strategy aimed at white voters), described 'outreach to black voters' as his 'number one goal', while the vice-presidential candidate in 1996, Jack Kemp, had long argued for efforts to win support from African Americans. Black organisations within the party or within the conservative movement have been highly active, but, with some localised exceptions, increased black support for the

Republican Party has remained an elusive aspiration. It remains the case, however, that party managers are likely to continue to pursue it (*USA Today* 6 November 1998; Carter 1995: 218; Ashbee 1999a: 236, 254, 238–48; Edsall with Edsall 1992: 221–2).

Party leaders have also proved hesitant to emphasise racial issues, both because of an unwillingness to alienate moderate voters and because it might stymie any attempt to increase support among African Americans. Thus, in the aftermath of Dole's defeat, articles in the memorably entitled 'Special Recriminations Issue' of *National Review* were to attack him for the tardiness of his support for the California Civil Rights Initiative, an anti-affirmative action measure that had won with 54 per cent of the vote. Kemp, one writer complained, had even decried it as 'a wedge issue' that he would not allow to 'tear up' the state. Elsewhere, similar attacks were launched both in *Chronicles* and in a recently launched monthly, *Middle American News*. Nor was the Dole campaign the only section of the party to come under criticism. The following year, another conservative publication, *Citizens Informer*, attacked Gingrich for his reluctance to endorse a bill ending affirmative action in federal employment and public contracts (*National Review* 9 December 1996; *Chronicles* April 1997; *Middle American News* December 1996; *Citizens Informer* Summer 1997).

Two further factors need to be borne in mind in considering the role of race in modern conservatism. One concerns a point already noted above, the contemporary existence of a black conservatism. This development has often been associated with an enthusiasm for the market and an opposition to affirmative action that it shared with white conservatism. This, however, has tended to obscure the existence of elements that suggest a rather more distinct dynamic. Rather than merely echoing white conservative priorities, some black conservatives have been highly critical of racism among their white counterparts, and there has also been a tendency to argue that the assumption that integration is the goal has resulted in a downplaying of the importance of building black businesses and fostering black schools. At the same time, some among both black and white conservatives have shown an interest in extending their search for alliances beyond Christian groups to the growing number of black Muslims, only some of whom identify with the Nation of Islam. Black conservatives do not speak with one voice nor, even more importantly, have they been successful in persuading blacks, many of whom hold conservative views on such questions as homosexuality and school prayer, that they should attach themselves to a more generalised conservatism. Their very existence, however, is a challenge to the assumption that modern conservatism can be explained through white resentments (Mobley 1996: 3, 8–9; Ashbee 1996: 6–9, 12, 1997b: 155–6, 1999a: 250–52, 259–60).

If the existence of black conservatism is surprising, the final development is even more noteworthy. Both the Edsalls and Carter argue that the clash between government and evangelicals at the end of the 1970s was particularly rooted in a wish to retain Christian schools as segregated institutions. While the Edsalls' account accepts that this was not the only concern, it nonetheless makes a suggestive argument that in this, as in other cases, race may have made an impact even where it was not immediately evident. (Indeed, it is also worth noting that opposition to busing was an important issue not only for the New Right but for Christian Voice too.) However, it is equally important to recognise how conservative evangelicals see race today. In 1995, the Southern Baptist Convention marked its 150th anniversary with a public apology for its previous support of racism, the leading charismatic magazine published a series of articles on 'racial reconciliation', and the Christian Coalition sponsored a conference on the subject. The following year the Coalition raised $750,000 to help repair black churches suffering from a spate of burnings and in 1997 it both launched the Samaritan Project, an attempt to encourage initiatives against poverty in African-American and Hispanic communities, and organised its own one-day Congress on Racial Justice and Reconciliation (Edsall with Edsall 1992: 131–3; Carter 1996: 56–7; Viguerie 1981: 186; Crawford 1980: 146; Diamond 1998a: 51; Watson 1997: 68–9).

Amidst these different developments, one in particular has stood out – the rise of the movement known as the Promise Keepers. Conceived in 1990 to bring men together to proclaim 'their love for Christ and their commitment to their families', its rallies attracted numbers that grew from around 4,200 in 1991 to nearly a million at its Washington DC gathering in 1997. Set up by a college football coach, Bill McCartney, a number of critics have drawn attention to the support it gained from both James Dobson and Pat Robertson and the involvement in it of a number of figures (including McCartney himself) who have also been active in opposing abortion or homosexuality. Rather than see it as part of the Christian Right, however, it would seem more useful to view it as part of the broader socially conservative evangelicalism of which the Christian Right is a part. But this is not to deny the political implications of its efforts, not only in its stance towards women, to which we will return later, but also towards race (Abraham 1997: 17; *Nation* 7 October 1996; Bellant 1995: 81–5; Clarkson 1997: 187–202, 260–63; *Christianity Today* 18 May 1998).

As Ken Abraham has noted, McCartney's views on the issue initially met with a frosty response when he first raised them at his overwhelmingly white gatherings. By 1996, however, the organisation's 'Break Down the Walls' conferences were emphasising racial as well as denominational barriers, and a leading Promise Keepers official was arguing that 'to promote racism, either by our ignorance or by our blatant activity, is a sin against God'. McCartney himself declared in his speeches that there was 'a spirit of white racial superiority that exists in our land' and that 'white guys' had to break with their 'insensitivity to the pain of the people of color'. Critics have argued that such an approach ignores the structural inequalities in American society. What is crucial for our discussion, however, is the centrality the organisation has given to opposing racism (Abraham 1997: 124–31; *Nation* 7 October 1996).

Furthermore, as Amy Ansell has noted, while such figures as Grover Norquist believed opposition to affirmative action was 'the perfect issue' to use against the Democrats, divisions within the Republican Party in Congress ensured that the issue was put to one side as the 1996 election season approached. While many conservatives are attracted to such issues, they present real problems for the right, and both the Republican Party and the Christian Right have proved considerably more reluctant to identify with a racially-framed politics than we might expect. During his time at the helm of the Christian Coalition, for instance, Ralph Reed was particularly concerned to differentiate the Christian Right from the segregationism of many white evangelicals forty years earlier and explicitly noted that the present-day movement is wary of taking a stance against affirmative action. But, if we are unconvinced that race is as central to the conservative movement as some writers have argued, how are we to understand two recent developments (Ansell 1998: 182–3; Reed 1996a: 235–41, 1996b: 277)?

The publication in 1994 of Richard Herrnstein and Charles Murray's book, *The Bell Curve*, marked the revival of an argument that can be traced back to the 1960s and, in a somewhat different form, back to the heyday of eugenics in the early twentieth century. The average white person, they declared, had a higher IQ than 84 per cent of black people, and IQ differences were predominantly, although not totally, a matter of heredity rather than environment. That such a book should not merely appear but receive massive publicity has been seen by a number of commentators as evidence of an increasing hostility to racial minorities. Michael Lind, for instance, has argued that while Herrnstein received little support when he first raised such arguments at the beginning of the 1970s, the more favourable response that he and his co-author, a leading conservative writer, received from conservatives in the mid-1990s showed that the mainstream right was now willing to embrace a white supremacism that, it hoped, could create a conservative coalition of the wealthy and 'poor and middling whites'. We are recognisably back in the same territory as the arguments raised by the Edsalls and Carter, and, indeed, the book figures in the latter's recent work. But does the revival of eugenics by Herrnstein and Murray give sustenance to such an argument (Herrnstein and Murray 1994: 9–10, 343, 269, 105–8; Lind 1996: 194, 199–200, 206; Carter 1996: 111–17)?

It is certainly true that the book, and the extensive discussion that it provoked, was seen by sections of the right as a welcome development. This was most obviously true for such groups as the National Association for the Advancement of White People, established by David Duke after his departure from the Ku Klux Klan; but, significantly, the effect also stretched much further. *American Renaissance*, a conservative newsletter which saw itself as defending 'the essential, European nature of our nation', declared at the end of 1994 that the book had injected 'questions of race and intelligence into the mainstream' of American debate, while the paleo-libertarian Murray Rothbard held that until the book's appearance it had been 'taboo' to acknowledge the truth about race and IQ. The decision of the neoconservative magazine, *Commentary*, to both publish a favourable review of the book and invite Murray to reply to his critics represented a particularly crucial source of support within the conservative movement. A more complex response, however, can be found in a symposium on the subject published by *National Review* soon after the book's appearance. The veteran conservative Ernest van den Haag treated the book as a validation of conservatives' belief in inherent inequality, while the psychologist Arthur Jensen, who had been a key figure in earlier disputes on the subject, declared the book to be right in its argument that 'social pathology', from crime and drug abuse to illegitimacy and 'permanent welfare dependency', was disproportionately to be found among those with IQs below 75, and that this encompassed 5 per cent of the white population – and at least a quarter of the black. The black conservative Glenn Loury, however, declared his horror at the prospect of conservatism's adopting the book's stance (as its editor has recently recalled, he was to break sharply with *Commentary* on the issue), while the leading religious conservative Richard John Neuhaus, who in the late 1980s had been involved in a bitter argument with *Chronicles* over its 'nativist tendencies', described the book as 'mischievous' (Dobratz and Shanks-Meile 1997: 48–9; *NAAWP News* 92, n.d., *c*.1996; American Renaissance, n.d., *c*.1992; *Intelligence Report* Winter 1999; D'Souza 1995: 387–9; *Nation* 10 June 1996; Hardisty 1998b: 121, 142; *National Review* 25 January 1999, 5 December 1994; Diamond 1995: 284).

If conservatives reacted in different ways to the book's claims, it is even more important to question whether *The Bell Curve* had an impact on the policies pursued by the right. Ansell, for instance, has suggested the book functioned more as an extreme by which mainstream conservative arguments about race and welfare came to appear more moderate. From a somewhat different perspective, Murray himself has suggested that while arguments, including those on the right, go ahead without reference to his work, *The Bell Curve* should be seen as 'the stealth public-policy book of the 1990s'. It is a proposition that is, to say the least, somewhat difficult to verify. But while he claims that scholars know that he is right, 'What I never see is acceptance of any part of this message in the public-policy world.' His book did, indeed, represent an important shift in conservative argument. But just as it was not one that was universally welcomed on the right, it is not to be seen as representing a new orthodoxy in Republican policy (Ansell 1998: 185; *National Review* 8 December 1997).

If *The Bell Curve* represents an attempt to shift the right's intellectual assumptions, a more recent development concerns the links between the Republican hierarchy and an organisation that sees conservatism as centrally concerned with race. Both the prominent House Judiciary Committee member Bob Barr and the Senate Majority Leader, Trent Lott, it was revealed in late 1998, had addressed the Council of Conservative Citizens, an organisation formed in the mid-1980s by veterans of the old Citizens' Councils.

Barr, who had spoken at the body's South Carolina convention in the summer of 1998, was subsequently to declare that its views on race were 'repugnant'. Lott, for his part, had told a 1992 Council meeting in Mississippi that 'The people in this room stand for the right principles and the right philosophy.' After some dispute over a statement by his spokesman that he had 'no firsthand knowledge of the group's views', he denied reports of being a member (the 1992 speech had not been his only link with the organisation) and dissociated himself from its racism (*Village Voice* 29 December 1998; *Newsweek* 1 February 1999; Militia Watchdog 1999).

Claiming some 15,000 members, the Council was described by one of its executive members, the conservative journalist Samuel Francis, as 'the country's most effective conservative activist group'. Its paper, which it had inherited from the Citizens' Councils, included columns by a number of figures, from Pat Buchanan and Joseph Sobran to Trent Lott and even the original founder of the Citizens' Councils, Robert B. Patterson. Commenting on one of Patterson's columns, the leading figure in the organisation, Gordon Baum (himself a former organiser for both Wallace and the Citizens' Councils) lamented that he had 'tried to explain' to him 'that miscegenation is 1950s talk, it just doesn't work in our new context'. As the last remark would suggest, the Council had not lost its political roots. Initially created, in Baum's words, to represent 'working middle-class whites', a subsequent leaflet described it as seeking to speak for 'the no-longer silent conservative majority'. It involved, it declared, 'men and women whose political experience comes from every responsible social movement, conservative organization and effective political party in America', and was working to reduce big government, end 'reverse discrimination' and defend American traditions and family values. Articles in its newspaper and on its website, however, suggested its concerns reached somewhat further. While, as we have seen, the *Citizens Informer*'s front-page attack on the Republican leadership for refusing to prioritise such issues as affirmative action was consonant with the views of other conservatives, that it also attacked **'FORCED INTEGRATION'** indicates a more far-reaching agenda. Essays on its website were more strident still. Thus, while one attacked '30 plus years of unending anti-white propaganda from the liberal elites', another called for 'fellow white Americans' to 'find the faces like yours, and see them as your brothers and sisters. Find the fair-skinned babies and see them as your children' (*Washington Post*

17 January 1999; *Citizens Informer* Summer 1996, Summer 1997, May–June 1980, Summer 1985; Council of Conservative Citizens, n.d. (1990s); ADL 1998).

The Council of Conservative Citizens represents not the American right as a whole, but a particular strand within it, seeking to shift it in an explicitly 'pro-white' direction. (More accurately, it would appear to represent more than one strand. Where one of its leading figures, *American Renaissance* editor Jared Taylor, has argued for 'an unapologetic preference for the culture and way of life of whites', a recent furore over the Council's relationship with David Duke has led to the *Spotlight*'s attacking Taylor for his opposition to those within the organisation who would like to ally white supremacism with a support for anti-Semitism.) For other sections of the conservative movement, too, such issues as opposition to affirmative action are of vital importance. But we must not reduce American conservatism to a fixation with race, nor fail to recognise its divisions. If such caution applies to the relationship between African Americans and whites, it applies too to the more recent emergence within the conservative movement of arguments against immigration. In 1991, for instance, Pat Buchanan had declared that given a choice between the immigration of a million Zulus and a million 'Englishmen', it was right to give priority to the European roots of America. Buchanan, however, represents only one of the voices in the anti-immigration camp. Organisations such as the Federation for American Immigration Reform and the American Immigration Control Foundation have been particularly important, as have books by the *Chronicles* senior editor Chilton Williamson Jr. and the *National Review* senior editor Peter Brimelow (and, indeed, sections of *The Bell Curve* itself). Immigrants, it is claimed, take jobs from Americans and are a burden on already stretched social services. Nor is it only economic factors that are raised by anti-immigration campaigners. Mexican immigration, it is argued, threatens a *Reconquista*, the regaining of American territory by its southern neighbour, while the changing composition of Miami is a warning of the inevitable loss of America to another people if immigration is not stopped. But, once again, we are not witnessing a unified conservative response, nor are conservatives simply pursuing a white backlash electorate. Not only have Jack Kemp and the libertarian Cato Institute opposed an anti-immigration stance, but so too has both the conservative strategist Grover Norquist and the Christian Coalition. For the pro-immigration side, too, economic arguments – that new

arrivals contribute to economic growth and contribute more in taxation than they receive in benefits – do not stand alone. Immigrants, it
is argued, are often conservative and pro-family and, in wanting to
come to America, are showing what makes it great. And if we can
detect a concern for the needs of business in parts of this argument, we
can also see a more political concern – that Hispanic Americans had
turned away from the Republican Party in vast numbers in the 1996
election but, as George W. Bush had proved in winning the governorship of Texas, have the potential to be a significant part of a winning
Republican coalition. As with the conservative movement's relationship with African Americans, its response to immigration cannot be
seen as monolithic. The same caution, it should be emphasised, does
not only apply to ethnicity; we should bear it in mind too when we
consider another factor often raised in the discussion of the American
right, that of gender (*Washington Post* 16 December 1998; *Spotlight* 15
March 1999; Feagin 1997: 36, 42; Ashbee 1998: 73–80; Reimers 1996:
23–30, 34; Diamond 1996: 176–7; Herrnstein and Murray 1994: 341–2,
356–64; Chavez 1997: 68; *Middle American News* December 1996; *Reason*
October 1998; *National Journal* 3 August 1996; *National Review* 26
February, 1 July 1996).

As we have already noted, the Christian Right or, as it is sometimes called, the 'pro-family' movement, emerged at the end of the
1970s. It was not, however, the first social conservative movement on
the modern American right. An array of groups had already emerged,
for instance, in opposition to sex education. So, too, had a movement
in opposition to the Equal Rights Amendment (ERA). Passed by the
Senate in March 1972, the ERA declared that 'Equality of rights under
the law shall not be denied or abridged by the United States or by any
State on account of sex' and that Congress would 'have the power to
enforce, by appropriate legislation, the provisions of this article'. Yet
while it comfortably secured the two-thirds majority needed in the
Senate, in the ten years that followed it was unable to gain the ratifi-
cation of the three-quarters of state legislatures that was also needed,
falling three short of the thirty-eight required. Crucial in this defeat
was the mobilisation of a wide range of often local or state groupings,
of which the most important, led by the veteran Catholic rightist
Phyllis Schlafly, was the national organisation, STOP ERA. For
Schlafly, the proposed Amendment would destroy the rights of those
women who did not want to compete with men. It would make them
equally responsible for providing for the family, rather than its being

the husband's duty, and would make it impossible for any of them to remain 'a full-time wife and mother'. It would 'make women subject to the draft and for combat duty', end both single-sex schooling and laws that protected girls from 'predatory males' and make it impossible for women in industry to be protected from having to do overtime or carry out heavy or dangerous work. Furthermore, she declared, it would be used to legalise homosexual marriages and to make abortion constitutionally protected (Breasted 1970; Mansbridge 1986: 1, 29; *Advocate* 2, 18 November 1977; *Phyllis Schlafly Report* November 1972, July 1973, July 1975).

The battle against the ERA interacted with two other developments during the 1970s. The first, the International Women's Year Conference in November 1977, was described by Schlafly as 'the decisive turning point in the war between Women's Lib and those who are Pro-Family'. Coming as the culmination of a series of state conventions, the Houston gathering voted overwhelmingly in support of the ERA, lesbian and gay rights and abortion on demand, while opponents formed about 20 per cent of the delegates and supported a rival Pro-Family Rally on the second day of the Conference. This was followed shortly afterwards by preparations for the White House Conference on Families (to the horror of traditionalists, the Carter administration had deliberately changed the title of what had originally been envisaged as a conference on the family). This involved a large number of meetings at state and local level and three regional conferences at which, a conservative account later claimed, 'pro-family' forces had proved strong enough at least to 'prevent the official recommendations . . . from being a wish list of the radical feminists . . . and anti-traditionalist groups' (*Phyllis Schlafly Report* December 1977; Pines 1982: 142–50).

While Schlafly was particularly visible during this period, she was powerfully aided by the New Right and the Christian Right. Both the Conservative Caucus and Paul Weyrich's Committee for the Survival of a Free Congress vigorously opposed the ERA. The leader of the Moral Majority, Jerry Falwell, described it as striking 'at the foundation of our entire social structure', while another of its central figures, Tim LaHaye, accused feminists of destroying femininity and undermining men. Much of this opposition was fuelled by the belief that, in demanding equal rights, women, in Falwell's phrase, were defying their 'God-given roles'. The Bible, he declared, decreed that 'the husband is the head of the wife, even as Christ is the head of the church', and it was an argument that appeared across the anti-feminist movement. Thus for Paul Weyrich, feminism contradicted 'the biblically ordained nature of the family, with the father as head of the household and the mother subject to his ultimate authority', while for Howard Phillips, the natural order had been disrupted long before the modern feminist movement. As far back as the nineteenth century, he declared in 1980, it had been 'a conscious policy of government to liberate the wife from the leadership of the husband' (Faludi 1992: 263; LaHaye 1982: 144–5; Falwell 1980: 130–31; *New York Times* 30 July 1980; Radl 1983: 49).

Just as conservative opposition to feminism would continue into the next decade, so too would the belief that men needed to regain their rightful position in the home. It was expressed, for instance, by Pat Robertson and, in particular, as many commentators noted, it was a central feature in the rise of the Promise Keepers. Thus, writing in one of their key publications, one pastor decried what he termed 'the feminization of the American male', whereby men had become 'sissified' and abdicated their role of leadership. Husbands, he declared, should sit down with their wives and tell them 'Honey, I've made a terrible mistake. I've given you my role. I gave up leading this family, and I forced you to take my place. Now I must reclaim that role' (Boston 1996: 164; Abraham 1997: 105–7).

Gender, it can hardly be doubted, is crucial to major segments of the American right. Yet this is not the same as saying that it is central to the right as a whole, or to its electoral success. There is a further problem too, the problem of whether we are talking about a mobilisation of men – or of women. As we have seen, while male leaders have been particularly forceful on the ungodly nature of feminism, and in attributing a divine origin to patriarchy, we should not take this to mean that it is men to whom they are necessarily appealing. Promise Keepers is an all-male movement, but the Christian Right has stronger support among women than among men. Furthermore, the anti-ERA insurgency of the late 1970s has left in its wake two substantial anti-feminist women's organisations (Balz and Brownstein 1996: 304; Reed 1996b: 224).

The first, Eagle Forum, was established by Phyllis Schlafly in 1975, and while it both predates the Christian Right and has very much pursued its own priorities, it plays a significant part in pro-family campaigning. The other organisation, Concerned Women for America, was created at the end of the 1970s by Beverly LaHaye (Tim

LaHaye's wife), already a well-known figure among evangelical women for her talks and writing on marriage and 'the spirit-filled woman'. She did not see her organisation as a rival to Schlafly's, she declared in 1984, but instead saw it as providing 'ground troops . . . undergirding the whole movement'. Already, however, CWA was 250,000 strong, and by the next decade it was claiming between 600,000 and 700,000 members to Schlafly's 80,000 (*Advocate* 18 November 1977; Hardisty 1998a: 113–14, 116–17; Faludi 1992: 279–80, 282–4; *Moral Majority Report* April 1984).

Concerned Women for America is effectively the third most important group on the Christian Right, playing a crucial role in campaigns around homosexuality, sex education and other issues. LaHaye, like many male – and female – evangelicals, believes that husbands must lead in the home. This has not stopped her, however, from playing a prominent role in the Christian Right and, indeed, Linda Kintz notes, she has argued that 'Some men have embraced the serious misconception that all women are to submit to all men. Nothing could be further from the truth. Yes, husbands are to lead their wives and male pastors are to lead churches, but no, men are not to lead women!' (*Family Voice* June 1996, September 1995; Kintz 1997: 35, 31).

The existence of a substantial mobilisation of both men and women against feminism needs careful exploration to untangle its motivation. As we have seen in elaborating Schlafly's argument against the Equal Rights Amendment, it is not to be solely understood as the championship of male primacy. Where Barbara Ehrenreich has made the intriguing suggestion that female anti-feminism involves a profound distrust of men (she notes, for instance, Schlafly's argument that the ERA would free faithless men of the 'obligation' to support their faithful wives) Kintz sees LaHaye as valorising Christian women's choice to stay at home or work part-time in order to be with their children. At the same time, she argues, LaHaye is also making use of their consequent availability for political activity by calling on them to mobilise to defend 'God's truth . . . in our homes, in our schools, and in our country'. Even the Promise Keepers may need to be seen as something more than a resurgence of patriarchy. If evangelicals have often been favourably disposed to shifts in race relations, they have, as Debbie Daniels has noted, also often taken a more egalitarian attitude to gender than we might expect, and she has argued that even the Promise Keepers have been affected, avoiding calling for men to head the family in favour of a more ambiguous notion that 'de-emphasizes the connection between leadership and authority' (Kintz 1997: 36–7; Ehrenreich 1983: 147–8; Daniels 1998: 14–15; for a recent Christian feminist argument that the Promise Keepers have 'sent mixed signals' on the subject, see *Christianity Today* 6 September 1999).

If the importance of women in the Christian Right is one crucial factor, there are others too that need to be borne in mind when considering the relationship between gender and the right. One is the increasing importance of women within one of the Republican Party's most important allies, the gun lobby. While claims that gun ownership among women is growing have been disputed, it is certainly the case, as Elizabeth Nishiura has described, that pro-gun groups have in recent years supplemented their traditional concern with firearms ownership as a healthy expression of masculinity with a new approach that represents it as the way in which 'women can resist illegitimate, violent forms of (usually male) domination'. Through the 'Refuse to Be a Victim' women's self-defence seminar, the magazine *Women & Guns* and books such as *Armed and Female*, the right to bear arms argument has been deliberately extended in a way that uses such feminist slogans as 'the right to choose' and invokes such feminist arguments as the connection between 'Keeping a woman afraid' and keeping women 'subordinate' (Nishiura 1998: 12–14, 16, 19, 21; Sugarmann 1992: 157).

Women are also significantly involved in the Patriot movement. While James Aho found that less than 1 in 5 of the Idaho Patriots he studied were female, in her study of a California grouping Deborah Kaplan found that almost a third were women. The militias include both men and women (the Missouri 51st Militia, for instance, has claimed 1,000 members, some 30 per cent of them women) and Elinor Burkett has argued that it is often Patriot women, not Christian Rightists, who have been leading campaigns against what they see as anti-American and anti-family developments in the education of their children (Aho 1990: 148; D. Kaplan 1998: Table 2, n.p.; *Marie Claire* June 1997; Burkett 1998: 115–23).

Even the famous gender gap between Democratic and Republican voting patterns is different from what we might imagine. While it is true that women are considerably less likely to vote Republican than men (in 1998, 52 per cent of men voted for the Republicans, as against 46 per cent of women), alongside a gender gap, a marriage gap is also visible. Where 63 per cent of unmarried women voted for the

Democrats, only 44 per cent of married women did. Two years earlier 54 per cent of women who voted supported Clinton, as against 43 per cent of men. But where only 28 per cent of unmarried women voted for Dole, 43 per cent of married women had (*USA Today* 6 November 1998; Pomper 1997: 183–4, 179).

Just as some accounts of the rise of the right have focused on race, others have argued that gender antagonism is at its heart. Susan Faludi, for instance, has claimed that the New Right 'fastened on feminism, not communism or race' as its central concern, while both Rosalind Pollack Petchesky and Zillah Eisenstein see the New Right as centrally concerned with attacking women's rights. And, as we noted earlier, it has become common in recent years to combine the two issues together in the supposedly explanatory figure of the angry white male. It is an argument that can be found not only, for instance, in Daniel Junas's pioneering study of 'The Rise of the Militias', in which he puts considerable weight on a 'predominantly white, male, and middle- and working-class sector . . . buffeted by global economic restructuring' and simultaneously having its 'privileges and status' challenged by feminism and ethnic minorities. It can also be found too in the Edsalls' account, which, while it often appears to be asserting the primacy of race, is at times offering a more nuanced explanation. Thus, the first chapter opens by arguing that Republican success in presidential elections 'has been driven by the overlapping issues of race and taxes', while the book's subtitle refers to 'the impact of race, rights, and taxes', a trinity that, like the book itself, leaves space for other conflicts over the distribution of resources or prestige than that between blacks and whites. As the Edsalls note, Supreme Court decisions in the 1960s and 1970s brought such issues as school prayer and abortion on to the national political agenda, while movements seeking to extend rights to women, gays and others became increasingly associated with the Democrats, and their opponents with the Republicans. But then they close the argument in a particular way. Just as the economy began to stagnate in the mid-1970s, they write, 'the rights revolution assaulted the traditional hierarchical structure of society, and in particular the status of white men' (Faludi 1992: 263; Petchesky 1984: 255; Eisenstein 1984: 41, 87; Junas 1995: 21; Edsall with Edsall 1992: 3, cover, 69–70, 107–8).

Indeed, the conservative columnist Samuel Francis was to quote a later comment of Thomas Edsall, that it was white men who were taking the brunt of declining wages and cutbacks, to argue that their defection to the Republican Party in 1994 deserved to be rewarded. But, in his argument, it is important to note, that was precisely what the GOP was not willing to do. If the rise of the right cannot be explained by race alone, neither can it be explained by race and gender combined, and it is not surprising that, in a more recent discussion, Edsall should have included not only the impact of economic changes but the mobilising power of religious belief in his portrayal of the factors that underpinned the 1994 Republican landslide (*Populist Observer* December 1994; Edsall 1997: 136–9).

A fuller explanation, indeed, needs carefully to explore these – and other – factors in understanding the appeal of the right in general, or such strands as the Christian Right, the Patriot movement and the Buchanan movement in particular. It needs, for instance, a sensitivity towards periodisation, both in discussing America's changing role in the world economy and the experience of particular regions. Where Phillips, anticipating Republican success in the late 1960s, linked the rise of conservatism with the rise of the West and the South, other writers have linked the right not with groups enjoying economic prosperity but with those suffering economic decline. For Edsall, as for Junas, it is those who are losing, not those who are winning, who are particularly drawn to the right. But this too needs careful differentiation (Phillips 1970: 466).

In part, this is because it is not only the right that has captured such voters. In 1994, Ruy Teixeira and Joel Rogers argue, a combination of declining wages and Clinton's support for the North American Free Trade Agreement were important factors in the desertion of large numbers of non-college-educated white voters to the Republicans. This affected large numbers of women as well as men, and to ascribe the fall in Democratic support to male anger, they suggest, is to miss 'a good part of the picture'. Two years earlier, however, non-college-educated whites had expressed their economic fears – and their economic nationalism – not by voting Republican but by supporting Ross Perot. But not only is there no necessary connection between falling income and defection to the right, there are also some elements of the right who continue to draw significant support from those who are benefiting from economic change. In 1996, for instance, Buchanan supporters tended to have a lower income than those of other Republican candidates. (One estimate suggested that 32 per cent of those who supported Buchanan earned less than 30,000 dollars a year and a further 35 per cent between 30 and 50 thousand. The comparable figures for Dole supporters were 27 and 26 per cent, and for Forbes supporters 22 and 32.) Conversely, the Christian Coalition's membership has been described by Ralph Reed as 'mostly middle class' and 'employed in managerial occupations' (Teixeira and Rogers 1998: 232–3, 228–9; *Wall Street Journal* 8 March 1996; Reed 1996b: 193).

If economic change has had a differential impact, so too has religious belief. As early as the beginning of the 1960s, writers were already drawing attention to the importance for the right of what was then described as fundamentalism. But it was not until the end of the following decade that the conservative movement was to incorporate significant sections of white evangelicalism, and it would take longer still before that religious grouping would in turn reshape the social bases of both the Republican Party's membership and its electoral coalition. Yet while this group has so influenced the concerns that the party has taken up, this does not mean that opposition to abortion or homosexuality is of the same importance to the evangelical voter as it is to the evangelical conservative activist. Nor is the Christian Right to be identified with white evangelicals in another way. It not only does not speak for them all, it also speaks, although to a lesser degree, for groupings within America's other religious traditions. The Christian Coalition, for instance, has claimed that 16 per cent of its members are Catholic and 'about' 3 or 4 per cent are African Americans (Danzig 1962: 291–8; Bell 1962: 24–7; Watson 1997: 67–8).

In questioning an over-reliance on whiteness and maleness in explaining the rise of the right, this discussion has sought to do no more than clear the ground of obstacles to a better understanding of the right in general and certain strands of it in particular. We need not deny the preponderance of white men in the militias, for instance, to appreciate that when the Missouri militia officer, Kay Sheil, rejects the 'angry white male' label, declaring that the movement's 'concern about the constitutional republic . . . cuts across gender', she is raising an important issue that needs exploring rather than dismissing. This is even more the case when the black militia activist, J. J. Johnson, complains that the label 'has been gratuitiously assigned to us by . . . the same press that has painted black males as illiterates, drug addicts and gang members' and 'black women as welfare mothers, prostitutes and junkies'. If we need to think more carefully about what motivates Patriot activists, we need to apply this same caution to others on the right. In the following chapters, we will examine three of the key questions that absorb right-wing energies – opposition to gay rights, to gun control and to abortion. Each is importantly linked both to the arguments raised in this chapter and to the chapters devoted to particular movements. In discussing the gun lobby, we will be concerned, in part, with the links between the militias and racism. Opposition to homosexuality, it can readily be seen, links religious belief, gender and the right. So too does abortion – but, it will be argued, in rather different ways from those that have often been assumed (*Washington Post* 9 September 1995; Mulloy 1999: 361).

Gay rights

Before the emergence of the Christian Right at the end of the 1970s, three of the issues closest to its heart were already matters of contention. Abortion was being strongly opposed by the 'pro-life' movement, in an effort to which 'pro-family' activists were to bring vital reinforcements. Feminism was being opposed by the anti-ERA campaigning of Phyllis Schlafly and others. The third issue was that of gay rights.

The rise of a gay movement during the 1970s, like the rise of the feminist movement, inevitably met with opposition from among those who argued that such a development was incompatible with family values and Biblical injunction. In part, opposition to the two movements was intertwined, and as early as September 1974, the greater part of an issue of the *Phyllis Schlafly Report* was devoted to the argument that the ERA would be used to legalise homosexual marriages, while its account of the 1977 International Women's Year Conference gave prominent place to what it saw as the dominant role of lesbians in the feminist movement. Predominantly, however, the argument took place at local level around attempts to pass measures introducing – or opposing – gay rights (*Phyllis Schlafly Report* September 1974, December 1977).

While the battles occurred in a number of localities, one was of particular importance. This, in Dade County, Florida, saw the emergence of a well-known Christian singer, Anita Bryant, at the head of a campaign against the decision of the county commissioners to pass a gay rights ordinance. Unable to persuade them to drop their plans, she turned instead to organising a referendum to reverse the decision and, in June 1977, defeated the proposal with 69.3 per cent of the vote. Her campaign then took on a national role, and in 1978 she supported an effort by California state senator John Briggs to ban gay teachers from the classroom. Opposed by then governor Ronald Reagan as likely to lead to false charges against teachers, the Briggs initiative was unsuccessful, losing by 3.9 million votes to 2.8 million. Local struggles continued, however, and were crucial for laying some of the key foundations of the future Christian Right. Firstly, the issue drew Tim LaHaye into increasing prominence as a 'pro-family' campaigner. Secondly, although initially little noticed, it was to lead to the executive director of Briggs's 1978 campaign, Lou Sheldon, launching the Traditional Values Coalition, an organisation that prioritised opposition to homosexuality. Though preponderantly based in California, the Coalition would reach into other states and become one of the more important Christian Right groupings. Finally, struggles in California against gay rights would be the catalyst in the emergence of Christian Voice in 1978, some months before the inception of Moral Majority (Bryant 1977: 16, 85, 125; Gallagher and Bull 1996: 17–18; LaHaye 1980b: 199–200, 212–15; Jefferys-Renault and Sloan 1993: 72; Diamond 1995: 171; Diamond 1989: 62, 60).

Christian Voice remained vitally concerned with opposing the gay movement, and during the 1980 presidential election campaign its political subdivision, Christians for Reagan, achieved considerable publicity through the use of television advertisements, one of which accused President Carter of advocating 'acceptance of homosexuality' while the Republican candidate stood 'for the Traditional American Family'. In subsequent years, it continued to foreground the issue in a particularly strident way. Thus, during the 1984 elections, for instance, one of its direct mail letters declared that the Democratic Party leadership had turned away from 'God and Country and bowed down to the lustful, sinister, and perverted demands of militant homosexuals'. A victory for the Democrats, it warned, would 'turn our "one nation under God" into "one nation under GAYS"' (Moen 1992: 19; Hill and Owen 1982: 60–61; Christian Voice n.d. (1984)).

The Moral Majority too had opposed the gay movement from its beginning. Homosexuality, Falwell declared in 1980, was being presented as normal. In fact, however, it was 'Satan's diabolical attack upon the family'. It was an issue that continued to be central to his concerns. In 1984, for instance, he declared that 'militant homosexuals . . . have their eyes on our schools . . . our churches . . . our government . . . and our precious children'. It took the gradual realisation of the dimensions of the AIDS crisis, however, for anti-gay campaigning to gain greater prominence still, and, surprisingly, for it to turn against a senior official in the Reagan administration itself (Falwell 1980: 157–9; Jorstad 1987: 87).

In 1986, C. Everett Koop, a prominent pro-life evangelical who had been appointed to the post of Surgeon General some five years earlier, issued a report on AIDS. Given his background, he might have been anticipated to argue that the only way to avert the spread of AIDS was a commitment to abstinence before marriage and fidelity afterwards. But while Koop did believe this to be the ultimate answer, he also believed that education in the use of condoms was vital if AIDS was to be defeated. That Koop should support sex education for the young and be unwilling to condemn either the use of contraception outside marriage or homosexuality infuriated his former supporters, and the latter days of the Reagan administration were marked by constant attacks on him. In early 1987, Phyllis Schlafly and others, including Paul Weyrich, Howard Phillips and the American Life League's Judie Brown, launched a Coalition for Teen Health, which declared that an attempt was being made to legitimise both heterosexual and homosexual promiscuity. Koop, it demanded, should advocate abstinence rather than 'sodomy' (Martin 1997: 238–40, 249–50; *Christian News* 23 March 1987).

Drawing on internal memos, Chip Berlet has shown how during this period Weyrich's Free Congress Foundation drew up a plan to produce and promote a book arguing that AIDS was helping gay campaigners to the 'detriment of family life and our culture.' Different Christian Right organisations were carefully targeted, with Focus on the Family agreeing to promote it, the Moral Majority arranging to take 5,000–10,000 copies, and Concerned Women for America's Beverly LaHaye providing an endorsement for the book, while her organisation would offer it as part of an 'Action Kit' to 'Fight the Gay Lobby'. Soon after, the Moral Majority ceased to exist. For the other two groups, however, the issue would remain a key priority (Berlet 1993: 46–7).

If the Reagan administration came under fire for its chief medical officer's stance on AIDS, anti-gay campaigners were even more critical of the Bush administration. In part, this revolved around the funding policies of the National Endowment for the Arts, which attracted considerable criticism for its support for the gay artist Robert Mapplethorpe, the production of films presenting positive gay images and other works, most controversially Andres Serrano's *Piss*

Christ. A number of organisations, from Eagle Forum to the American Family Association, were involved in the fray, and the newly-established Christian Coalition placed advertisements in *USA Today* and the *Washington Post* daring members of Congress to 'Vote for the NEA appropriation'. 'There may be', the Coalition suggested, 'more homosexuals and pedophiles in your district than there are Roman Catholics and Baptists . . . But maybe not.' Eventually, Bush forced the resignation of the NEA director, but only after Pat Buchanan's airing of a TV advertisement during the presidential primaries showing images from a documentary on gay black men subsidised by the Endowment. The Bush administration, the advertisement declared, had 'invested our tax dollars in pornographic and blasphemous art too shocking to show . . . Even after good people protested, Bush continued to fund this kind of art' (Diamond 1995: 254–5; Cantor 1994: 28; *Socialist Review* 1996; *International Herald Tribune* 28 February 1992).

But the administration also came under fire from both the Christian Right and other conservative evangelicals for what was seen as a deliberate attempt to court gay support. Gay and lesbian groups had been invited to Bush's signing of a Hate Crimes Bill in April 1990, and in July AIDS activists were present when he signed an Americans with Disabilities Act. Then, in early 1992, as the presidential election approached, the Bush campaign held a meeting with gay and lesbian group leaders. Bush subsequently held a meeting with a number of prominent evangelicals. Emphasising that he was opposed to 'the same-sex marriage thing', he was able to dampen some of the criticism, but good relations were not fully restored until the adoption of the Republican platform. In 1988, as Duane Oldfield notes, the party platform had been 'silent on gay and lesbian rights'. The draft 1992 platform, however, declared its support for what would soon become a highly controversial issue, the continued banning of gays from the military, and was then amended during the platform hearings also to oppose gay rights legislation and same-sex marriages and adoptions (Martin 1997: 314–15; Gallagher and Bull 1996: 66; Oldfield 1996: 195, 201).

If social conservatives had seen Bush as half-hearted in his opposition to gay rights, then, as Buchanan's speech to the 1992 Republican convention made clear, Clinton was seen as representing 'the most pro-lesbian and pro-gay ticket in history'. Nor was this the only such intervention. Echoing the Christians for Reagan campaign of twelve years earlier, one anti-gay group, the Christian Action Network, attempted to avert his election by airing an advertisement that declared 'Bill Clinton's vision for a better America includes: Job Quotas for Homosexuals, Special Rights for Homosexuals, Homosexuals in the Armed Forces'. But if the issue played a part in the Presidential election campaign, it was far more important elsewhere. Two state measures to defeat gay rights legislation both came to the ballot on election day and drew a phenomenal amount of public attention (Buchanan 1992; *Radical America* September–December 1990 [actually published April 1993]).

Crucially, they took very different approaches and met with different fates. The Oregon campaign, organised by the Oregon Citizens Alliance, a conservative grouping that had emerged in the late 1980s and had already won a popular vote to overturn an executive order promoting gay rights, drew up a ballot measure that not only forbade the state to recognise sexual orientation, but also instructed government bodies to set 'a standard for Oregon's youth that recognises homosexuality, pedophilia, sadism and masochism as abnormal, wrong, and perverse . . . behaviours . . . to be discouraged and avoided'. In contrast, Colorado for Family Values, which had been established only the year before its initiative went to the vote, deliberately limited it to forbidding the state from adopting 'any statute, regulation, ordinance, or policy whereby homosexual, lesbian or bisexual orientation' would be the basis of any claim for 'minority status, quota preferences, protected status, or claim of discrimination'. Colorado's Amendment 2 was successful, receiving 53.4 per cent of the vote (subsequently, and to the fury of anti-gay campaigners, it was struck down by the Supreme Court). The Oregon measure, however, was defeated, gaining only 44 per cent support (Strinowski 1993: 6–7; Herman 1997: 139–57).

In a political atmosphere in which anti-gay activity was already crucial for the Christian Right, the decision of the Clinton administration soon after coming to office to attempt to end the ban on gays in the military brought the issue more prominence still. The day on which Pat Robertson urged viewers of his television programme, *The 700 Club*, to phone Congress with their objections, a record 436,000 calls were received by the switchboard. After Clinton's retreat on the issue, Ralph Reed noted how he had tried to dissuade a journalist from focusing on the Christian Right's involvement. It was active and retired service personnel who were particularly opposed, he argued, and 'I emphasized that we had no intention of leading the fight, which would hand Clinton an opportunity to change the subject by making us the issue.' Others, however, were more than willing to claim credit. A letter to Family Research Council supporters in the summer of 1993, for instance, claimed that the lifting of the ban had only been defeated because 'grassroots, pro-family Americans' had 'jammed the phone lines into the Capitol', written to Congress, called into talk radio programmes – and 'contributed to Family Research Council so we could do battle' (Reed 1996b: 164–5; Balz and Brownstein 1996: 102; Bauer n.d., 1993).

It was not the only battle on the issue in which the Christian Coalition had been involved. In May 1993, following a campaign that had led to the dismissal of the city schools chancellor, the organisation, in a surprising alliance with the Catholic Church, had also distributed large numbers of voters' guides for the New York City school board elections. The chancellor, Joseph Fernandez, promoted a multicultural school curriculum that supported 'acceptance of homosexuality', and many of the candidates the Coalition supported were successful. Beneath the surface of events, however, the issue was causing problems. As we shall find later, leading Republicans already had grave doubts about the political usefulness of an uncompromisingly anti-abortion stance. Similarly, while the issue of gay rights has been crucial for many on the right, there were reservations too about the effects of an anti-gay stance. Thus, in an interview that appeared in a gay weekly following the 1994 election, Gingrich announced that the party's position towards homosexuality should be 'toleration'. Most 'practicing homosexuals', he declared, were 'good citizens . . . So why would you then say that, of all the different groups you can pick on, this is the one group you're going to single out?' It was a position that, when reiterated during a television interview, led to one gay magazine's arguing that, regardless of his frequent comparison of homosexuality with alcoholism, Gingrich at least appeared to recognise that issues dear to the Christian Right were better avoided rather than running the risk of alienating moderate (or libertarian) voters. In the preceding year, conversely, Bob Dole tied himself in knots over the issue during his campaign for the Republican presidential nomination, finding particular difficulty over the appropriateness of accepting a campaign contribution from a gay Republican organisation (*Christian American* July–August 1993; *Christian News* 5 December 1994; *Out* March 1995; Gallagher and Bull 1996: 249–52).

But if leading Republicans had doubts about identifying with an anti-gay stance, there were changes afoot within the Christian Right itself. As we have noted, in 1993 Ralph Reed published an article in the Heritage Foundation's journal calling for a repositioning of the pro-family movement. Crucially, the article argued that while abortion and homosexuality were 'vital moral issues, and must remain an important part of the message', the movement needed to recognise that what had proved 'important in attracting activists and building coalitions' could prove ineffective in attracting the support of a majority of voters. A close examination of the article made it clear that homosexuality would continue to be significant for the Coalition – Reed specifically cited the New York City fight against 'instruction about the gay lifestyle' as an example of how the Coalition could extend its support. But the article did mark an important shift in emphasis that would lead to responses both from within the Christian Right and from its opponents (*Policy Review* Summer 1993).

This came sharply into view when, in 1995, the Coalition issued its *Contract with the American Family* and chose to exclude homosexuality from the ten issues it raised. As an article in the *Nation* was to indicate, the decision appeared to suggest the existence of strains within the Christian Right. In a poll of Coalition members, it observed, opposition to 'the agenda of the homosexual lobby' had been one of the issues they had most wanted in such a document. After it had failed to appear, a spokesman for the organisation claimed that since no national gay rights legislation was likely there was 'no reason to address it nationally'. Yet the Concerned Women for America, the Christian Action Network and Jerry Falwell all also borrowed the idea of a contract from the Republican party, and each of them, unlike the Christian Coalition, emphasised opposition to homosexuality (*Nation* 19 June 1995).

The *Nation* article was not the only one to question what this new departure denoted. One gay publication, for instance, cited not only the omission of homosexuality from the *Contract with the American Family* but Reed's declaration at a New York meeting that 'rhetoric that singles out gays for attack' was 'inconsistent with Christ's gospel'. On issues of sexuality that did not involve violence, he had declared, 'our policy is one of tolerance, although not necessarily approval', and when asked if such a view might be criticised from within the Christian Right, he had replied 'I don't think I'll take hits from our followers. I'll take hits from other conservative leaders who are raising money from that issue.' Such a stance, it suggested, might be part of the same process of moderation as appeared to be affecting his views on abortion. However, just as the article in the *Nation* had seen the Coalition as still pursuing an anti-gay agenda, so too did this article. Most lesbian and gay leaders, it noted, saw Reed as hypocritical, and his claim that he would not 'put the Christian Coalition out front on gay issues' did not accord well, it suggested, with either the rhetoric of his organisation's fund-raising mail or the role of Coalition activists in anti-gay campaigning (*Nation* 19 June 1995; *Out* August 1996).

Indeed, in 1995 Coalition officials had told journalists that 'they wanted to leave that issue to the states', and at local and state level, struggles over the question were continuing to break out. The Oregon Citizens Alliance, which was briefly the Christian Coalition's state affiliate, broke away again and created Citizens Alliances in Idaho and Washington. Both the Oregon and Idaho groups met with defeat in 1994, as did campaigners in Maine the following year. Some local campaigns were successful, however, and in early 1998 the Christian Coalition, now under new leadership, claimed credit for the repeal of gay rights legislation in Maine. But it was developments in Hawaii that were to propel the issue back on to the national stage (*New York Times* 18 May 1995; Strinowski 1993: 6, 8; Herman 1997: 148; Diamond 1995: 302; *Washington Post* 18 February 1998).

A trial was about to begin, Focus on the Family reported in early 1996, that could legalise same-sex marriage throughout the country. Following a decision by the Hawaii Supreme Court that the state's refusal to issue gay marriage licences was incompatible with Hawaii's previous adoption of the Equal Rights Amendment, the appeal of three couples against the state's policy had been sent back for a full hearing that was scheduled to begin on 1 August. Rather than await the decision, which, if favourable, would result in other states' having to accept any such marriages as legal, anti-gay campaigners had begun to move measures through state legislatures refusing to recognise same-sex marriages performed elsewhere. At national level legislation on the issue was also being prepared (*Focus on the Family Citizen* 22 April 1996).

The Defense of Marriage Act, which, after its passing by Congress, was signed into law in late September, gave states the right to refuse to recognise same-sex marriages and defined marriage 'for federal purposes' as the union of a man and a woman. But while anti-gay campaigners had successfully challenged the drive for gay marriage at national level, this was not to mean that they were strong enough to reverse gay movement gains in general. Defeated at the polls in Oregon and by the judiciary in Colorado, they were even more disturbed by other developments (*Advocate* 11 June 1996; *Focus on the Family Citizen* 25 November 1996).

The media, they complained, were '"desensitizing" America to the wrongness of homosexuality' and cultural elites, including members of the clergy, were increasingly regarding it as either an alternative lifestyle or an inborn characteristic. In particular, it was the last development that exercised them. While the gay movement was divided as to whether homosexuality was innate, considerable publicity was given to scientific research claiming to discover either a gay gene or a specifically gay configuration of the brain. Such findings, anti-gay campaigners frequently declared, deserved no credence and in some cases had already been disproved. Instead, they held, homosexuality was the result of failings in socialisation and could be conquered. Special ministries had emerged as early as the 1970s committed to persuading gays to abandon their sexual orientation, and in late 1995, in response to what one gay group called National Coming Out Day, the Family Research Council, the Traditional Values Coalition and other groups sponsored a National Coming Out of Homosexuality Day. This approach attracted considerably more attention when, in late 1998, the national director of the Center for Reclaiming America, an organisation set up by the leading evangelical D. James Kennedy, approached a number of other groups to fund a newspaper advertising campaign focusing on 'ex-gays' (*Family Voice* July 1992; *Focus on the Family Citizen* 16 November 1992, 22 September 1997; Herman 1997: 49, 69–72, 210–11; *Christianity Today* 13 November 1995, 7 September 1998).

Opposition to homosexuality, gay groups argued, fuelled attacks on and even murders of gays. It was a claim that anti-gay groups indignantly denied; and when, in early 1999, President Clinton called for stronger laws against hate crimes and announced plans for a national school programme where children could 'learn about the harmful impact of intolerance', the Christian Right reacted sharply. Andrea Sheldon, the executive director of the Traditional Values Coalition, accused the president of launching a 'war on Christian parents and children', while Robert Knight, a leading figure at the Family Research Council, declared that Clinton was intending 'to invade America's middle schools and colleges with the homosexual agenda'. The advertising campaign organised by the Center for Reclaiming America suggested that attacks on such figures as Senate Majority Leader Trent Lott, who (like Gingrich before him) had compared homosexuality with alcoholism, was proof that it was those who defended homosexuality who were intolerant. It was a claim that they continued to make, and plans for a new wave of advertisements were just one of the Christian Right's responses to what they saw as the threat of homosexuality (*Focus on the Family Citizen* December 1998; *Washington Times National Weekly Edition* 12–18 April 1999; *New Republic* 10 May 1999).

The Christian Right's and other social conservatives' opposition to homosexuality has a number of elements. One particularly prominent aspect is a reading of the Bible as specifically condemning sexual relationships between either men or women. Another is quite simply a revulsion against both same-sex relationships and certain forms of sex associated, although not exclusively so, with homosexuality. This, in turn, is seen as supported by the findings of a number of researchers into homosexuality, above all the extremely controversial figure of the psychologist Paul Cameron. Allied to this intermingling of religious prohibition, deep-seated hostility and appeals to scientific support are two highly symbolic associations – that between predatory males and vulnerable children and that between immorality and social dissolution.

We have already seen much of this in some of the pronouncements we have already cited. Invocations of Scripture were particularly common in such early writings as Tim LaHaye's 1978 book, *The Unhappy Gays*, reissued two years later as *What Everyone Should Know About Homosexuality*; but they can be found too, for instance, in a book published by Focus on the Family in 1995. As for revulsion against homosexuality and certain kinds of sexual activity, it has rarely been so explicitly championed as it was by Pat Buchanan when he declared in 1991: 'A visceral recoil from homosexuality is the natural reaction of a healthy society wishing to preserve itself. A prejudice against males who engage in sodomy with one another presents a normal and natural bias in favour of sound morality.' But opposition to homosexuality does not rest solely on Scripture or deep-seated antipathy. In addition to encouraging 'ex-gay' ministries, anti-gay campaigners also support the National Association for Research and Therapy of Homosexuality, a 700–strong group, some of whose members have been highly visible both in 'treating' and arguing against homosexuality. The best-known source of research support for the anti-gay cause, however, is Paul Cameron, the founder of the Institute for the Scientific Investigation of Sexuality, subsequently the Family Research Institute. Cameron achieved considerable notoriety with his claims that gays were responsible for half of all sex murders, were ten to twenty times more likely than heterosexuals to molest children and were far more likely to contract sexual diseases and to die young. Expelled from the American Psychological Association in 1983, he was involved with both the Oregon and Colorado campaigns and has been cited in many of the various anti-gay publications (LaHaye 1980a: 105–16; Burtoft 1995: 93–100; *Washington Inquirer* 29 March 1991; *Focus on the Family Citizen* 22 September 1997; *New Republic* 3 October 1994; Herman 1997: 77–8).

The link between opposition to homosexuality and images of innocent and endangered childhood takes more than one form. In some versions, it is linked in turn with fears about the socialisation of the next generation. While Falwell argued in 1980 that men's failure to lead and women's failure to be submissive resulted in children's being unable to develop proper sex roles, so James Dobson and Gary Bauer have more recently objected to the efforts of gay and lesbian teachers to influence the content of textbooks used in California schools. If 'traditionalists' don't resist such moves, they declared, then 'their sons and daughters will soon be sitting in fourth or . . . eighth grade social studies classes, reading about the wonderful exploits of their homosexual and lesbian forefathers'. But as we saw both in discussing Falwell in the mid-1980s and Cameron more recently, the link is often to the individual homosexual as predator. It is a link that can be traced back to the earliest days of anti-gay activity, in the decision by both Anita Bryant and John Briggs to title their campaigns 'Save Our Children', and it explains, in part, why anti-gay campaigners expend more energy in attacking male homosexuality than they do lesbianism. While sometimes portrayed as effeminate, gay men, Didi Herman has argued, are far more frequently seen by the Christian Right as aggressive and hypermasculine, and while lesbianism has come under fire from social conservatives (Cameron, for instance, has even claimed that lesbians are 12 times more likely than heterosexual women to have had an oral infection from heterosexual sex) it is frequently, as with our earlier reference to Schlafly, because of a perceived link between lesbianism and feminism. Thus, in an interview in 1995, Robert Knight of the Family Research Council declared that 'lesbianism is the animating principle of feminism. Because feminism, at the core, is at war with motherhood, femininity, family, and God. And lesbians are at war with all these things' (Falwell 1980: 159–60; Dobson and Bauer 1990: 31–2; Diamond 1995: 171; *California Save Our Children Bulletin*, n.d., c.1977; Herman 1997: 80–82, 98–104).

If children are seen as threatened by homosexuality, so too is society. This is already clear in Dobson and Bauer's argument, just as it is in the Traditional Values Coalition's contention that the legitimising of homosexuality would destroy the 'moral boundaries' that sustain civilisation. But it is evident too in anti-gay campaigners' invocation of the fate of errant nations in the Bible. Thus for Pat Robertson, the natural disasters that have hit America in recent years are signs of God's anger with a nation that has legalised abortion, banned school prayer and encouraged homosexuality, while for Tim LaHaye, 'when sodomy fills the national cup of man's abominations to overflowing, God earmarks that nation for destruction' (Robertson 1993: 298–9, 295; *Traditional Values Report* Summer 1996; LaHaye 1980a: 202).

While much anti-gay argument has remained constant, two important changes have taken place in recent years. The first is the emergence of a new element – the claim that rather than being associated with homophobia, Nazism should be seen as crucially linked with homosexuality. This allegation appears to have originated in the early 1990s. An article on the subject appeared in a 1992 issue of Cameron's *Family Research Report*, while in the same year another anti-gay campaigner, Gene Antonio, declared that, far from gays' being the victims of the Nazis, 'the Nazi movement – the New World Order of its day – was put on the map by militant homosexuals'. It would not be until 1994, however, that a book-length treatment of the issue appeared from two anti-gay writers, Kevin Abrams and Scott Lively. Abrams had already developed the argument in some detail in a magazine devoted to anti-gay material (the article was also reprinted by Colorado for Family Values the following year), while Lively, the Oregon Citizens Alliance's membership director, had been putting it forward at OCA meetings. It is the book, however, through which such claims can be best understood (Magnuson 1994: 57, 179; Cantor 1994: 131; *Lambda Report* August 1994; *Harvard Gay and Lesbian Review* Summer 1995; *New Republic* 14 November 1994).

Carrying recommendations from several anti-gay activists, *The Pink Swastika* was described in Abrams's preface as 'a response to the "gay political agenda" and its strategy of portraying homosexuals as victims of societal and Nazi persecution'. The book, he argued, documented how 'homosexualism, elevated to a popular ideology and combined with black occult forces, not only gave birth to Nazi imperialism but also led to the Holocaust itself'. The Nazi Party, it was claimed, had its roots in 'a number of groups in Germany which were centers of homosexual activity' and had even initially met in 'a tavern frequented by homosexual roughnecks'. How, then, was the persecution of gays that the Third Reich subsequently engaged in to be explained? For Lively and Abrams, it was to be seen as a factional struggle between militaristic gays, such as the paramilitary SA leader Ernst Roehm, and those homosexuals they considered effeminate. (Roehm's death at the hands of the SS soon after the party came to power, however, was interpreted as wholly political and unconnected with his sexuality.) Rather than anti-gay, indeed, the Nazi hierarchy was almost wholly gay itself, and when it denounced homosexuality, it was only in order either to persecute its rivals within the gay movement or to discredit political opponents (Lively and Abrams 1995: back cover, iv, 2, 1, 5–6, 102, 79–85, 95–100).

In the closing sections of the book, the authors turned their attention from Germany to the USA. Under the heading, 'American Nazis', they moved from noting the presence of homosexuality among some modern American Nazis to the claim that the leading gay publication, the *Advocate*, promoted Nazi images in its advertisements. One former leader of the militant gay group, ACT-UP, they declared, had admitted its use of 'fascist tactics', and although America had not 'experienced the wide-scale atrocities perpetrated by the Nazis in Germany', it had suffered horrific serial killings, 'reminiscent of the worst SS butchers', usually the work of homosexuals. Like pre-Nazi Germany, America had undergone a sexual revolution, the rise of 'homo-activism' and a resurgence of paganism, and its only hope, they concluded, lay in 'a Judeo-Christian renewal' (Lively and Abrams 1995: 143–6, 169, 174, 177–8, 194).

Such claims were to prove highly attractive to a number of anti-gay campaigners. Speaking in late 1994, for instance, Pat Robertson declared 'Many of those people involved with Adolf Hitler were satanists. Many of them were homosexuals. The two seem to go together', while one issue of a social conservative publication, *Culture Wars*, devoted its lead article to a seven-page excerpt from the book, and accompanied this with a further two-page review of the book, praising the 'yeoman's job' Lively and Abrams had done in 'bringing this . . . important information to the public forum' (Gallagher and Bull 1996: 276; *Culture Wars* April 1996).

It represented, however, a very different direction for anti-gay campaigning from that espoused by others in the movement. Here, we need to turn to focus not on the arguments made by Lively's group, the Oregon Citizens Alliance, but on those of the other key state organisation, Colorado for Family Values.

In early 1993, an article in the Concerned Women for America monthly contrasted the fate of the two groups' measures. In Oregon, the author noted, 'many had doubts from the onset about the group's strategy'. Including references to 'things like sadism' and 'casting homosexuality as a moral evil', particularly in a socially liberal state, had been a mistake, and the approach of Colorado for Family Values (CFV) had been far wiser. They had not asked voters 'to condemn homosexuality' nor had they dwelt on 'degrading homosexual sex practices' but had concentrated on arguing against the claim that gays were a disadvantaged minority comparable with America's blacks. The Colorado group, the article noted, had used some material on 'homosexuals' debauched lifestyle', and had also argued that gay rights would take away the rights of others; but they had concentrated on showing that gays were a 'counterfeit majority', and where the Oregon group had sought to 'legislate . . . traditional values onto a population', CFV had taken the more 'subtle' position that people should not have their values denied by 'politically correct courts' (*Family Voice* March 1993).

In understanding the Colorado group's approach, and its influence on other anti-gay campaigners, we need to see it in the light of the efforts of one of its leading figures. In early 1992, before the Colorado measure went to the polls, Focus on the Family published an article by CFV's co-founder, Tony Marco. In it, he argued that courts and civil rights authorities had defined minority groups in three ways. Firstly, a history of discrimination evidenced by low income, poor education or lack of cultural opportunity. But gays, he claimed, had a high average household income, were significantly above the average in the rate of college graduation and were far more likely to hold professional or managerial positions. The second criterion, he went on, was to exhibit clear distinguishing characteristics that defined them as a distinct group. Yet claims of scientific proof for physical differences between homosexuals and heterosexuals were not convincing, and as both a study by the Kinsey Institute and work on prison behaviour had demonstrated, many people moved in and out of periods of homosexual activity. Finally, a group deserving special protection had to demonstrate political powerlessness. But the record of gay success in achieving legislative and other changes, Marco declared, was proof that 'homosexual activists' had risen 'to a position of almost irresistible influence in today's America' (*Focus on the Family Citizen* 20 April 1992).

Some of these points were to be raised in the article in *Family Voice* the following year, and Marco was to argue along similar lines in an article in the Christian Coalition's paper in the same period. But, as Herman notes, he had resigned from CFV soon after its inception, although he had continued to advise it. As she also notes, despite 'CFV's professed embracement' of Marco's approach, during its campaign it nonetheless 'fell back on provoking outrage' by arguing that homosexuality posed dangers to both children and public health. This was a vital source of tension between the CFV leadership and Marco himself. Marco argued that if CFV continued with such an approach, it would allow gay activists to portray its proposals as 'hateful' and 'fear-mongering'. The CFV's leading figure, Will Perkins, however, replied that Marco had 'the right to his own opinion' but that the strategy would not be changed (*Christian American* February 1993; Herman 1997: 143–4, 123–4; Gallagher and Bull 1996: 123).

Marco's attempt to persuade anti-gay campaigners to recast their argument against homosexuality did not take place in isolation. One reason why it received such favourable attention from national organisations was that it coincided with a broader shift in the Christian Right's discourse, so that, rather than speaking in the language of the evangelical subculture, it could find ways of appealing more broadly. In 1991, Focus on the Family published a looseleaf book intended to arm local activists in the fight against the gay movement. 'You know', it declared, 'that homosexuality is wrong, and you believe it is wrong because the Bible says so.' But to oppose the homosexual agenda effectively, it continued, arguments were needed that could convince those who did not believe in the Bible. In part, the arguments were those championed by Marco. (His 1992 article had not, it is important to note, been his first attempt to argue along such lines.) Gay rights laws, it declared, ignored the fact that homosexuals already had the same rights as everyone else, and sought to extend to a group that could change its behaviour a status intended for such innate groups as races and sexes. But, as with the CFV itself, this was linked to the older arguments that Marco had sought to abandon. Gay rights measures, the book argued, stopped people having 'the right to discriminate' when homosexuals were dangerous to the health of others. Furthermore, it claimed, they were disproportionately responsible for child molestation and serial murder (Focus on the Family n.d. (1991): 9–12, 15; *Focus on the Family Citizen* 20 April 1992).

Following its victory at the polls, Colorado for Family Values itself was to organise two conferences, the more ambitious of which drew from states ranging from Alaska to Texas and from organisations from Focus on the Family and the Christian Coalition to Kansas Education Watch and New Mexico's Mothers Against Bad Government. Among the publications coming out of these gatherings was a 'Practical Workbook' of 'Winning Plans, Strategies and Observations for engaging the Militant Homosexual Agenda' in which it emphasised its rejection of what it saw as the 'conventional wisdom' among anti-gay campaigners, that they had to concede civil rights to their opponents and appeal instead to 'people's God-given revulsion towards homosexuality'. Instead, it declared, by making what it called 'a civil-rights argument for denying homosexuals protected status', CFV had given 'people a chance to access their religious and visceral feelings', deepening the support that the organisation's more judicious approach had succeeded in winning (*Freedom Writer* August 1994; *Freedom Watch* July–August 1994; Colorado for Family Values n.d., *c.*1993: cover, II-1-2).

Just as Reed's attempt to downgrade anti-gay activity was only partially successful, the same can be said for Marco's attempt to reconfigure the anti-gay argument. Indeed, there is evidence that a particularly draconian attitude continues to exert influence in at least some parts of the movement. As we have already noted, one of the most commented-upon aspects of the form of socially conservative Christianity known as Reconstructionism is its advocacy of capital punishment for blasphemy, adultery and homosexuality. Such an approach is by no means unique to Reconstructionists. In the late 1970s, the Indianapolis pastor Greg Dixon, subsequently a leader of the Moral Majority, preached a sermon calling for the death penalty for homosexuality, while Tim LaHaye was to note that homosexuality had not only been condemned in the Bible but had been treated as a capital offence. 'Who', he went on, 'is *really* being cruel and inhuman – those whose leniency allows homosexuality to spread to millions of

victims . . . or those who practised Old Testament capital punishment?' By the early 1980s, however, a California spokesman for the
Moral Majority was to be repudiated by Falwell after he declared that
homosexuality deserved the death penalty. Yet sympathy for such
views within the Christian Right has not totally disappeared today.
Thus one book, published in the early 1990s and recommended by the
Christian Coalition, found it useful to cite a thirteenth-century law
code prescribing the death sentence for men 'having intercourse with
each other, against nature and natural custom' as evidence of the med-
ieval church's continuation of 'the honored tradition of the ancient
church in its forthright condemnation of homosexuality' (Peron 1981:
7, footnotes (n.p.); LaHaye 1980a: 107; Lienesch 1982: 418; Grant and
Horne 1993: 213; *Christian American* January–February 1996).

Furthermore, if, in some quarters, the death penalty has been
defended, another penalty has also received attention. During a television programme in the late 1980s, Paul Cameron was to observe that
Jefferson, 'one of our most liberal thinkers in the western world', had
favoured castration for male homosexuals, while 'homosexual
females' were to have a 'hole drilled through the cartilage of their
nose'. It is somewhat more startling, however, to find Focus on the
Family also offering as evidence of 'the accumulated wisdom of centuries' the observation that until 1861 homosexuality had been a
capital offence in England, while Jefferson's support for male castration and female mutilation had specified in the latter case that the hole
be 'no less than one-quarter inch in diameter' (Diamond 1989: 101–2;
Focus on the Family n.d. (1991): 18).

If the Christian Right has continued to regard opposition to
homosexuality as among its most important priorities, it has not been
the only anti-gay group on the American right. We have already noted
the involvement of such figures as Paul Weyrich. The most important
radical right group, the John Birch Society, has also been strongly
antagonistic to gay rights, as is well illustrated by its publication in
late 1986 of an enthusiastic review of a book that, it claimed, deserved
'a place on every Americanist's bookshelf'. *AIDS: A Special Report*,
was co-authored by three men, two of whom, David Noebel and Paul
Cameron, would subsequently be central figures in Colorado for
Family Values. Its 52 recommendations, which the reviewer held
should be studied by every policy-maker at federal, state and local
level, ranged from the closing down of gay bars and bookstores and
the quarantining of those testing HIV-positive to the reaffirmation of

God's creation of male and female and the advising of all gays 'to return quietly and hastily to the closet and cease all homosexual activity' (*New American* 29 September 1986; Herman 1997: 141, 143, 77).

At first sight, the Patriot movement is similarly opposed to homosexuality. In the late 1970s, for instance, the *Spotlight* was an enthusiastic supporter of both Anita Bryant and the Briggs campaign, while in 1991 Populist Party members in New York and New Jersey launched the American Conservative Alliance in order 'to network with different conservative, patriotic and nationalist groups'. Over the next two years, the party's paper subsequently reported, alliances were made 'with groups that we thought we could never work with', in a process of networking that included co-operating with 'black and white conservative groups' against homosexuality. Yet if the vision of Populist Party members working with black (and, as was also noted, conservative Jewish) groupings is somewhat surprising, so too is the debate that rocked sections of the Patriot movement in the same period (Diamond 1995: 156, 362; *Populist Observer* April 1993).

In the run-up to Bo Gritz's 1992 presidential election campaign Identity leader Pete Peters had helped fund the distribution of Gritz's book, *Called to Serve*; but their relationship was to sour following Gritz's announcement that he was not 'personally' in support of the death penalty for homosexuality. In response, Peters published a pamphlet advocating such a punishment, and Gritz subsequently reported that Peters was telling supporters not to vote for him because 'I will not support the persecution of homosexuals . . . I don't support homosexuality. I'm a Christian. But I don't think they should be persecuted' (*Soldier of Fortune* September 1992; Crawford *et al.* 1994: 2.23, 43).

Dedicated to 'my Colonel friend who inadvertently inspired me to write this', Peters' pamphlet emphasised that the Bible had declared that 'If a man also lie with mankind, as he lieth with a woman' then both had 'committed an abomination; they shall surely be put to death'. To sign 'petitions to stop the advancement of homosexuals', as the 'lukewarm Judeo-Christians' of Colorado for Family Values were seeking to do, was not enough. Indeed, Peters observed, its chairman had claimed that the CFV measure would not deny homosexuals 'the same basic constitutional rights' as other Americans, or deny them the right to 'live with whomever they wish'. Forty years ago, 'family values in America' had denied these rights, 'and thus, the homosexual was afraid to come out of the closet'. Now, however, supposed Christians wanted homosexuals to have rights when the Bible allowed no such thing (Peters 1992: n.p., i, iii–iv; for other Identity calls for the death penalty for homosexuals, see Crawford *et al.* 1994: 2.23–24; Bushart, Craig and Barnes 1998: 78–9).

Significantly, Gritz had also drawn fire during his campaign for expressing doubts on whether it was right to ban either marijuana use or prostitution. For others in the Patriot movement too, a libertarian impulse struggled with a moralist one. In some cases, it was libertarianism that ultimately lost out. Thus in the mid-1990s one Patriot magazine, the *AntiShyster*, published an extended extract of an article by Paul Cameron, 'Medical Consequences of What Homosexuals Do', preceded by a long explanation by the magazine's editor (who had previously been a Libertarian Party election candidate) on how he was now persuaded that gay rights were 'dangerous', having long believed that what adults did sexually with other adults was up to them (Novick 1995: 257–8; *AntiShyster* 6.2, n.d., c.1996; Militia Watchdog 1996).

The previous year, however, the contrary impulse appears to have won out, when an alliance between the Idaho Citizens Alliance and the United States Militia Association proved to be short-lived. The ICA claimed that it had decided to break with the USMA. The militia leader, Samuel Sherwood, however, declared that having read the ICA's proposed ballot initiatives on homosexuality, abortion and education he had concluded they 'violated the Declaration of Independence' (Yurman 1995).

Yet, if some in the movement have doubts about the anti-gay cause, others do not. The *Free American*, for instance, has published several articles on the 'Homosexual Agenda', while the newsletter of the Virginia Citizen's Militia has even declared that 'ABORTION AND ESPECIALLY HOMOSEXUALITY ARE THE GREATEST MORAL EVILS OF OUR DAY!' Indeed, in 1995 it was reported that Kevin Tebedo, a leading figure in Colorado for Family Values, had joined up with Patriot leader Eugene Schroder and state senator Charles Duke in a campaign against what it saw as government abuses of power. The homosexual lobby clearly wanted the family redefined, Tebedo declared, and what was there to stop the state's Governor from using his emergency powers to declare that both homosexuality and polygamy were protected? As a result of his growing involvement in the Patriot movement, however, Tebedo resigned from CFV, explaining to a press conference that he and its executive board had agreed 'that my personal beliefs and motivations have expanded beyond the scope of CFV's mission' (*Free American* October, December 1997, August 1998, June 1999; *Southern Ranger* January–February 1999; *Turning the Tide* Winter 1995–6; Burghardt and Crawford 1996: 29).

More needs to be said about the links between the Patriot movement and libertarianism and those between libertarianism and gay rights, and we will be returning to both later. We can already see, however, some of the problems that anti-gay campaigning have thrown up for the right. The Christian Right has continued to find the issue central to its concerns, but remained uncertain both as to how best to oppose gay rights and of how reliable either the Republican leadership or some in their own ranks would prove in carrying the fight to success. For Patriots, for their part, it was not always so certain what stance they took on the issue. It has both brought elements of the right together and divided them, and in the next chapter, we will turn to another issue through which the same process and the same complexity can be observed – the fight against gun control.

4

Gun rights

While it has been the subject of considerable discussion in recent years, it is somewhat surprising that little has been written on the relationship between the fight against gun control and the right. Studies of the gun lobby have given little attention to its links with conservative politics, while studies of conservatism have almost completely ignored the importance of opposition to gun control. Only in some of the discussion of the far right in America has the guns issue received the attention it deserves, and then too often in isolation from both the mainstream of the gun lobby and the Republican right. In this chapter, I want to explore the rise of the gun lobby in America, the arguments it makes and the role it has played in right-wing politics. I want then to turn to one of the most publicised aspects of the firearms controversy in recent years, the emergence of the militias. In examining their origin, I will be particularly concerned with arguments about the militias' links with the racist right; but I also want to examine the extent to which they are linked not only to disputes over the regulation of gun ownership but to the gun lobby itself.

The argument over guns in the United States cannot be understood without referring to the celebrated Second Amendment of the American Constitution and the contested nature of its phrasing. Drawn up in the aftermath of the revolt against the British and amidst considerable dispute as how to secure new-won liberty, the second of the ten Amendments that made up the Bill of Rights declared 'A well-regulated militia being necessary to the security of a free state, the right of the people to keep and bear arms shall not be infringed.' As an examination of documents of the time makes clear, the Amendment was underpinned by a distrust of government. But it was connected too to the belief that a standing army was a danger to freedom and that only an armed people could be trusted to resist oppression. It is at this point, however, that the gun lobby and its critics diverge (Bijlefeld 1997: 2–16; Spitzer 1995: 28–35).

Advocates of gun control and, indeed, the Supreme Court on several occasions, have sought to argue that the Amendment refers not to individuals, and the private possession of firearms, but to state militias, and their ability to mobilise in defence of state and nation. Such a concern, it is argued, is now obsolete in an age not of muskets and militiamen, but advanced technology and professional armed services. Militias in the original sense had gradually eroded in the years following the passing of the Second Amendment, and the decision in 1903 to inaugurate a National Guard meant that states could now call on some of their citizens to perform the tasks once assigned to the people. There is another reason too for seeing the Amendment as no longer pertinent, since the militia had in fact not been composed of the people as a whole, but only of able-bodied white males aged between 18 and 45 (Bijlefeld 1997: 18–19; Spitzer 1995: 35–45).

Nonetheless, the Amendment continues to be part of the Constitution and has been used to champion not one but two distinct rights. The first, to which we will return, is the right to create an armed militia. The second, and the dominant aspect of the gun lobby's argument, is the right of individuals to own firearms for recreation or defence, free of government restrictions.

In the twentieth century, the principal defender of gun ownership has been the National Rifle Association (NRA). Established in 1871, the Association has grown to an organisation of around 3 million members, which, alongside its shooting competitions, firearms safety courses, insurance packages and other membership services, has concentrated on lobbying against restrictive legislation and intervening in elections in an attempt to ensure that its allies are elected and its enemies defeated. In 1980 it endorsed Reagan (he addressed the NRA convention the year before the 1984 contest), while in 1988 it campaigned for the election of George Bush. Capable of mobilising considerable support, it has played a highly visible role in many contests. In the 1994 congressional elections, for instance, it spent $5.3 million in campaign contributions, independent expenditures on behalf of favoured candidates and internal campaigns aimed at its own members telling them how to vote. Some 79 per cent of the campaign contributions and 87 per cent of the independent expenditures went to support Republicans, with gun owners providing a third of Republican candidates' votes. In the late 1980s, an article in the

Heritage Foundation journal complained that the NRA was refusing to work with conservatives in their efforts to shift the composition of the Supreme Court. It was also at fault, the article declared, in following an electoral strategy more calculated to punish the Bush administration, with which it was in dispute, than to strengthen links with conservative Republicans. Five years later, however, the NRA was taking part in meetings of Grover Norquist's conservative coalition, seen both by him and the Republican hierarchy as crucial to challenging Democrat incumbents in potentially Republican districts (Shaiko and Wallace 1998: 156–8; *Newsweek* 23 August 1999; Sugarmann 1992: 25–6, 170, 63; Davidson 1993: 142–5; *Mother Jones* July–August 1996; Balz and Brownstein 1996: 197–8, 181–2; *Rolling Stone* 31 October 1996; *Policy Review* Summer 1989; Dreyfuss 1996: 204).

An organisation whose members have included several Presidents, the NRA has been involved in a wide range of battles since gun control became a significant issue in the aftermath of the assassination of President Kennedy in November 1963. For the NRA, 'antigunners' are pursuing an agenda that threatens gun owners and 'gun rights', and their arguments have particularly centred around two questions: what restrictions can be put on purchasing a firearm and whether certain types of gun are too dangerous to be allowed in private ownership (Sugarmann 1992: 16; Davidson 1993: 150).

The first of these disputes, as we might expect, has a special link with the Kennedy assassination. The ease with which a gun could be purchased by mail order was already the subject of Congressional investigation when Kennedy was killed by just such a weapon. But an attempt to ban such purchases was successfully defeated, and it was only after the murders of Martin Luther King and Robert Kennedy in 1968 that legislation was passed to stop the interstate sale, first, of handguns, and then of rifles and shotguns. In 1986, however, in a very different political environment, a bill was passed reversing the latter measure. Arguments for restrictions, however, did not stop in 1968 or remain linked with purchasing by post. For those in favour of gun control, easy access to weapons is both advantageous to criminals and a contributory factor in the escalation of domestic quarrels into manslaughter or murder. The imposition of compulsory waiting periods, during which background checks can be carried out, formed the central plank of one of the most controversial gun control measures, the Brady Bill, named after the White House press secretary who had been seriously injured in the 1981 shooting in which President Reagan had been wounded. In 1988 the gun lobby ensured that the first attempt to pass the Bill failed. In 1991, however, both chambers passed the measure, but the Senate's decision to attach it to a controversial crime bill made progress impossible; and only in 1993, with the support of the new administration, did it eventually pass (Sugarmann 1992: 35–42; Spitzer 1995: 149, 157–62).

If the introduction of waiting periods has been a key issue for the NRA, it was even more exercised by proposals to ban the ownership of certain weapons altogether. Criminals' use of weapons able to fire a large number of rounds led during the late 1980s to calls from police and others for their removal from private hands, and in 1989 the Bush administration announced an import ban on five kinds of semi-automatic assault weapons, a move that was subsequently expanded to cover a further thirty-eight makes. This development was to prove particularly damaging to the NRA, forcing it into conflict both with a Republican administration and the police. An enthusiastic proponent of tougher sentencing and a stronger law and order stance in general, the NRA had already come into conflict with law enforcement organisations earlier in the decade for its defence of so-called cop-killer bullets. (They were eventually banned in 1986.) Having been accused of putting police lives at risk over bullets that could pierce bulletproof clothing, the NRA now faced the same charge over assault weapons, and while attempts in 1990 and 1991 to follow the import ban with a bill aimed at domestically manufactured weapons were successfully beaten off, in 1994 a measure to ban the sale and possession of nineteen types of assault weapon was finally passed. Just as Bush's stance on the import of assault weapons was to cost him the NRA's support in 1992, Dole's decision to abandon his pledge to the NRA that he would pursue a reversal of the assault weapons ban led it to decide not to support his candidacy in 1996 (Sugarmann 1992: 205–8, 183–7, 211–14; Spitzer 1995: 152–6, 106; Woodward 1996: 123; *National Review* 14 October 1996).

The NRA has often been described as a formidable lobbying force. Legislators who have considered supporting gun control measures have frequently been unwilling to take on the Association, and in 1997 the business magazine, *Fortune*, surveyed over 2,000 members of Congress, White House officials, professional lobbyists and others to find which lobby groups were considered the most powerful. The NRA was ranked sixth (the Christian Coalition was seventh, the National Right to Life Committee tenth). But if the NRA is so powerful, why, then, has it suffered significant defeats in recent years? In part, it has been argued, its electoral strength has been overstated; not only were other issues involved on occasions in which it deserved credit for the defeat of particular candidates, but many of those it supported either would have won anyway or actually lost. There has also been, as we have suggested, a breach with allies in law enforcement and the Republican Party followed by the coming to power in 1993 of a Democrat gun control supporter. As Robert Spitzer notes, between 1968 and 1988 no Congressional gun control bill ever made it to the vote. Since then, that has been far from the case. Nonetheless, not only can it still play a significant role in some elections; it has not lost on the widespread ownership of firearms. It feels itself beleaguered, but, unlike the anti-abortion movement, for instance, it has not seen what it believes in comprehensively defeated and that defeat still not in prospect of reversal (Davidson 1993: 141, 145–7; *National Right to Life News* 18 November 1997; Spitzer 1995: 117, 129, 152).

The NRA has argued its views in many outlets, from its own magazines and those produced commercially for gun enthusiasts to press advertisements and even its own radio show. In 1994, its executive vice-president and most influential figure in recent years, Wayne LaPierre, produced a book in order to equip supporters with the organisation's arguments, and it is to this that we can most easily turn for the NRA's views. In part, these address the key areas of conflict between the gun lobby and gun control supporters in recent years. Millions of Americans, he argued, owned semi-automatic weapons. To ban such weapons would not reduce crime; they were rarely used by criminals and could be obtained illegally anyway. As for waiting periods, these too did not deter criminals, but would 'prevent law-abiding people from purchasing handguns without delay when they needed firearms the most – for self-protection' (Shaiko and Wallace 1998: 160, 162; Davidson 1993: 238, 250–51; LaPierre 1995: 60, 57–9, 42–3).

The book also discusses an issue that has arisen more recently, the passing of laws in a number of states allowing 'law-abiding citizens' to carry concealed weapons in public. This measure, LaPierre argues, has had a marked effect on the willingness of criminals to approach the possibly not so defenceless. But, as we would expect, his opposition to gun control proposals is not merely argued on a case-by-case basis. Instead, it is placed within an overarching argument, that the

Second Amendment defends the right to own guns (though not, he adds, bazookas or nuclear devices) and that any attempt to restrict this is not only unAmerican, but represents 'just one more step in the march toward national disarmament'. In arguing against gun control, LaPierre holds that the real solution to crime is tougher sentencing. But he also makes an argument to which we will return when we discuss the militia movement. In 1993, he notes, President Clinton announced that he saw the Brady Bill as 'only the beginning' of gun control and instructed the Justice Department to examine proposals for the registration of guns. But registration, he declared, would result in confiscation, and 'a people disarmed is a people in danger'. In Nazi Germany, 'firearm registration helped lead to the holocaust' and one of the reasons why such a horror could not happen in America was the Second Amendment – 'the ultimate safeguard against despotism and genocide'. It was a view that was stated even more starkly in an NRA fund-raising letter sent out by LaPierre a few days before the Oklahoma City bombing, in which he declared that 'You can see . . . our freedoms slowly slipping away when jack-booted government thugs, wearing black, armed to the teeth, break down a door, open fire with an automatic weapon, and kill or maim law-abiding citizens.' As the Weaver case and Waco had shown, he argued, under Clinton, 'if you have a badge' you can intimidate or even commit murder. 'America's gun owners will only be the first to lose their freedoms. If we lose the right to keep and bear arms, then the right to free speech, free practice of religion, and every other freedom in the Bill of Rights are sure to follow' (LaPierre 1995: 29–39, 15–18, 51, 126, 84, 86, 167; Stern 1996: 110–11).

The NRA has long suffered from internal disagreements on how it should best defend gun owners' rights. As Dan Balz and Ronald Brownstein remark, 'like a banana republic', the NRA 'combines palace intrigues, contending factions, lots of guns, and periodic coups'. Most famously, in 1977, suggestions that the organisation should move out of Washington and concentrate on providing recreational facilities for its members led to a revolt at its Cincinnati conference in which a hard-line group took control of its board of directors. One of the leaders of the revolt, Neal Knox, was to be removed from his position as head of the organisation's Institute for Legislative Action in the early 1980s, and his subsequent decision to campaign against the organisation's position on a proposed bill led to his removal from the board. But the Association's problems, both

financial and political, gave Knox his opportunity at the organisation's 1991 convention when, at the head of a militant slate for the
elections to the board, he was to return to power. Under his influence,
the NRA took a particularly hard-line stance, as was well demonstrated when in late 1994 the organisation circulated an article by him
in which he noted that a recent incident in which shots had been fired
at the White House was but the latest of a whole series of outrages,
ranging from the Kennedy and King assassinations to the Hungerford
massacre in England, that had led to gains for the gun control cause.
They had happened too often to be coincidental, he suggested, but
'with drugs and evil intent', some of them could have been deliberately engineered 'for the purpose of disarming the people of the free
world' (Balz and Brownstein 1996: 192; Sugarmann 1992: 48–51, 61,
64–5, 230–33, 239–40; *E Pluribus Unum* January 1995).

Disputes over how the NRA was managed and whether it should
pursue a purist strategy or a pragmatic one was to lead to a bitter conflict between Knox and LaPierre. LaPierre (whose approach was compared by one conservative journalist to that of Ralph Reed) held that
the organisation needed to be 'positioned in the mainstream' if it was
going to survive. The NRA, he held, faced a 'watershed moment' in
which it had to choose whether or not to embrace the 'fringe' ideology of the militias. Knox, who had replied that if the organisation
were ever in the mainstream then 'our gun rights will be a thing of the
past', fought hard to remove LaPierre from office but, at the 1997
annual meeting, his candidates were defeated and he was removed
from his position of first vice president. The NRA in the aftermath of
his departure continues to take what many would describe as a hard-
line stance. (The NRA's President, Charlton Heston, was subsequently to tell a conservative gathering that a 'cultural war' had been
launched against white Protestants, heterosexuals and gun owners.)
Attempts by gun control forces to put forward limits on gun ownership in the aftermath of a wave of killings in the late 1990s have met
with concerted opposition. But the organisation has both had to
manoeuvre in attempting to defeat these and other attempts and, as
its refusal to support the 1996 Dole candidacy indicated, has also
experienced problems in its relationship with leading Republicans.
As with the Christian Right or, as we shall see, the anti-abortion movement, the leading group in a movement rarely escapes criticism, and
rival groups have emerged that argue that the NRA has refused to
pursue an intransigent enough position. During the Brady Bill debate,

for instance, the NRA supported an instant background check before a gun could be bought, a position which, the *Spotlight* later observed, had 'infuriated many Second Amendment purists' (*American Spectator* May 1997; *Washington Post* 6 May 1997; *Wake Up Call America* September–October 1998, March–April 1999; *National Review* 14 June 1999; *Newsweek* 28 June 1999; *Gun Owners* 31 December 1996; *Free American* September 1998; *Spotlight* 5 July 1999).

Three groupings in particular have proved attractive to such purists. The Gun Owners of America was founded in 1975 by Bill Richardson, a California state senator and former John Birch Society organiser. In recent years, claiming 150,000 members, it has been led by the equally conservative Larry Pratt, a former Virginia state legislator and a leading figure in the 1996 Buchanan campaign. Another grouping, the Citizens Committee for the Right to Keep and Bear Arms, established in 1974 by Alan Gottlieb, a conservative activist and direct mail expert, is also highly active, with over 100 members of Congress among the organisation's Advisors, while a third organisation, the American Pistol and Rifle Association, long involved in the Patriot movement, has recently merged with Gun Owners of America (Sugarmann 1992: 130–38; Stern 1996: 117; Zeskind 1995: 61; Flynn and Gerhardt 1989: 228–9; *Wake Up Call America* March–April 1996).

The rivalry between these groups and the NRA has been an important, and neglected, dynamic in gun lobby politics. But it has implications for another question too. As we noted earlier, the rise of the militia movement and the subsequent Oklahoma City bombing have been much discussed, but in ways that have not always been helpful. In particular, we need to look again at the vexed question of the relationship between the militias and racism. And, as we shall see, this is closely connected to another question – the links between the militias and the gun lobby.

While the emergence of paramilitary groups in early 1994 initially attracted little interest, this was to change dramatically following the federal building bombing in April of the following year. The two men eventually convicted of the attack, Timothy McVeigh and Terry Nichols, held anti-government views and read Patriot literature and, while they had not joined any militia, many accounts linked the terrorist attack with the armed movement that was now visible nationally. Each of the precipitating factors in the creation of the movement were linked with guns. The events at Ruby Ridge, Idaho, in August 1992 came about after Randy Weaver had refused to inform on the racist group, Aryan Nations, in order to avoid prosecution for a fire-arms offence. The massive loss of life at Waco had come about after an abortive raid by the Bureau of Alcohol, Tobacco and Firearms (BATF) in pursuit of illegal weapons. Early the following year, when the two most important groups, the Militia of Montana and the Michigan Militia, were set up, another factor had come into play, the Brady Bill and the imminence of the assault rifle ban. Guns were crucial in the rise of the militia movement, as an examination of its pronounce-ments makes very clear (*New York Times* 15 June 1997; *USA Today* 8 January 1998; Stern 1996: 191–9, 21, 38–9, 58–60).

Thus Norman Olson, the pastor (and gun-shop owner) who initi-ated the Michigan Militia, argued that 'the Second Amendment is really the First in our country, because without guns for protection from tyrants, we would have no free speech', while the Militia of Montana declared that Jefferson had been right that the 'strongest reason for the people to retain the right to keep and bear arms' was to protect them-selves against a tyrannical government. Nor were such views confined to the best-known groups. Most militias had been formed by private citizens; but in late July 1994, the conservative periodical, *Human Events*, reported that, in response to 'the intensifying national assault on gun ownership', the Board of County Commissioners in Santa Rosa County, Florida, had passed a resolution establishing a militia. Three other counties had done likewise, and the establishment of hundreds of militias across the country, the magazine declared, demonstrated how 'gun ownership rights' had become a crucial popular issue. Both Larry Pratt of the Gun Owners of America and John Snyder of the Citizens Committee for the Right to Keep and Bear Arms were cited in the article, Snyder declaring that militias were 'a primal expression of frustration' against the Clinton administration's plans for gun control. Indeed, the month before the libertarian magazine, *Freedom Network News*, had reported a mass rally in the state capital calling for militias to march on Washington in support of the Second Amendment (*Northern Express* 22 August 1994; Militia of Montana n.d.: 2; *Human Events* 22 July 1994; *Freedom Network News* June–July 1994).

But if opposition to gun control was a central feature of the mili-tias, it was not the only one. As we shall explore later, they can only be fully understood in the context of the Patriot movement of which they are part. Here, however, it would be appropriate to examine one of the most influential accounts of the emergence of militias. Larry Pratt, as we shall see, had long advocated the creation of such organisations. In arguing this, he had spoken before audiences whose views extended considerably beyond the rights of gun owners, and it was at one such gathering, it has been argued, that the militias had their origin, an origin that ties them to a firmly racist agenda.

In October 1992, in response to the Weaver shootings, a meeting took place in Estes Park, Colorado. Organised by Christian Identity pastor Pete Peters, it has been described by one of the key writers on the extreme right, Leonard Zeskind, as marking 'the birth of the modern militia movement'. During his address to the meeting, Pratt had argued that people like Dick Armey were needed to offer leadership within Congress. He had declared too that, while more needed to be done, the NRA was beginning to move in a more hard-line direction. But what he had also done, surrounded by white supremacists, was to call for 'an armed militia able to organize quickly and effectively'. In part, Zeskind's article on the meeting discussed the NRA's stance towards the militias, a subject to which we shall return. But its main focus was to argue for the seminal role of the Estes Park meeting. A closer examination of both the gathering and the militia movement itself, however, poses a series of problems for this interpretation (Zeskind 1995: 55, 60, 56–7).

The gathering was attended by 160 'concerned Christian men', who, Peters subsequently wrote, had come together, listened to speakers and then established a series of committees to 'take counsel' and report back to the entire assembly. A number of topics were discussed, ranging from taking part in radio phone-ins to the possibility of taking legal action. But of the five committees, the two that are of most relevance for our purposes were the Divine Ways and Means Committee, whose responsibilities included an examination of 'Bible prerequisites to direct action', and the even more dramatically titled Sacred Warfare Action Tactics (SWAT) Committee, established to 'evaluate what our people would be forced to consider should tyranny and despotism become the order of the day and no other recourse is available' (Peters n.d. (1992): 1, 4, 7, 8).

The first of these committees had concluded that 'a Christian civil body politic' would emerge first at local level, and then more generally. It would have the power to 'punish all disobedience to God's Laws'; but, the committee argued, there was also both Biblical precedent for what had been termed 'vigilante action' and clear guidance as to how Christians should deal with oppressive government. It should first be petitioned with 'specific grievances', and then charged with acting against the Constitution and God's Laws; and, finally, it was declared, action should be taken along the lines proposed by the SWAT Committee. Careful consideration should also be given, the committee added, 'to the concept of church militias', which had been 'common with our Christian forefathers in the 17th and 18th centuries'. (Peters n.d. (1992): 12–13).

The Divine Ways and Means Committee recommended the proposals of the SWAT Committee. What were they? It is evident that the report was not as forthcoming as it might be, since its chairman, Identity leader Earl Jones, told the gathering that 'angry' committee members had brought more information than could be found in a 'Special Forces manual', but that they had been careful to avoid producing a document that could result in the government's bringing conspiracy charges against 'the whole bunch of us'. Nonetheless, while the committee recommended non-violence 'for the time being', the report noted that it had discussed the idea of leaderless resistance. The better to explain this notion, which, it suggested, should be understood in the light of 'the body of believers' acting individually under the instructions of Christ's 'word and Holy Spirit', it included an edited version of an article on the subject by Louis Beam. Beam's article, aimed at those who 'love our people, culture, and heritage', argued that the federal government would not allow organised opposition. The answer was to adopt the cell structure as used by Communists, but with one vital difference. Where the Communists retained a centralised leadership, the committees of correspondence in the American Revolution had not. Those who sought 'to defeat state tyranny' today, Beam declared, must adopt the latter approach. Newspapers, leaflets and computers could be used to inform the movement, but each cell or individual would act in their own way. 'No one need issue an order to anyone' (Peters n.d. (1992): 17–23; Dees with Corcoran 1996: 49–50, 63).

Peters's Report was not the only account of the gathering circulating among racist activists, and one that appeared in the Identity publication associated with Louis Beam is of particular interest. It summarised a number of contributions, ranging from Pratt's defence of the 'God-given right to keep and bear arms' to Beam's call for unity against the New World Order. It did note that one speaker had called for the creation of militias, but this was not Pratt but a Baptist Pastor, Greg Dixon, who had 'admonished his listeners to establish Constitutional militias within their churches – as he had done'. The Sacred Warfare Action Tactics committee, the paper noted, had discussed leaderless resistance, which the writer defined as 'a concept wherein Yahweh gives each man his inspiration for defensive action'. But this report did not emphasise the call for militias, and the leaderless resistance espoused by the Identity believer and former Klansman Louis Beam and the church militias championed by the former Moral Majority leader (and critic of Identity), Greg Dixon, were significantly different both from each other and from the eventual form the militia movement took over a year later. This is not to deny that some militia groups have shown interest in Beam's organisational ideas. To describe the movement as leaderless, however, would be to mistake fragmentation and organisational rivalry for a conscious rejection of the very command structures that Beam had argued had to be abandoned, but that the militias were to retain (*Jubilee* November–December 1992; Dees with Corcoran 1996: 87; on Dixon, see Georgianna 1989: 12; *BEHOLD!* February 1997).

If the militias that actually emerged were organisationally different from those envisaged at Estes Park, they were often also multiracial. The co-founder of the Michigan Militia, for instance, declared 'We've been recruiting blacks, Jews, Hispanics, and other minorities into the militias. We sure wouldn't be doing that if we were racist', while one Midwestern leader, asked about his group's membership rules, had replied, 'The first time I see a swastika, the first time I hear the word "nigger", the first time I hear the word "Jew" in a bad way, that's it. They're out.' This is not to deny that the militias were predominantly white or that racists were highly active within them. (Indeed, it is somewhat ironic that a newspaper article citing a Texas militia commander's advocacy of recruiting ethnic minorities was to be reprinted in the main extreme right paper, the *Spotlight*.) What it does mean, however, is that racists were forced to struggle for hegemony within the movement, and it was not theirs from its inception (*New American* 6 February 1995; *Christian Science Monitor* 20–26 October 1995; *Wake-Up Call America* February 1995).

If we are to argue that the militias are markedly different from what was envisaged at Estes Park, the extended gap between the gathering and the subsequent emergence of a paramilitary movement also deserves far more attention than it has so far received. Evidence for links between Estes Park participants and the rise of the militias remains scanty. Most importantly, one of the key militia figures, John

Trochmann, had worked with Louis Beam and another attender, the former Bo Gritz organiser Chris Temple, in an organisation set up to publicise the Weaver case, the United Citizens for Justice. But it was only after disputes had broken out over that organisation's strategy that Trochmann turned instead to organising the Militia of Montana.

Not only is it highly debatable whether, as one account suggests, Estes Park 'established a working structure' for the subsequent militia movement; earlier attempts to bring such bodies into existence had long predated the Colorado gathering. Thus as early as 1968 a group involved in the far right Constitution Parties of the United States had sought to organise what it termed a parallel government, including state militias based on 'family units of honest citizens'; while in the mid-1970s, an American Militia Organization had issued a pamphlet urging a combination of a campaign to elect sympathetic sheriffs, county commissioners and state officials with preparations for the large-scale concealment of arms and provisions and the creation of 'a formidable militia' to resist 'the traitors who control our federal government' and 'those international conspirators who clearly plot our subjection'. In the following decade the idea spread yet further. One group, the Committee of the States, had an Unorganized Militia attached to it that engaged in military training in preparation for the day it was called on 'to take this nation back'. Similarly, an attempt in Idaho in 1982 to establish a 'Civil Body Politic' for 'the preservation, protection, and sustenance of our Aryan Race' included the formation of a Militia to act 'in accordance with our customs as defined by God's Law and our own private Courts, Judges, and Juries'. Militias also existed in Oregon and New York and other groupings too, including the Christian-Patriots Defense League and the White Patriot Party, described themselves in such terms (Dees with Corcoran 1996: 79, 49, 97, 62; Zeskind 1995: 56; Martin 1968, 1970; Sargent 1995: 360–66; Seymour 1991: 312–15, 20, 26; Butler et al. 1982: 1–2; Aho 1990: 10; Spotlight 28 March 1983; Finch 1983: 100).

Indeed, agitation for the creation of militias continued into the period immediately preceding the Estes Park gathering. One activist, as he later noted after joining the Militia of Montana, had already published a book in 1989 calling for a 'rising of the militia'. In the early 1990s, another writer was calling for militias to be mobilised, 'willing to spill blood in the defense of liberty and justice'. Finally, during the 1992 presidential election, Bo Gritz had urged the creation of militias, and one of his supporters, Eva Vail Lamb, was involved in organising such a body in Idaho. What links existed between all this early activity and the movement that came into existence in 1994 remains unclear. We know, for instance, that one of the more important modern militia groupings, the US Militia Association, grew out of a Constitutional Militia Association that had been formed in 1991. Rather than see Estes Park as the origin of the modern militias, it would seem more useful to see it as one of many Patriot initiatives that anticipated, but only in some cases influenced, the emergence of a new wave of paramilitary groups in 1994. But there is another line of influence too, which stretches between the militias and the more militant sections of the gun lobby (*Spotlight* 9 January 1995; Campbell n.d. (1991): 7, 9; Stern 1996: 36; Anon. 1995a: 3; Anon. 1995b: 10).

While Zeskind noted Pratt's comments on the increasingly hardline stance of the NRA, he had been cautious as to how far its radicalisation had gone. At its 1995 conference, held shortly after the Oklahoma City bombing, Wayne LaPierre formally apologised for calling BATF agents 'jack-booted government thugs' and he had declared that there was 'no room at the NRA' for anyone who supported terrorism or treason. But, Zeskind also observed, the organisation had awarded its Law Enforcement Officer of the Year Award to Sheriff Richard Mack, who had formed a militia in Arizona, and when a pro-militia resolution had been put forward from the floor, the leadership headed it off with a substitute resolution declaring that, while it had 'not been involved in the formation of any citizen militia units, neither has the NRA discouraged nor would the NRA contemplate discouraging exercise of any constitutional right' (Zeskind 1995: 58).

Before the widespread creation of militias, NRA publications were already highly critical of the federal government over both the Weaver case and Waco. Furthermore, while in 1995 LaPierre was forced to apologise for his attack on government agents, this was not, in fact, the first time the NRA had cast them in such a light. In 1981, Neal Knox had produced an anti-gun-control film for the NRA in which a board member had described the BATF as 'a jack-booted group of fascists'. Rather than, in John Bruce and Clyde Wilcox's phrase, the NRA using 'rhetoric borrowed from militia groups', both were drawing from the same pool of anti-government sentiment, and it was the gun lobby, not the militias, that had first used the language to which others took such exception (Spitzer 1995: 178–9; Sugarmann 1992: 122–3; Bruce and Wilcox 1998: 15).

Yet, while it is highly likely that NRA rhetoric prepared the ground for the creation of militias (and certainly NRA members were crucial in their development), this is not the same as arguing that their emergence can be put at the NRA's door. What of its rivals in the gun lobby? We noted earlier the somewhat dismissive response of one of the leading figures in the Citizens Committee for the Right to Keep and Bear Arms to the 'primal' outrage against gun control he saw in the rise of militias. (The 'more sophisticated' approach, he claimed, would be to vote against gun control.) In the mid-1980s, however, when one Patriot group, the Alaska Common Law School, was calling for the creation of state militias to resist the federal government, it drew in part on the writings of the central figure in the Citizens Committee, Alan Gottlieb. Nonetheless, it appears undeniable that it is the director of the rival Gun Owners of America who has been the most important figure in the gun lobby in encouraging the spread of militias (*Human Events* 22 July 1994; *Upright Ostrich* November 1986).

Larry Pratt argued in a book published in 1990, *Armed People Victorious*, that where the United States had abandoned its 'reliance on an armed people', other countries, such as Guatemala and the Philippines, had rediscovered its value. (His praise for what have rather more frequently been described as death squads was subsequently to fuel the attacks on him.) He has continued to defend militias since the Estes Park gathering, arguing in 1994, for instance, that semi-automatic rifles should be in the hands of as many Americans as possible, because unless government feared the people, it would carry out such atrocities as the murder of Sammy and Vicki Weaver and the slaughter at Waco. The emergence of militias, he held, was 'one of the most hopeful signs for the preservation of liberty in our time' (*Village Voice* 23 May 1995; *Preparedness Journal* July–August 1994).

Pratt is linked in turn with another grouping in which militias have been advocated. In 1990, the Coalition on Revival, a grouping that bought together Reconstructionists with other religious conservatives, including such prominent Christian Right figures as Tim and Beverly LaHaye and American Family Association leader Don Wildmon, established a National Coordinating Council. This body called not only for the abolition of the public schools, the Internal Revenue Service and the Federal Reserve but, inspired by Pratt, also urged the creation of militias. Pratt himself had long been involved in Reconstructionism and had called for militias in a 1983 Reconstructionist publication. But it is also important to note that not only did several of the most prominent figures subsequently resign,

concerned at the degree of Reconstructionist influence in the organisation, but, just as proposals made at Estes Park markedly differed
from what followed, the militias envisaged in the 1990 document
were to be set up at county level under the control of the sheriff and
Board of Supervisors, a precondition not usually present in the subsequent militia movement itself (Clarkson 1997: 97–9, 103, 243;
Clarkson and Porteous 1993: 12, 287).

If both Pratt and, to a lesser degree, the NRA have been important in the spread of militias and the central role they give to resisting
gun control, what links exist in turn between the extreme right, the
gun lobby and the militias? One suggestion, as we noted earlier, has
been to postulate an important connection between the militias and
William Pierce's *The Turner Diaries*. First published in 1978 (although
it had earlier been serialised in the National Alliance's paper), *The
Turner Diaries* is the story of a white revolutionary, Earl Turner, and his
role in a guerilla war that eventually escalates to the launching of
nuclear, biological and chemical warfare against the enemies of the
white race throughout the globe. Within its genocidal plot, the theme
of gun control is particularly crucial; it is the attempt by the Jewish
rulers of America to disarm whites that first sets resistance into
motion, and, as we have noted, commentators have linked Oklahoma
bomber Timothy McVeigh's enthusiasm for the book with the terrorist attack he later launched (Macdonald 1980: ii–iii, 209, 190–91, 210,
1–2, 181; *Attack!* January 1975).

A decade earlier, the book also played a seminal role in the creation of the terrorist group, The Order. But to suggest that particular
figures in the Patriot movement have been influenced by Pierce's
book is not the same as arguing that the strategy followed by Earl
Turner is that pursued by the militias. *The Turner Diaries* describes a
centralised racist organisation engaged in guerilla warfare. Just as the
militias do not accord with Beam's notion of leaderlessness, they do
not accord with the approach described in Pierce's novel. Instead,
there is an altogether more complicated relationship. As we shall see,
while both the gun lobby and the militias offer opportunities to
figures such as Pierce, they have also presented the racist right with
problems. In part, this concerns the attempts of both militias and gun
lobby organisations to reach beyond white support. But it also concerns the influence within both the Patriot movement and the gun
lobby of an argument that links anti-Semitism not to the argument for
guns, but to the argument against (Flynn and Gerhardt 1989: 174, 235).

In 1989 a Vietnam veteran, Aaron Zelman, formed Jews for the Preservation of Firearms Ownership (JFPO). The organisation soon achieved a notoriety both among gun control supporters and, as we shall see, some on the opposite side, for its claim that gun control was a fascist doctrine. Most vividly illustrated by a poster of Hitler with his arm outstretched in a Nazi salute, and the caption, ALL IN FAVOUR OF GUN CONTROL RAISE YOUR RIGHT HAND, the organisation's argument was developed in most detail in a massive tome bringing together the texts of gun laws from seven countries, ranging from Turkey and Germany to China and the Soviet Union. In each of these countries, it declared, large numbers of people had been murdered by the government, and the key to that genocide was the passing of gun control laws that made successful resistance impossible. The fate of the Jews in Germany, it claimed, had been decided not with Hitler's accession to power but five years earlier, when the German parliament passed a 'Law on Firearms and Ammunition'. The Nazis had been able to use firearms registration lists to establish who had guns, and in 1938 they enacted a law introducing handgun control, and then issued regulations forbidding Jews from owning any weapon whatsoever. The 1938 law, JFPO sensationally claimed, appeared to be the basis of the American gun control legislation passed thirty years later (Sugarmann 1992: 139–40; *Rolling Stone* 15 June 1995; Simkin, Zelman and Rice 1994: 7, 2, 11).

As we have already seen in discussing the book by Wayne LaPierre, it was an argument that has enjoyed considerable circulation among gun rights supporters. The NRA's Neal Knox, for instance, has described the 1968 legislation as modelled on the Nazis', while the Michigan Militia's Norman Olson, commenting on the 1938 law, claimed that it was 'hard to avoid the conclusion that the powers then are the same powers as now'. It was not an argument, however, that has proved agreeable to those opponents of gun control who are also supporters of the Third Reich (*American Spectator* May 1997; *Northern Express* 22 August 1994; for other militia invocations of the Nazi era as a demonstration of the evils of gun control, see Stern 1996: 116).

Writing in 1994, William Pierce argued that the Clinton administration's attempt to 'disarm Americans' presented his organisation with a window of opportunity to gain support among those who were angry at the threat to their guns. Such people, he lamented, did not understand why the government was trying to take away their right to defend themselves, but their hatred of 'the gun-grabbers' meant they could be highly receptive to the National Alliance's message. This would involve, however, being careful about how it was put forward. To book a table at a gun show and then erect a banner declaring 'Jews Are Behind Gun Control', he suggested, would lead to instant eviction. But it was possible, as activists in both New York and Florida had recently demonstrated, to be allowed to sell material at such events, and although they had eventually been ejected, other members had encountered almost no problems at all (*National Alliance Bulletin* February 1994).

In his article, Pierce complained that not only did gun rights activists usually lack any understanding of why gun ownership was under attack, but that some had been persuaded by 'Jewish disinformation agents or conservative cranks' that gun control was 'a Nazi scheme'. As an article in the concurrent issue of *National Vanguard* made clear, this was a complaint aimed at the arguments made by Jews For the Preservation of Firearms Ownership. This group, the article complained, had already persuaded one leading gun magazine that the original architect of gun control was Adolf Hitler. But the Third Reich's 1938 German Weapons Law was not a measure to disarm Germans. Instead, the Alliance claimed, it represented a less restrictive stance than the legislation passed by Socialist and Catholic politicians five years before Hitler had come to power. For a journal with such a record of sympathy for National Socialism, the German law posed somewhat of a problem. Not only did it insist on a handgun permit, something the article suggested was not 'ideal . . . from the viewpoint of today's beleaguered American patriot', but it also only allowed it to be issued 'to persons whose trustworthiness is not in question and who can show a need'. Such requirements, the writer commented, were 'troubling', but not only had they been carried over from the pre-Nazi legislation, they had been 'interpreted liberally' by the new regime. The 1938 law, as the article admitted, had included a provision for denying a handgun permit if 'persons' were 'known to be engaged in activities hostile to the state'. Seeking to appeal to an audience concerned with its rights, however, *National Vanguard* sought to present National Socialism not as their antithesis, but as their protector (*National Alliance Bulletin* February 1994; *National Vanguard* March–April 1994).

The problem was not a new one for Pierce's organisation. Over twenty years earlier, one of the early issues of its paper complained that opponents of gun control were wrong to claim that 'it happened in Germany, and it can happen here'. Under Hitler, it declared, 'German citizens were completely free to own and bear firearms.' It did not name those who, as it put it, were 'in the unfortunate habit of describing proposed firearms laws as "Hitlerian"', but such claims were not restricted to such organisations as the NRA. The year before a Patriot pro-gun publication, *Armed Citizen News*, had not only described Hitler as a proponent of gun control, but presented him as a typical socialist for doing so! (*Attack!* January 1973; *Armed Citizen News* July 1972).

The confluence of anti-Nazi sentiment within the gun lobby and the multiracial (if overwhelmingly white) make-up of the militia movement has been crucial in forming extreme right views of the opportunities and problems both movements offer. We have already seen this in the case of the gun lobby. Three publications from the year after the militia movement took national form are of particular interest in the latter regard.

In early 1995, one extreme right group, the National Socialist Vanguard, argued that while many militia members had 'the instincts for White racial self-preservation', militias were 'becoming somewhat of an embarassment' because of their leaders' claims that neither they nor their organisations were racist. Nonetheless, it suggested, it was 'important to keep the militias alive', both because they provided both 'a pool for future recruiting into the White Nationalist Movement' and as 'a gathering point' for those who were already racist. 'Given the militia situation as it is, the White Nationalist Movement's most practical course of action would be to encourage fellow White Nationalists to infiltrate the militias, get to know each other and establish cores of racist militias within the grassroots militias so that one day, when the weak and incompetent grassroots militia leaders fall along the wayside, the racist militias will emerge' (*NSV Report* April–June 1995).

Another grouping, the National Socialist White People's Party, describing the militias as 'a very promising development', argued that they were the first example of mass white alienation to move beyond electoral politics. Nonetheless, only some were close to National Socialism. Others were religious, some were multiracial, and many were ultra-conservative. It was likely, the article argued, that they would be infiltrated by government *agents provocateurs* and their members 'imprisoned on trumped-up gun charges'. But some groups might survive to become 'the future nuclei of the armed forces of the revolution' and any 'Party comrades' who wished to 'get involved with a quality, racially-oriented militia in their locality' should go ahead (*Resistance* February 1995).

Other sections of the extreme right, usually those already rooted in the Patriot movement, have been more optimistic as to the potential of the militias as a whole. One long-term activist, Eustace Mullins, has described them as 'the only organized threat to the Zionists' absolute control of the U.S.', while an article by a Militia of Montana supporter noted that 'Our friend Louis Beam recently pointed out that a man can join the armed forces and serve the United Nations or he can join the militia and defend America.' But the approach taken in the two explicitly Nazi publications, to regard the militias as an opportunity, but to be sceptical about the existing politics of significant sections of the movement, was also that of William Pierce, who explained in the National Alliance internal bulletin in late 1995 that a Militia Project had been launched to facilitate members' making contact with a militia in their area. 'Some of the militia groups in the United States', he declared, were 'being badly misled in the ideological realm and are in need of some Alliance input' (*Washington Post* 27 August 1996; *Spotlight* 9 January 1995; Dees with Corcoran 1996: 202; for attacks on the militias in two other racist publications, see *American Viewpoint Monthly* February 1995; Dobratz and Shanks-Meile 1997: 152, 30).

As we discuss further in the chapter on the Patriot movement, it is no easy matter to distinguish the non-racist right from the racist right. To claim, as one militia officer has done, that 'Nothing in the Militia Movement ever had anything to do with racism or anti-Semitism' is an insupportable contention. But so too is the claim that the movement is an expression of white supremacism. Instead, the militia movement is a site of both co-operation and conflict between different strands of the right. To take one particularly illuminating example, we could instance the heated exchange that took place in 1997 between two activists, Alabama militia leader Mike Vanderboegh and the former editor of *The Modern Militiaman*, Martin Lindstedt, as to whether neo-Nazis and Identity believers were a crucial part of 'the overall Resistance movement' or, as Vanderboegh claimed, should be seen as incompatible with the beliefs of the militias. If we are to see the movement to which they both belong as bringing together racists and non-racists, at one and the same time potentially uniting them against the federal government and potentially turning them on each other, this is a very different approach from the one that so often been put forward. But it sheds a different light too on how we might understand Larry Pratt (*Taking Aim* January 1998; *John Doe Times* 14 July 1997).

Zeskind argued not that Pratt was a racist, but that Estes Park represented the forging of an alliance between racists and others on the far right, of which he was a key example. During the 1996 election campaign, in which Pratt became a co-chairman of Pat Buchanan's presidential effort, he was the subject of a critical report that drew attention to his attendance not only at Estes Park but at other events involving white supremacists. Pratt's reply centred partly on the argument that 'To speak to a group does not mean you sign up for their agenda'. But he also claimed that he was an anti-racist. One of his pastors was an African-American, his wife a Central American and he was a member of both the Congress of Racial Equality and Jews for the Preservation of Firearms Ownership. Indeed, at the Estes Park gathering, he declared, he had explicitly championed the work of Jews for the Preservation of Firearms Ownership. Such a reply did nothing to rebut either criticism of his politics or his choice of speaking engagements. What it did do, however, as does so much about the gun lobby, the militias and the right, is remind us how complicated the relationship between them is (Zeskind 1995: 56; *New York Times* 16, 17 February 1996; *Preparedness Journal* March–April 1996).

5

Abortion and the right

If the 1950s marked the beginnings of the modern American right, they also marked another development – the beginnings of a move-ment to liberalise abortion law. It was not until the following decade, however, that a counter-movement emerged. In 1967, concerned at the growing strength of demands for reform, the Family Life Division of the National Conference of Catholic Bishops launched a national campaign to disseminate the Church's teaching on abortion. The Church also encouraged the creation of anti-abortion groups at state and local level, and in 1971 sought to link them together through 'a loosely knit information clearing house', the National Right to Life Committee (NRLC). By the beginning of the 1970s, abortion oppo-nents were already a significant force. In New York, for instance, the passing of a liberal law in 1970 was to lead to such strong resistance that two years later only the governor's veto would stop the legisla-ture from repealing it, while in 1972 anti-abortion activists also suc-cessfully campaigned against the liberalisation of the law in Minnesota. But it was not they, but those who sought to liberalise the law, who were to welcome the Supreme Court ruling in the case of *Roe v. Wade* in January 1973. In a majority of states, the Court declared, it was a crime to procure an abortion except to save the life of the mother. Such a stance, however, was contrary to the Constitutionally guaranteed right of personal privacy, and as such could not be upheld. The State did have a legitimate interest, it ruled, in ensuring that a fetus capable of 'meaningful life' outside the womb should be protected, except when abortion was necessary to preserve the mother's life or health. But in the first three months, abortion was a matter only for the medical judgement of the pregnant woman's doctor, while after the first trimester, when terminations became more difficult, states could regulate the procedure in the interests of maternal health. The Supreme Court, by a majority of 7 to 2, had declared that abortion could no longer be banned. In the years that followed, a movement would emerge committed to the reversal of the decision, with the NRLC as its most important component (Merton 1981: 43; *Front Lines Research* November 1994; Francome 1984: 190–91; Lader 1973: 198–9, 206, 178; Craig and O'Brien 1993: 1, 23–30).

At its first conference in June 1973 the NRLC declared that it was now an independent organisation. Given the predominance of Catholics within its membership and the continued involvement of the Church in anti-abortion activity, however, claims that it was seeking to impose Catholic teaching on those outside the faith were to continue to bedevil it, and the large-scale entry of evangelicals into anti-abortion activity from the late 1970s onwards was to have a paradoxical affect. The intensity of their religious commitment ensured that opposition to abortion was still popularly identified with religion, if not with Catholicism as such; but the anti-abortion movement itself was not as affected by their influx as might be thought. Some joined the NRLC or other early anti-abortion organisations, and in the late 1980s the rapid growth of anti-abortion militancy, particularly the rise of Operation Rescue, marked a veritable explosion of evangelical pro-life activity. But a major part of evangelical opposition to abortion has not gone into the existing movement. Instead, it has been channeled into the multi-issue religious conservative organisations of the Christian Right (Paige 1983: 57, 82–3; Francome 1984: 191; Jaffe, Lindheim and Lee 1981: 73–85; Martin 1997: 193–4).

As we have seen, the Christian Right did not emerge until several years after the anti-abortion movement, and where the latter describes itself as the pro-life movement, the former defines itself as pro-family. It opposes abortion, and makes exactly the same central argument as the anti-abortion movement, that the fetus is an unborn human being with the right to life. But its opposition to abortion is only one of a series of stances it has taken up in defence of the family and Christian sexual morality. The Moral Majority, for instance, emphasised opposition to abortion, homosexuality and pornography in the early 1980s, and one can find similar priorities with other organisations. But for much of the Christian Right, these issues are then linked with other questions, questions that can range from the damaging effects of gambling to calling for the introduction of an anti-missile defence system (Falwell with Dobson and Hindson 1981: 195–8; Dobson and Bauer 1990: 140–43; *Conservative Digest* July 1981;

Christian American July–August 1996; *Concerned Women for America News* September 1986).

The Christian Right is to be distinguished from other strands within conservatism because it foregrounds an evangelical sexual politics. It should be distinguished too from evangelical Churches or denominations that oppose abortion, or sex education, but do not identify themselves with the conservative movement. But the Christian Right is also different from the pro-life movement. Although often described as single-issue, organisations such as the NRLC are not solely concerned with abortion. Their argument about the right to life is brought to bear on three other issues: cases where doctors or parents have decided to end the lives of babies with disabilities, embryo experimentation, and euthanasia. In each of these issues, the Christian Right is also to be found on the same side, but this agreement does not extend to the Christian Right agenda as a whole. Certainly, many anti-abortion activists may oppose premarital sex or see abortion as a symptom of a sexually immoral society. But the NRLC does not campaign on anything other than right to life issues, and seeks to present these issues in ways that will enable the movement to maximise its appeal (Andrusko 1983: 7–8; *National Right to Life News* 19 February 1999; Leahy *et al.* 1983: 32, 35, 38–9; Petchesky 1981: 228–30, 245).

On occasion, NRLC material reflects a commitment to a traditionalist sexual morality. But the core of its argument is a focus on the status of life, not the defence of a particular form of family. Opposition to abortion is deliberately framed in the language of human rights and compared to the anti-slavery movement and the fight against Nazism. The former, it is argued, was eventually successful despite a Supreme Court ruling that saw the slave as unentitled to rights, while the Third Reich, like 'today's abortionists', systematically denied the humanity of those it sought to destroy. The battle against abortion, it is argued, is a fight to defend the weak from those who would deny their most basic human right. It is an argument that can be made from a number of different political positions. Thus in the same issue of *National Right to Life News* that proudly announced that the NRLC had been invited to a meeting with Reagan two days after his inauguration, a report of the annual March for Life noted that its participants 'spanned the political spectrum from left to right', from the anti-war Prolifers for Survival to the conservative Catholic group, Tradition, Family and Property. One of the groups that it cited, Feminists for Life, is particularly important in this regard. Originating in 1972, it emphasises the opposition to abortion of leading nineteenth-century feminists and calls for amending the Constitution to ban both abortion and discrimination against women. Similarly, in 1994 the March for Life included a contingent from the Pro-Life Alliance of Gays and Lesbians, which distributed an open letter to fellow-marchers, arguing that 'the message of the Lesbian and Gay community' and that of the movement was 'the same: All human life deserves protection and respect simply because it is human' (Lippis 1978: 17–18; Andrusko 1983: 153–67, 215, 14–15; *National Right to Life News* 27 January 1981; *Focus on the Family Citizen* February 1999; *Mother Jones* May 1989; *Life Advocate* March 1994).

Unlike the Christian Right, the pro-life movement has avoided political identification with conservatism. But, as we shall see, the need to distinguish between two movements that are often collapsed together has to take into account two complications. Firstly, a shared opposition to abortion has forged links between the pro-life movement and major sections of the right. Secondly, groups have emerged within the movement that have not confined themselves to those issues that concern the NRLC, and bear a marked resemblance to the Christian Right in their generalised attack on sexual permissiveness. However, both their origins outside the Christian Right, and their denunciation of contraception (the Christian Right campaigns against the promotion of birth control in schools, but does not oppose it as such) should dissuade us from declaring that their existence proves there is no analytical distinction between the pro-family movement and the pro-life movement. On one side of the divide lies a constellation of organisations, predominantly evangelical, whose focus on the family and morality encompasses opposition to abortion. On the other side is to be found another cluster of organisations, largely Catholic, which focus on abortion but include groupings that argue that abortion cannot be successfully opposed without the restoration of a Christian moral framework. It would be tempting to suggest that, for this section of the pro-life movement, campaigning against abortion is a vehicle for orthodox Catholics unwilling to transfer their allegiance to a movement defined by another religious tradition. As we shall see, however, some of those most strongly arguing for extending the pro-life agenda, to the extent even of opposing contraception, are themselves evangelicals. (For the Christian Right and contraception in schools, see Dobson and Bauer 1990: 43–55; for a recent attempt, however, by Bauer's organisation to question conservatives' acceptance of 'the contraceptive culture', see *Family Policy* September–October 1999.)

In the years since its inception, the NRLC has been by far the largest section of the movement. (Estimates of its membership, however, have diverged dramatically, with on one occasion, a claim to have between 11 and 13 million being quickly followed by an admission that whole churches were included in this number if the pastor was sympathetic!) It has been a significant force not only in supporting pro-life candidates in presidential, Congressional and other elections but in seeking to get bills passed in state legislatures restricting abortion by, for instance, enforcing compulsory waiting periods between attending a clinic and obtaining an abortion, or insisting that a girl under the age of 18 has to have parental consent before her pregnancy can be terminated. We have already remarked on the emergence of groups within the movement committed to linking abortion with a more general moral conservatism. But their dispute with the NRLC is also linked to a critique of the legislation it has pursued and the candidates it has supported. The Committee, its critics claim, is too compromising, committed to a gradualist strategy of reducing abortions when all of them must be stopped. Thus a willingness to vote for restrictions on abortion that allow exceptions for rape or incest or the health of the woman is seen as a betrayal, while for the organisation to call for the election of politicians who have voted for particular compromises in Congress is similarly treated as failing to stand for a full pro-life position. Of the more intransigent groups, the most important is the American Life Lobby, subsequently the American Life League, an organisation that in recent years has reportedly achieved a membership of some 300,000. In turn, the arguments made by the League and other critics of the NRLC connect to a second set of contentions. Lobbying, it is argued, has not stopped abortion, and the only thing that will is direct action. Although present from as early as the late 1970s, this argument only came to the fore with the emergence of Operation Rescue in the late 1980s. For the proponents of direct action, clinics needed to be physically stopped from functioning. For most, this meant sit-ins and blockades, tactics that increasingly drew prison sentences. For a smaller number, non-violence was itself a betrayal. Instead, clinics had to be destroyed and, for the most uncompromising of all, doctors had to be shot (Merton 1981: 201; O'Connor 1996: 137; *National Right to Life News* 24 February 1997; *Human Events* 31 May–7 June 1996; Kaplan 1993b; Risen and Thomas 1998).

How does the development of this substantial and decades-old movement relate to the different strands of the right? In the discussion that follows, we shall examine how the Republican Party has sought to deal with the abortion issue and the resultant tensions that have emerged between it, the Christian Right and the pro-life movement. We shall then look at the rise of direct action within the movement, both in its non-violent and violent forms, and examine to what degree more militant sections of the American right have supported it. Finally, we shall turn back to a key moment in the early development of the movement to address one of the most important arguments that have been put forward about abortion and the right – that the efforts of the New Right to shape the direction of anti-abortion politics in the late 1970s and early 1980s should be seen as symptomatic of a meshing together of a nominally independent anti-abortion movement and the right.

Whether intervening in election contests or seeking to achieve legislative gains, the anti-abortion movement has been successful in finding a number of sympathetic Democrats. Overwhelmingly, however, it is in the Republican Party that its arguments have gained most purchase, and while the 1976 GOP platform for the presidential election combined a recognition of disagreements and uncertainty among Republicans on the issue with support for a constitutional amendment to reverse the Supreme Court's decision, the reference to Republican disagreements on the issue was weakened in the 1980 platform. By 1984 it had disappeared altogether, with the party now calling not only for a constitutional amendment but also for Supreme Court justices and federal judges to be appointed only if they respected 'traditional family values and the sanctity of innocent human life' (*National Right to Life News* 14 November 1996; O'Connor 1996: 73; Craig and O'Brien 1993: 166–7).

This position has not been universally popular among Republican members of Congress or others in the party. Just as some Republican Senators or Representatives continue to vote in favour of abortion rights, there have been several attempts to change the party platform either to support the pro-choice view or, at the least, to recognise publicly the existence of diverse views within the party. The emergence in 1989 of a Republican abortion rights group, preponderantly made up of moderates, was followed by the creation the following year of another pro-choice group, this time led by a former New Rightist. The latter group had emerged after a discussion with the party chairman,

Lee Atwater, who had become convinced that a continuation of the party's hard-line stance on the issue threatened to lose it support among economically conservative but socially libertarian voters. His solution to this dilemma, to present the party as a big tent, open to a diversity of views, was a red flag to those who feared any weakening in the party's commitment (Melich 1996: 243–5; McKeegan 1992: 172–5).

The Family Research Council leader Gary Bauer issued a four-page open letter, threatening the party with dire electoral consequences if it retreated from its anti-abortion stance, and towards the end of 1990 he, the Eagle Forum leader Phyllis Schlafly and the Concerned Women for America leader Beverly LaHaye announced the creation of the Republican National Coalition for Life. The new organisation would ensure, Schlafly declared, that the party did not abandon its opposition to abortion; and, working alongside the Christian Coalition and other groupings, it was successful in retaining a strong stance on the issue in the 1992 platform. The issue, however, did not go away, and Schlafly, Bauer and others were already organising in 1995 for the 1996 platform fight. The NRLC too urged pro-life Republicans to plan 'for their 1996 state caucuses, conventions and primaries' and where initially several pro-choice governors were expected to lead the attack on the pro-life position, in the event it was the Dole campaign that was particularly active in trying to modify the platform's position on abortion to include a reference to the tolerance of different views. The situation was complicated yet further by fears among some in the pro-life camp that the Christian Coalition, which had been so crucial in defending a pro-life platform in 1992, might now be willing to accept a modification of the party's position. In the event, however, this did not come about, and an alliance of Schlafly, Bauer, the Christian Coalition and the Buchanan campaign worked together successfully to retain a hard-line stance in the party platform (*Lifeletter* 1990, 1; *National Right to Life News* 12 February 1990; McKeegan 1992: 174, 208; Melich 1996: 268–71; *New York Times* 4, 5 May 1996; *Focus on the Family Citizen* 17 April 1995, 23 September 1996).

The issue has played a part too in deciding which of the different candidates would be victorious in the primaries. Reagan in 1980 was decisively pro-life, while his vice-presidential candidate, George Bush, had to renounce his earlier pro-choice views. In 1996, some, including the American Life League's president, Judie Brown, believed that Bob Dole was insufficiently committed to the cause and that Pat Buchanan should be supported for the Republican nomination in his stead. In a direct mail letter addressed to 'Dear Fellow Pro-Lifer', Buchanan declared that while he stood for no compromise, the other main candidates were either pro-choice or evasive on the issue. Such a stance did not win him the party's nomination. But only candidates who are acceptable to at least the dominant force in the pro-life movement have been nominated since the issue became part of the party's agenda (Melich 1996: 140–42; Buchanan n.d. (1995)).

If Republican presidential candidates have consistently been pro-life since the beginning of the 1980s, does this mean that, if elected, they have pursued the movement's agenda? Here, there is room for argument. The Supreme Court Justices successfully nominated by Reagan and Bush have moved the Court to a greater sympathy for states' efforts to restrict abortion. But the Court has not voted to abandon the 1973 decision, and, to the horror of pro-lifers, while supporting increased restrictions in 1992, three Republican nominees also argued that to reverse such an important ruling would undermine faith in the Court. If some states' restrictions have proved acceptable to the Supreme Court, and have subsequently been adopted by other state legislatures where pro-life influence is strong, anti-abortion measures have also come through the Republican Party's control of federal government. In 1987, family planning facilities in receipt of federal money were forbidden to carry out abortions or refer clients for abortions, while in 1984, Agency for International Development funding was removed from non-governmental organisations that were involved in abortion abroad. But, despite the efforts of some within the Reagan administration, under Title X of the 1970 Public Health Service Act, government money continued to be allocated to the main family planning organisation, Planned Parenthood, loathed by the more hard-line anti-abortionists because of its promotion of contraception and opposed by all of them for its involvement in abortion provision (Craig and O'Brien 1993: 329, 337–8, 341; *Christian American* September–October 1992; O'Connor 1996: 123–4, 132–3, 158, 160–61; McKeegan 1992: 117–18, 197, 86, 79, 90, 41–2, 63–4, 113–17; Glasow 1988: 25–7).

There were other disputes too. The Reagan administration's decision in 1981 to nominate Sandra O'Connor to the Supreme Court, despite her denunciation by leading pro-lifers for her votes on abortion in the Arizona state legislature, resulted in particularly bad relations between Administration and movement. Despite a furious response by abortion opponents (the president of the NRLC, for instance, declared that O'Connor's inclusion on the Supreme Court 'would be the most devastating blow to the pro-life movement' since *Roe* v. *Wade*), Reagan continued to support her, and the Senate endorsed her unanimously (*Conservative Digest* August 1981; McKeegan 1992: 132–3; Melich 1996: 156).

Both O'Connor's pro-life votes on the Supreme Court and the measures introduced by Reagan served to close much of the gap between pro-lifers and the Administration. So too did Reagan's attempt to influence the result when, in 1982, the Senate voted on a bill introduced by Senator Jesse Helms that declared that human life began at conception and sought to strip federal courts of the power to strike down anti-abortion legislation. The President, *Conservative Digest* reported, had given strong support to the lobbying of Senators in support of the Helms bill. He had personally met with pro-life leaders in an extended strategy session before the vote, and, Judie Brown commented, while the White House intervention had been left till too late, the bill's defeat had not been due to Reagan (*Conservative Digest* September 1982; Craig and O'Brien 1993: 139–40).

Indeed, Brown attributed defeat to divisions in the movement. Rival proposals to Helms's had also emerged, of which the most important was one from another Republican Senator, Orrin Hatch, to introduce a constitutional amendment returning the issue to the states. For the American Life Lobby and others in the more hard-line contingent of the movement, Helms's approach was the right one. Hatch, however, was supported by the Catholic Church, the NRLC and others. Hatch supporters argued that the Helms bill would not pass and was 'patently unconstitutional' in its attempt to limit federal courts. Helms supporters held that Hatch's amendment failed to recognise the right to life and would allow states to pursue liberal abortion policies. To render the situation even more complicated, the NRLC itself was bitterly divided, with a number of state leaders opposing its support for Hatch. His measure too would be defeated in 1983 (*Conservative Digest* September 1982; Craig and O'Brien 1993: 139–47; *National Journal* 20 March 1982).

The defeat of these two measures represented the high-water mark of pro-life hopes to reverse *Roe* v. *Wade* through Congress. Brown, despite her favourable comment about Reagan's 1982 intervention, was particularly critical of what she dubbed an 'apathetic Administration'. While the different sections of the movement continued to believe that the ultimate answer was a constitutional amendment to ban abortion, they could neither agree how it should be phrased nor what lesser measures might also deserve support, nor, more important, could they find the two-thirds support among Senators that any such amendment would need to be passed. (Even then, of course, it would have to successfully negotiate three-quarters of the state legislatures.) Attention has shifted to attempting to pass restrictions at state level, to continued efforts to influence the composition of Congress, and, most recently, to a campaign against a particular form of abortion, described by pro-lifers as partial-birth abortion, which, they argue, has shifted the abortion debate on to terrain less favourable to those who argue for unrestricted access to abortion. Much of this became harder, however, with the ending of the Republican control of the Presidency. Despite pro-lifers' reservations, Bush held to the anti-abortion line of his predecessor. Clinton, however, opposed the movement strongly, issuing executive directives reversing a number of anti-abortion measures introduced in the 1980s and subsequently vetoing the bill to ban partial-birth abortion (*National Review* 4 February 1983; Committee on the Judiciary 1983: 1072, 1179–81; Rice n.d.; O'Connor 1996: 116, 139–40; *Christian American* March 1993; *National Right to Life News* 12 October 1998, 21 October 1997).

Within Congress, the Republican Party has chosen not to prioritise abortion. As we have noted, this has been crucial in the development of a major division between the more pragmatic Christian Coalition and the more uncompromising approach of James Dobson and Gary Bauer. The American Life League has also been highly critical of the Coalition, attacking the condemnation of abortion in its *Contract with the American Family* as 'deceptive and misleading' when compared with its willingness to settle for lesser measures, and while the pro-life and pro-family movements remain separate, there are significant parallels between those who criticise the NRLC within the pro-life movement and those who criticise the Christian Coalition within the pro-family movement. Both, in turn, are also highly likely to criticise the Republican hierarchy, something which the larger groups are also willing to do, but far less frequently. In early 1995, for instance, the NRLC accused Gingrich of capitulating to pressure from 'pro-abortion' Republican House members and stopping an anti-abortion measure from being brought to a vote. Considerably more typical, however, was its praise for the party's Congressional leadership three years later, and in 1990 even Atwater's call for the GOP to adopt a big tent strategy was seen in a sympathetic light (*Christian News* 7 August 1995; *National Right to Life News* 6 April 1995; *American Spectator* July 1998; *Lifeletter* 1990, #1).

But if the NRLC is at pains to maintain its good relationship both with the Republican Party and the Christian Right (in 1995, for instance, it took a far more favourable view of the Christian Coalition's stance on abortion than had the American Life League), this should not obscure the potential for conflict; and one recent development in this area is particularly illuminating. In 1994, as we have discussed, the House Republicans committed themselves to a *Contract With America*, one item of which concerned welfare reform. Calling for the transfer of much of the responsibility for welfare to the states, the *Contract* argued that the existing welfare system 'bred illegitimacy'. Skyrocketing 'out-of-wedlock births', it declared, were 'ripping apart our nation's social fabric', and what was needed was the denial of Aid to Families with Dependent Children (AFDC) payments to unmarried mothers under the age of 18, with states having the option to extend the prohibition to those aged between 18 and 21. The money saved could be used to reduce unmarried pregnancies, to encourage adoption or for other purposes, but could not be spent on abortion. In addition to discouraging teenage pregnancies, the *Contract* also envisaged discouraging illegitimacy in general. Any mothers receiving payments for children, it declared, would be denied any additional amount for any other children born outside marriage (*National Right to Life News* 15 June 1995; Gillespie and Schellhas 1994: 65–6, 70–71).

In taking such a stance, Gingrich and his colleagues were drawing on an argument that had been increasingly raised within conservative circles from the Reagan years onwards. Associated with a number of figures, above all the writer Charles Murray, it accused the welfare system, in the words of the *Contract*, of telling 'young girls' to have 'an illegitimate baby and taxpayers will guarantee you cash, food stamps, and medical care, plus a host of other benefits'. What was needed, it held, was 'to change the incentives and make responsible parenthood the norm and not the exception'. It was an argument that had already proved highly controversial, and it did not take a profound knowledge of politics to predict that it would come under heavy fire from Democrats inside Congress and liberal groups outside it once it reached the legislative stage. What would be more surprising, however, would be who else would oppose it (Joffe 1998: 293–4; Balz and Brownstein 1996: 265–83; Gillespie and Schellhas 1994: 75).

The House, *National Review* reported in April the following year, had at last passed a welfare bill that gave greater leeway to the states and was aimed at moving welfare recipients into work and reducing illegitimacy. Where, it declared, it had originally been envisaged that any girl under the age of 18 who had a baby outside marriage would be permanently barred from receiving benefits, the bill had been changed to allow her to receive aid once she had passed 18. But the final version did, at least, move 'toward stigmatizing out-of-wedlock births' by giving states higher block grants if they reduced illegitimate births without an equivalent increase in abortions. The bill's stand against illegitimacy had been supported by 'most pro-life and pro-family groups', from the Christian Coalition to the Concerned Women for America. It was unfortunate, however, that it had been attacked by the NRLC, armed with the 'curious argument' that penalising out-of-wedlock births would encourage young women to abort (*National Review* 17 April 1995).

As a subsequent letter made clear, the Committee's President, Wanda Franz, was less than pleased by the report. The House bill, she argued, contained three provisions that would increase abortion, the rewarding of states for reducing illegitimacy, the prohibition on cash assistance for children born to 'unmarried minor mothers' and the notion of a family cap, by which women already receiving money for a child would be denied it for any more that were born. Conservative supporters of the bill, she noted, had admitted that it would lead to increased abortion, although they claimed that this would only be temporary. Even if this were true, which was unlikely, abortion was always evil. 'Being born out of wedlock didn't make it into the Ten Commandments – killing did' (*National Review* 29 May 1995).

The exchange made it very clear that a heated, and revealing, argument had broken out. At the end of January, a meeting had already been held between pro-life members of Congress, the NRLC and a number of other organisations in which concern was expressed over the effects of the proposals. In the months that followed, the Committee fought for amendments, first in the House, and then in the Senate, to allow the payment of vouchers both to women who had a further child and to under-18 mothers provided they lived under adult supervision and remained in school. They continued, too, to oppose the payment of an 'illegitimacy ratio bonus' to states. In the House, they complained, two of the amendments they favoured had been blocked from being actually voted on by the Republican leadership, while 'many legislators who usually vote pro-life' had 'succumbed to pressure' from party leaders 'and from multi-issue conservative groups which have made the prevention of out-of-wedlock births a priority'. In the Senate, however, they found greater sympathy from the Majority Leader, Bob Dole, and, after negotiating both the divisions in the party and Democrat resistance (which included President Clinton's use of his veto), welfare reform was eventually to be passed in August 1996. The use of incentives for states to discourage out-of-wedlock births was retained, but with the important proviso that the abortion rate must not rise, while the provision of welfare for under-18 mothers and women who had a further child on welfare, rather than being forbidden, was left to states' discretion (*National Right to Life News* 3 February, 16 March, 6 April, 22 August 1995; *Congressional Quarterly Weekly Report* 23 September, 9 December 1995, 3 February, 3 August 1996; Joffe 1998: 290, 298, 297).

Ironically, the exclusion of abortion from the *Contract with America* led the Republican leadership to emphasise the moral aspects of welfare reform, placed in the *Contract* in part as a signal to the Christian Right that their concerns were not being ignored. Conversely, the dilution of the original proposals in the Senate also involved political undercurrents, in which Dole, having rejected the House's position on teenage mothers, felt bound to support at least some version of the family cap in order to remain on good terms with the Christian Coalition as the 1996 presidential election approached. It had proved a nightmare, however, to find a position that could satisfy both those who prioritised the 'pro-family' argument and those who found that it clashed with the centrality they gave to a 'pro-life' stance (Balz and Brownstein 1996: 281, 289–92).

In concentrating our attention on the NRLC and the American Life League, we have been concerned to explore the dynamics of the two main organisations within the pro-life movement. But there have been other important developments too. While the NRLC has continued with its gradualist strategy, sharply criticised by the American Life League, many in the movement have chosen to focus their energies on pregnancy care centers, where women are counselled against abortion and given material support if they agree to carry through the pregnancy. Some take this attempt to dissuade women from abortion a step further and stand outside clinics, urging women not to enter. What has been noticeable first in the early 1980s and then, more dramatically, since the latter part of the decade, has been the rise of a more confrontational approach. Drawing both on the experience of earlier movements of civil disobedience and the biblical injunction for Christians to rescue those in mortal danger, groupings such as the Pro-Life Action League, the Pro-Life Action Network and, above all, Operation Rescue brought a new militancy into anti-abortion activity. Opposed by the NRLC, direct action was welcomed by the American Life League and leading figures on the Christian Right. But legal actions against the leading organisations, the effect of jail sentences, often repeated ones, on activists and the passing of a law making it a federal offence to block access to clinics ensured that non-violent direct action had peaked by the early 1990s. An array of direct action organisations have continued to exist, however, and while differing from the American Life League in the centrality they gave to civil disobedience, such groups frequently share with it a commitment to a more general moral conservatism (*National Right to Life News* 10 June 1999; Scheidler 1985: 19–23; Risen and Thomas 1998; Diamond 1989: 92; *A.L.L. About Issues* May 1988).

The League had long argued that a society that encourages contraception will also accept abortion. That such figures as Judie Brown, a committed Catholic, hold such views is less surprising than the opposition to birth control also expressed by the evangelical activists, Randy Terry and Matthew Trewhella. Adherents of both religious traditions make other links, too. In recent years, Operation Rescue has attacked homosexuality, sex education and the sale of what it regards as pornography by major bookstores. A number of splits have developed within this wing of the movement, and Terry no longer leads Operation Rescue. But the politics of this strand are nonetheless particularly well caught in a speech he made to an anti-abortion rally in 1993: 'It's a given that all of us want legalized child-killing to be crushed . . . But beyond that, what else do we want? What else does our vision for this nation encompass? . . . What would be, for example, the status of the sodomite movement? What about pornography? . . . Now, if you are envisioning reformation along the areas that I have just spoken of, then what you are hoping for is a Christian culture, dare I say a Christian nation . . . We are the resistance! We are those who say, 'Over our dead bodies will this country go into hell!''

(*Christian News* 14 May 1984, 10 February 1992, 20 May 1996; *Village Voice* 4 May 1999; Risen and Thomas 1998: 308–14; *Mother Jones* November–December 1993).

Operation Rescue and kindred groups represented one form of anti-abortion militancy. In their shadow, another far smaller movement has also grown, one that used such terms as 'defensive action' – and even 'justifiable homicide' – to encapsulate the moral rightness of putting lives at risk by the bombing or burning of clinics, or taking them by the murder of doctors. A number of publications, including a remarkably well-produced monthly magazine, *Life Advocate*, carried the arguments of those who held that the comparison of the fight against abortion to that against slavery or Nazism should also extend to the methods that should be used. Meanwhile, the Army of God manual gave a detailed description of the manufacture of explosives and the use of noxious chemicals in order 'to disrupt and ultimately destroy Satan's power to kill our children'. It was a development that was condemned not only by the mainstream of the movement, but by Operation Rescue too. But not all the non-violent direct action groups were prepared to condemn the use of force, and Operation Rescue's insistence that those it worked with disavow any such sympathy has been a major factor in the continued fragmentation of the militant wing of the movement (*Life Advocate* March, April 1995; Kaplan 1995: 153–5, 142–4, 160; Planned Parenthood 1995; Risen and Thomas 1998: 339–71; *USA Today* 12 March 1993; while the Army of God manual had originally been clandestinely circulated, for its reprinting in a militant anti-abortion newsletter see *Media Bypass* January 1999).

If a number of sympathisers with violence have emerged within groups such as the American Coalition of Life Activists, links also exist between anti-abortion violence and the Patriot movement. One of the main publications of those who view the killing of doctors as justifiable homicide, *Prayer + Action Weekly News*, has linked one of the key concerns for Patriots, opposition to the environmental movement, to its own fight against abortion by calling for the creation of militias to resist government attacks on 'our farmers, loggers, miners, fishermen, small businessmen, patriots, and the unborn' while the leading Christian Identity periodical, the *Jubilee*, declared its support for a former Presbyterian minister, Paul Hill, following his killing of a doctor and his bodyguard outside a Florida clinic. A Patriot activist, wanted for several bombings, including an abortion clinic and a lesbian bar, has been the subject of an extensive FBI search, while the leader of the Oklahoma Constitutional Militia and two associates were sentenced for a bomb conspiracy whose targets again included abortion clinics and gay bars. As Sandi DuBowski and Frederick Clarkson have demonstrated, other links exist between Patriot and anti-abortion activity. Nonetheless, we would be mistaken if we assumed that it is the Patriot movement that is responsible for most anti-abortion violence. Instead, the reservoir from which those who have actually resorted to force is drawn seems far more to be found among those who find Biblical support for their feelings of anger and frustration about the persistence of abortion and the failure of the mainstream anti-abortion movement than among those already mobilised in a movement that sees America as endangered by a globalist conspiracy. There is, however, one party that appeals both to sections of the Patriot movement and supporters of both the violent and non-violent direct action wings of the anti-abortion movement (Risen and Thomas 1998: 360; Planned Parenthood 1995; Crawford *et al* 1994: 3.19; *Media Bypass* January 1999; Anon 1997: 11; DuBowski 1996: 1–11; Clarkson 1998: 8–12; for further discussion of the roots of anti-abortion violence, see Kaplan 1995: 128–63; Maxwell and Jelen 1995: 117–31; Maxwell 1995: 1–20).

Where the NRLC supported Bob Dole's candidacy in 1996, Judie Brown first supported Buchanan and had then called for a vote for 'the only pro-life candidate – and party – that exists in our country today . . . Howard Phillips and the U.S. Taxpayers Party'. The Taxpayers Party has had a particular attraction to anti-abortion militants. The most important example, Operation Rescue founder Randy Terry, told the 1996 party convention to prepare 'for the collapse of the godless two-party system', while another key proponent of direct action, the Missionaries to the Preborn leader Matthew Trewhella, called for the formation of militias while addressing the party's 1994 Wisconsin state convention. The church which he pastored, he declared, was already holding firearms classes. In addition to Terry, other Operation Rescue veterans are involved in the party, which has also received support from Michael Bray, a Lutheran pastor convicted in connection with clinic bombings in 1985 and subsequently the author of a defence of the use of violence in the anti-abortion struggle. Phillips's party has drawn support from within a number of different movements, from Patriot activists such as the former Populist Party organiser William Shearer and the anti-banking campaigner Byron Dale to Reconstructionists, notably its central figure, R. J.

Rushdoony, himself, ironically, a critic of Operation Rescue, for, as he saw it, behaving in an unbiblical way by rebelling against authority. But, amidst that diverse support, it has clearly developed an identity that attracts at least some of the militant anti-abortionists (*National Right to Life News* 21 August 1996; *Wanderer* 10 October 1996; *Progressive* October 1996; *Front Lines Research* August, November 1994; Risen and Thomas 1998: 86, 99; *Life Advocate* December 1994; *Christian News* 2 January 1989).

For much of the right, abortion has been a crucial issue. It has been a central feature of the Christian Right agenda and of Pat Buchanan's campaigns for the presidency. It was a vital part of the New Right's move into mass politics in the late 1970s, and from the 1973 Supreme Court decision, or even earlier, it has concerned the radical right and the extreme right too. An early John Birch Society pamphlet, for instance, described abortion as only part of a 'total conspiracy' against America, while the National States Rights Party's response to the Roe v. Wade decision was to demand a constitutional amendment to defend 'the rights of the unborn'. But if opposition to abortion is widespread on the right, should we conclude that the anti-abortion movement is being disingeneous in claiming to be politically independent? (Gordon and Hunter 1977–1978: 12; *Thunderbolt* March 1973).

We have already argued against the assumption that opposition to abortion is inherently right-wing. It is perfectly possible, as we have seen, for people of different political inclinations to identify with the pro-life position, and, conversely, for those on the right, the libertarian argument that abortion is a woman's right or the less elevated belief that opposition to abortion can cost votes have generated periodic bursts of resistance to pro-life hegemony within the Republican Party. But the fact of that hegemony, and the crucial role of the New Right in bringing the abortion issue into conservative politics, remain highly significant, and while a number of writers have sought to explain the connection, the most elaborate attempt to do so is to be found in an article that appeared in 1981 by the feminist political scientist, Rosalind Pollack Petchesky.

If there was anything new in the New Right, she argued, it was its 'focus on reproductive and sexual issues'. If once the right had seen Communism as the greatest threat, now it was feminism and homosexuality that it most feared, and of all feminist demands, abortion was seen as the most threatening. The anti-abortion movement provided the right with both a potent issue and access to an organised mass constituency. Its mass mobilisation, including a hard-hitting electoral strategy, served as a model for the New Right and at the same time had helped to create a consciousness that was to prove amenable to the arguments of a pro-family conservatism. As a result, from 1978, the New Right had set about organising its own pro-life and pro-family organisations (Petchesky 1981: 207, 211–12, 215).

Just as 'the Reagan forces', with their different priorities, used the New Right, she argued, so the New Right used the anti-abortion movement. But this did not mean that the New Right did not care about abortion. Replying to accusations about attacks on abortion clinics, Dr J. C. Willke, the NRLC's president, declared that, by encouraging promiscuity, undermining the family and denying men the right to stop their wives from aborting, it was those who supported abortion who were the real source of violence 'to our beloved nation'. In making such a statement, Petchesky argued, he was revealing why both the New Right and the pro-life movement opposed abortion. It was not the fetus they were centrally concerned about, but 'patriarchal dominion' (Petchesky 1981: 208, 220–21).

Where, in some accounts, the NRLC has been described as part of the right, Petchesky's account was more nuanced. The relationship between the two movements, she acknowledged, was complicated, involving both links and tensions. New Right organisers had worked with anti-abortion groups, providing their expertise in direct mailing and the targeting of candidates. But their concerns went far beyond abortion, and not only did some pro-life leaders resent attempts to absorb abortion into a broader right-wing agenda, but the movement itself used a language of rights intended to appeal to liberals, and even included a number of left-wing activists. It was an argument she substantially retained when the article appeared in a revised form as part of a book three years later. In this version, however, rather than the New Right's being seen as creating its own constellation of organisations separate from the mainstream pro-life movement, it was now described as engaged in a process of absorbing the movement as a whole (Diamond 1995: 352–3; Calhoun-Brown 1997: 121; Diamond 1998b: 2, 110; Petchesky 1981: 218–20; Petchesky 1984: 256).

To evaluate this argument, we need to separate out two strands, the link between opposition to abortion and what might be called sexual conservatism and that between the movement and political conservatism. Petchesky's argument drew in part on what she

described as a study of pro-life activists that had found a strong cor-
relation between opposition to abortion and a morally conservative
stance. (Unfortunately, however, the study in question had actually
been of national survey data on the question, and examined opinion
at large rather than in the movement itself.) She suggested too that a
traditionalist sexual morality was evident not only in Willke's pro-
nouncement but also in the comments of participants at both a
national and a local pro-life convention (Petchesky 1981: 228–30, 245;
Granberg 1978: 414–29).

   In making such an argument, Petchesky had offered a possible
reason for joining the movement. Furthermore, as we have already
noted, other evidence exists of pro-life support for a conservative
sexual morality. But if this is the central motivation for activists in
general, why did the movement so frequently submerge that stance
beneath a discourse that foregrounded the status of life, not the protection of the family, as the reason for mobilisation? Anti-abortionists,
she argued, were concerned not with the endangered fetus, but with
an endangered patriarchy. But, in arguing this, she collapsed together
views on the rightful place of sex with views on the rightful place of
men, when the very study of abortion attitudes she had cited had concluded that there was only a 'slight' link between opposition to abortion and anti-feminism, and that only among Protestants. (Indeed, in
a subsequent article, its author had reported that NRLC members
usually supported women's equal rights, while another study from
the same period, this time comparing the official Catholic Church
stance on abortion with that of a Catholic prayer group, argued that
the two took a different approach to the issue, with only the latter pri-
oritising a link between the unborn and the family. Neither group,
however, linked the issue to either opposition to homosexuality or the
Equal Rights Amendment.) In equating opposition to abortion, to
sexual permissiveness and to feminism, Petchesky made it difficult to
see why anti-abortion activists joined the pro-life movement rather
than the Christian Right. In focusing on Willke's remark on the rights
of husbands, she had made it harder to understand a movement preponderantly made up not of men but of women. Nor, finally, had she
resolved whether the movement as a whole or a particular section of
it was to be understood as part of the New Right (Granberg 1978: 423,
1981: 162; Neitz 1981: 265, 271–3; Luker 1984: 138, 145).

   Certainly, just as the New Right had been instrumental in the
inception of the Christian Right, it had also played an important part

in the development of the anti-abortion movement in the late 1970s. The American Life Lobby had originated in a split from the NRLC in 1979, a split which had coincided with the breakaway of another organisation, led by Judie Brown's husband, the Life Amendment Political Action Committee (LAPAC). Already, before the break, she had been attending strategy meetings organised by Paul Weyrich for organisations concerned with the 'social issues'. He subsequently acted as an adviser to the American Life Lobby, and when the Browns called a conference in late 1981 in an unsuccessful attempt to unite pro-lifers around the Helms bill, Weyrich, Richard Viguerie and Howard Phillips were all among those who attended (*Human Events* 31 May–7 June 1996; Merton 1981: 162–4; Paige 1983: 147–50, 229).

But rather than representing the irrevocable annexation of part of the movement, let alone the beginnings of the capture of the movement as a whole, the New Right's relationship with pro-lifers was to prove highly problematic. Shortly after the break with the NRLC, one of the LAPAC's leading figures had declared that while the Committee was 'afraid of being called a tool of the New Right', his organisation was not. But, he added, the New Right was also 'a tool of ours'. The disappointments of the Reagan years, and the two movements' different priorities, were gradually to weaken this mutual dependence. In 1986, commenting on Reagan's support for a pro-choice Senator against a pro-life challenger, Judie Brown declared that pro-lifers should not rely on the President, the New Right or anyone else who 'espouses the pro-life message on occasion'. By 1991, while acknowledging the importance of advice from Weyrich and others on the right, she was arguing that the League worked 'very hard' to avoid 'the label "conservative" . . . We can't afford to be the tool of any group' (Merton 1981: 164; *A.L.L. About Issues* April 1986; McKeegan 1992: 170, 206–7).

While the League has become wary of the priorities of the American right, it appears to have remained closer to it than the last quotation would suggest, and in 1996, for instance, was one of the sponsoring organisations of an annual gathering of right-wing activists, the Conservative Leadership Conference. The NRLC has also forged links with the right, the most striking example of which caused some furore when it was revealed that it had accepted $650,000 from the Republican National Committee during the 1996 election campaign. But while the US Taxpayers Party suggested that this could be seen as 'political prostitution' on the part of the NRLC, it would be

more accurate to see it as compelling evidence of a mutually benefi-
cial relationship between a party wanting to encourage pro-life activity against Democrats and a movement which, even while it
sometimes supports Democrats or opposes Republicans, is bound to
be more sympathetic to the Republican Party than to its opponent. It
was not an inevitable relationship. As the 1980 election approached,
Jack Willke used his column in *National Right to Life News* to argue that
where once the Democrats had been the party that had cared for the
poor and defenceless, the Republican Party's taking up of the rights
of the unborn ensured that now it was the party that deserved to be
elected. Only, he declared, if the Democrats abandoned their support
for abortion could they return to their 'deserved central . . . place in
the American political scene.' We need not concur with this argument
to recognise that it offers a vital clue to the relationship between the
right to life movement and the right. Many pro-lifers do, indeed, see
the Republican Party as their ally. For some, such as the American Life
League, the relationship has proved disappointing. But it is an alliance around the issue that brought the pro-life movement into existence, and it is that, rather than the inherent nature of the movement's
itself, that has led to a politically heterogeneous movement's finding
its greatest chance of success to lie with the American right (*American
Enterprise* November–December 1996; *Washington Post National
Weekly Edition* 27 October 1997; Phillips, n.d.; *National Right to Life
News* 18 August 1980).

6

The Christian Right

We have already discussed a number of aspects of the Christian Right. In this chapter, we propose to consider three questions. Firstly, what it is that the Christian Right actually wants? Does it have a theocratic agenda, or is it considerably more modest in what it seeks to achieve? Secondly, what relationship does it have to other forms of right-wing politics? To what extent are there points of contact, and to what degree are there differences? Finally, in the light of the furore over Pat Robertson's writings, what role does conspiracy theory play in Christian Right thinking, and would we be right to see Robertson, and perhaps other figures on the Christian Right, as anti-Semitic?

In arguing that the Christian Right is pursuing a theocratic agenda, opponents have held that it presents a fundamental threat to a pluralist society. From the republic's founding, they contend, the dangers of a triumphant religious sectarianism have been kept at bay by laws and practices that protect the rights of believers and non-believers alike. Above all, the First Amendment erects a 'wall of sep-aration' between Church and State. The Christian Right, it is claimed, is seeking to impose its religious convictions on America and to replace a secular state with an evangelical authoritarianism (Boston 1996: 20; Cantor 1994: 1–3, 145–6; Clarkson 1997: 1–7).

A number of arguments have been put forward to counter such contentions. Two particularly deserve discussion. The former con-cerns the movement's origin, the latter its agenda. In the first, made in different ways by the neoconservative Nathan Glazer and the New Rightist Paul Weyrich, the Christian Right is seen not as arising in order to impose its views on society, but as a defensive movement against the 'successes of secular and liberal forces'. In Glazer's reading, school prayer did not enter the political arena until the Supreme Court banned it, abortion did not become an issue until liberals overrode state laws against it, and arguments about Christian schooling only arose because the state sought to impose restrictions on it. For Weyrich, it is the last of those which is crucial. The Christian Right, he observes, did not emerge in the aftermath of the 1962 Supreme Court decision on school prayer or the decision on abortion eleven years later. Instead, it was the federal government's attack on the rights of Christian schools that awoke the sleeping giant of evangelicalism (Glazer 1987: 250; Cromartie 1993: 25–6).

There are considerable difficulties with both of these arguments. Glazer views the Christian Right as a response to what was seen as secular aggression. But it is America as a whole, and not just the evangelical subculture, that was affected by court rulings and cultural change. To say that the views of traditionalist Christians were being overridden is certainly true. But for evangelicals to attempt to ensure that government took a certain stance on abortion or school prayer cannot convincingly be described as simply defensive when, if they had been successful, it would have been their views that had been imposed on others. As for Weyrich's argument, which, as we saw earlier, was espoused in *Conservative Digest* at the very moment that he was involved in bringing the Christian Right into existence, to say that the attack on Christian schools provoked its mobilisation is not to say that is solely what motivated it. This is even more the case when we consider the content of the schooling that the Christian Right was seeking to defend. Christians were being taught that abortion was wrong as such, and that homosexuality was wrong for evangelicals and non-evangelicals alike; and when we look at the initial priorities of groups such as the Moral Majority, we are seeing a movement whose activities stretched far beyond defending evangelicals' rights. Indeed, Weyrich has on at least one occasion given a different emphasis, in which the Christian Right is seen as precipitated by the government's intervention into Christian schools, but within the context of a more wide-ranging reaction to the social changes of the 1960s. What was crucial, he argued, was that the changes to which evangelicals objected in the broader society were now threatening their right to educate their own children. Such a reaction, however, did not and could not take a merely defensive form (Glazer 1987: 252; *National Review* 23 May 1986).

But if the Christian Right cannot be seen as simply protective, are we to conclude instead that it represents an attempt to impose a particular kind of Christianity on the polity as a whole? Here, we encounter the second attempt to refute accusations of theocracy. In part, as we saw earlier, this entails an expansion of the movement's putative constituency, from evangelicals to encompass, in Ralph Reed's formulation, 'people of faith' in general. It also involves, as we have noted, not only an attempt to deal with racism but an emphatic philo-Semitism, in which Robertson and many other figures in the Christian Right have long been involved in a defence of the state of Israel against its enemies. But it also entails a particular construction of the movement's agenda. In 1995, commenting on the *Contract with the American Family*, Reed declared: 'As religious conservatives, we have finally gained what we have always sought: a place at the table, a sense of legitimacy, and a voice in the conversation that we call democracy.' This has been a recurring theme in the Coalition's pronouncements. In describing its Road to Victory conference later the same year, for instance, Mike Russell, its communications director, was similarly to announce that with 'with the success of the conference . . . we have accomplished what we set out to do six years ago: get a seat at the table' (Reed 1996a: 11; *Christianity Today* 17 July 1995; *Human Events* 22 September 1995).

It is an argument that has been put forward by Reed at some length. The First Amendment, he argues, forbids the creation of an official religion, not the bringing of religious conviction to public debate, and believers wanted a place in society commensurate with their numbers. They had a 'unique contribution' to make to the building of a better country; but it was vital that they made it clear that their objective was 'not to dominate, but to participate'. Such a view can also be found elsewhere on the Christian Right. Thus, in a recent collection of essays produced by Focus on the Family, the editor explicitly rejects the suggestion that constitutional and legislative measures could – or should – Christianise America. When the public square is devoid of religion, he argues, then secularism itself becomes its religion. But if the public square, instead of being naked, is made sacred, then an imposed Christianity would violate the proper separation of Church and State and the rights of conscience. Instead of either, he concludes, America needs a principled pluralism, an affirmation of diversity in which competing truth claims can be debated and 'ultimate truth' freely sought (Reed 1996a: 77–9, 23, 40, 222; Crippen 1996: 36–7, 39–41).

This relatively modest interpretation of the Christian Right's agenda has interesting points of contact to two other arguments, one made by a conservative strategist, Grover Norquist, the other by one of the leading academic analysts of the movement, Matthew Moen.

We noted earlier Norquist's role in organising a conservative coalition in the early 1990s. It was described by Norquist as the 'Leave Us Alone' Coalition, and what united taxpayers, property owners, gun owners and small business, he declared, was that they all wanted to be left alone by government. The Christian Right too, he argued, was part of this coalition, both because it originated as a defensive response to government interference in the late 1970s and because it was essentially a parents' rights movement opposed to government interference and its use of 'their own tax dollars' in ways that insulted and attacked 'their values and their faith'. If Norquist's argument refers both to agenda and origin, seeing them as united, Moen treats them separately, arguing that the movement has been transformed since it first arose. Where the first wave of the movement, he argues, spoke in an explicitly Christian language, calling for the moral redemption of America, the second wave has turned instead to a more sophisticated strategy of presenting itself as a persecuted minority and framing the issues with which it was concerned in the liberal language of rights (*Imprimis* May 1996; Moen 1992: 119–37).

Here, again, there are problems. Reed's argument, as we have seen, represented a certain period in the development of the Christian Right that appears to have been seen as too compromising, not only by James Dobson, Gary Bauer and others outside the Christian Coalition, but by elements within it. In addition to what still remains an open question, how the Christian Right will develop after Reed's departure, there is also the question of how well how the movement addresses those outside its ranks matches what is argued within. Where Moen suggests that the movement has become more realistic and more accepting of ruling political norms, it may be that this overstates the degree to which the movement as a whole has moderated its demands. As Justin Watson has argued, the Christian Coalition need not be seen as consciously deceptive in trying to hold together two impulses, one to represent an interest within the world of interest group politics, the other, in the image we shall explore later, to 'take America back' (*New Republic* 26 May 1997; Moen 1992: 157–9; Watson 1997: 175–9).

Indeed, while Moen has suggested that early notions of a secular humanist conspiracy have been replaced by 'more scientific approaches to public policy', this would certainly seem to overstate the evolution that has taken place. In 1980, Tim LaHaye argued that humanists were leading America 'down the path of moral degeneracy' and the creation of a 'socialist state similar to Russia'. Ten years later, such views were still strong, with Pat Robertson arguing that humanists who sought a socialist society and one-world government were responsible for the promotion of promiscuity in the media and James Dobson contending that conservative Christians were under attack by secular humanism, now the dominant force in education, the media and government. There was 'a coordinated, well thought out strategy' in play, he declared, in which by isolating children from their parents and indoctrinating them with humanist values, the culture could be fundamentally changed (Moen 1997: 28; LaHaye 1980b: 143, 147; Robertson 1990: 13, 66–7; Dobson and Bauer 1990: 20–22, 35).

It is important, certainly, not to exaggerate the ambition of the modern movement. As we noted earlier, outside the Christian Right, though with some influence within it, a grouping has emerged that has criticised it for both its theology and its politics. If there is a tension in the Christian Right between defending an embattled enclave and seeking to restore a lost hegemony, no such tension exists among Reconstructionists. Created initially by the Presbyterian thinker (and John Birch Society activist) R. J. Rushdoony at the end of the 1950s, Reconstructionism has become an increasingly visible presence among conservative Protestants. An understanding of its argument necessitates some discussion of theology. Reconstructionists argue that God's mandate at the time of the creation, that man should subdue the earth and exercise dominion over it, is to be understood as an instruction for his followers today. In consequence, they are highly critical of the Christian Right, arguing it espouses what one of the leading Reconstructionists, Gary DeMar, has called 'a compromised Christian agenda' in which America is 'called back to morality but not necessarily to Christ'. Furthermore, he argues, the Christian Right has failed to pursue 'an offensive strategy'. This, it is claimed, is linked to a fundamentally flawed approach to Scripture. Within the Christian Right, and indeed among evangelicals more generally, there is a widespread belief in what is known as premillennialism, that Christ will return, lifting the faithful into the heavens in what is termed the Rapture. According to Reconstructionists, however, while it is indeed true that Christ will return, it will only be after an extended period of Christian government, based on Old Testament law. In arguing that the Second Coming follows, not precedes, the creation of a Godly order, Reconstructionists believe they have secured a sound basis for political action, while premillennialists cannot be fully committed to taking possession of social institutions, since they expect at any time to be rescued from a world that is in its Last Days (Cantor 1994: 120–21; Barron 1992: 23–5; *Christian News* 18 September 1989; *Biblical Worldview* March 1995; Clarkson 1997: 98).

Despite the ferocity with which this dispute has been conducted, it is difficult to be persuaded that the Christian Right's theology has proved so disabling. While believing in the imminent return of Christ, premillennialists have proved perfectly able to pursue a political agenda. Indeed, rather than succumb to what one of the leading Reconstructionists, Gary North, has called a 'Bugout theology', the Christian Right has been accused by critics of having come under the sway of Reconstructionism itself. But to underplay the tension between Christian Right hopes of dominion and less ambitious aspirations, or to ignore the conflict between Reconstructionists and Christian Right leaders, would be to misread the situation. The Focus on the Family book referred to earlier, for instance, explicitly rejects Reconstructionism, citing a leading evangelical's suggestion that chances of survival might be better under a radical Shi'ite regime, while Reed has characterised it as 'an authoritarian ideology' that the Christian Right should unequivocally oppose (Diamond 1989: 135; Clarkson and Porteous 1993: 93; Clarkson 1997: 77; Crippen 1996: 35; Reed 1996b: 262).

In Reed's case, the antagonism is mutual. DeMar has criticised him both for disavowing the need for a Christian nation and for characterising homosexuality as wrong while refusing to advocate the Biblical sanction for it – the death penalty. Another Reconstructionist, while declaring that many of the Coalition's grass-roots leaders were sound, has attacked him for merely claiming an equal say in politics when 'most politically active Christians don't want equal time with homosexuals, abortionists, animal worshiping pagans' and 'radical feminists . . . We want them silenced and mercifully disciplined according to the Word of God.' But what of Robertson himself? In distinction to their scathing attitude to many in the Christian Right, Reconstructionists have suggested that he represents, in North's formulation, a 'halfway house' between the two camps (or, in DeMar's even more intriguing phrase, that he is 'an operational Reconstructionist'). Certainly, he has declared his belief in dominion and his admiration for many Reconstructionist teachings. However, both because of what he sees as their unbiblical belief in a 'utopia here on earth' and their post-millennialism, he has disassociated himself from their overall argument (Watson 1997: 115, 119, 114; Lienesch 1993: 228; *Christian News* 27 January 1992).

Originating partly as a defence of a threatened subculture, but also as an attempt to displace the hegemony of a rival belief-system, the Christian Right continues to display both impulses. Robertson, for example, has portrayed America as threatened with collapse unless 'Christian conservatives' challenge 'the Radical Left' control of 'all of the citadels of power' and 'blast the enemy out of its positions'. Yet, if we can contrast this view with Reed's call for a place at the table, we can also contrast Dobson's criticism of Christian Coalition compromise with Focus on the Family's publication of a book calling for Christians to join in a public discussion in which all questions are open to debate. The Christian Right is neither a theocratic juggernaut nor the last gasp of an embattled enclave succumbing to modernity. Instead, it is torn between defending what is left and restoring what it has lost, just as it is torn between earthly compromise and heavenly transformation (Robertson 1993: 300–1).

We have already discussed the Christian Right's relationship with the Republican hierarchy. Electorally significant but also seen as potentially electorally damaging, the Christian Right has proved an important if difficult ally for GOP leaders. But what of its relationship to the conservative movement as a whole? Here, it is important to be careful. Rebecca Klatch, in her discussion of women on the right, had distinguished between *laissez-faire* and social conservatives, arguing that the first grouping takes a libertarian stance incompatible with that of the second. This cleavage, she argues, has long existed, distinguishing those drawn to non-economic issues from those committed to economic conservatism. But this is to equate economic conservatives with full-fledged libertarians, when those who occupy the first category may regard social conservatism as irrelevant to their concerns or to electoral success rather than fundamentally unacceptable. Certainly, economic conservatives may well view the incursion of the Christian Right into the Republican Party with horror, and in that way may be little different from those within the party who are still definable not as conservatives but as moderates. It is equally possible, however, that should economic conservatives conclude that without social conservative support they would be unable to prevail, then they would diversify their political agenda accordingly. This would appear to be a useful way to understand the efforts of both Gingrich and Norquist to incorporate the Christian Right within a broader coalition in which Christian Right priorities are subordinated but not overtly rejected (Klatch 1987: 6–9).

If we were to focus solely on libertarians, we would appear to be on safer ground in assuming diametrical opposition. Thus, in the early 1980s, an article in the leading libertarian periodical, *Reason*, described the Christian Right as authoritarians 'hell-bent on repealing the 20th century' while, later in the decade, *Libertarian Agenda*, the journal of libertarians within the Republican Party, indignantly denied that libertarians and the Christian Right could be seen as part of the same movement (Brudnoy 1982: 243; *Libertarian Agenda* February 1988).

This hostility continued into the next decade. In the late 1990s, for instance, discussing the recent advertisements arguing that gays could become heterosexual, an editorial in *Reason* commented on a recent television appearance of the co-ordinator of the campaign, Janet Folger of the Center for Reclaiming America. She had been forced to admit, it noted, that she favoured the imprisonment of gays. 'Her claim to speak for "tolerance" dissolved instantly.' Another writer the following month was even more concerned by what he described as the effects of Reconstructionism on 'the terms of discourse on the traditionalist right'. But, as we have noted, the libertarian movement is not wholly in agreement on social issues. Within the Libertarian Party, an argument has long raged on the status of the fetus and thus the legitimacy or otherwise of abortion, while for paleolibertarians there is an amount of common ground between their beliefs and those of the Christian Right. Most libertarians, Rothbard has suggested, think of Christian conservatives as seeking to impose a theocracy and wanting to 'break down bedroom doors to enforce a Morality Police upon the country'. In fact, he claimed, their central concern was instead to resist the efforts of 'a left-liberal elite' to destroy their culture and undermine minimal government in the name of rights. The ban on gays in the military, he argued, was good sense, not bigotry, while on abortion, although those libertarians who, like himself, supported the right to choose were diametrically opposed to the pro-life stance of the Christian Right, there was still room for co-operation around opposition to taxpayer funding of abortions and a return of decisions on the matter to state and local levels. Libertarians, he concluded, should see themselves as allies of the Christian Right. 'Once again, as before the late 1950's, libertarians should consider themselves people of the Right' (*Reason* October,

November 1998; Burkett 1998: 48; *Rothbard–Rockwell Report* February 1993).

If the relationship between the Christian Right and libertarians is more complicated than we might expect, so too is that between the Christian Right and the Patriot movement. One source of conflict, at least with some in the Patriot movement, concerns Christian Right support for Israel. In 1983, for instance, the *Moral Majority Report* accused the leading Patriot publication, the *Spotlight*, of deceit in its criticisms of Falwell's support for Israel. Describing the paper as 'well-known for its anti-Semitic leanings', the publication declared that reports of meetings between the Moral Majority leader and critics of his position had been fabricated, as had claims of massive falls in donations in protest at his stance on the treatment of Palestinians. Nor was Falwell the only prominent evangelical with which the *Spotlight* clashed. The same year, it published a four-part series criticising Robertson's views on Israel and carried a cover-article denouncing him for telling viewers of his television programme that they should not read the paper (*Moral Majority Report* May 1983; Cantor 1994: 15; *Spotlight* 2 May 1983).

There has been conflict too over evangelical belief in the Rapture, in which, reminiscent of the Christian Right's disputes with Reconstructionists, Christian Identity believers have argued that to anticipate being swept into the heavens denies the need for Christians to wage a final war against America's enemies on earth. But if there have been clashes, this does not mean that the two movements were wholly antagonistic. One concern that has reached into a number of sections of the right concerns environmental regulation. Much of this argument has been concerned with the effects of regulation on both employment and free enterprise, but Patriots have been particularly inclined to give a highly sinister interpretation to environmentalist calls for reducing population. Most importantly, they are particularly exercised by the role of the United Nations and other international bodies in promoting a global ecological agenda. It is a concern they share with sections of the 'pro-family' movement, which links, in turn, to the most important aspect of Patriot argument in recent years, the threat posed by the New World Order. As we have already noted, this entails the conviction that America is in danger of enslavement by conspiratorial forces. In this concern, Patriots are not alone. In late 1994, for instance, a critic described attending a Christian Coalition meeting in Ohio and hearing members claim that former military bases were being converted into detention camps, that UN troops were already stationed on American soil and that black helicopters had been sighted in the area. In the same period, the publication of a New York chapter of the Coalition included material from the *Spotlight* claiming that UN occupation was imminent (Barkun 1997: 106; Zeskind n.d., c.1987: 24, 33; Switzer 1997; Russell 1997: 86–7; *Free American* October 1997; *Wake-Up Call America* January–February, March–April 1998; *Media Bypass* August 1996; *Eagle Forum* Winter 1989; *Family Voice* May 1996; Boston 1996: 138–40).

All of these claims, as we shall discover in the next chapter, are central to Patriot writings in recent years. That sections of the Christian Right have been echoing Patriot themes is not to say that the two movements have coalesced, although, intriguingly, one study of a Patriot grouping in California in 1996 did find that 15.6 per cent of the people surveyed were also involved with the Christian Right. Often, it can be that the two movements, with their different priorities and strategies, represent alternatives. Thus, at a 1996 Christian Coalition gathering, one participant told a journalist that if it weren't for the Christian Coalition, he would be in the Michigan Militia. He had prayed and the Lord had showed him Scripture about honouring government. 'It's a tough battle', he told her, 'but I stay away from the men who are organized,' adding 'I don't know, though, what's gonna happen when push comes to shove' (Kaplan 1998: 3, 25, appendix n.p.; *Vogue* July 1996).

Certainly the two strategies are seen as alternatives by the Christian Coalition's leadership. Thus, according to the organisation's spokesman, Mike Russell: 'What we're hearing from militias is a conspiracy theory that the government is the enemy and it is best to withdraw from the civic process. That is not what the Christian Coalition or the religious conservative policy organizations are saying. They are working within the system, not trying to extricate from it. It's 180 degrees in the opposite direction from what the militias or the ultra-fringe organizations are trying to do' (*Washington Post National Weekly Edition* 29 May–4 June 1995).

Nonetheless, there remain points of contact. In part, this is because it is not actually the case that militias oppose working in the political process nor, come to that, that they are unconcerned with moral issues. We have already noted an Idaho militia's involvement in 'pro-family' petitioning, while the Virginia Citizens' Militia has suggested that a 'Resistance Movement' should be divided into a political arm and a military arm, the former to include 'those who are involved in Pro-Life organizations', gun rights groups, the home schooling movement and other organisations. The Militia of Montana, too, in describing how Militia Support Groups could be organised on a nationwide basis, has set out a detailed organisational structure including the position of Coalition Director 'responsible for developing a broad-based coalition of conservative organizations who will provide leadership and support in the moral community for pro-family efforts' (Militia of Montana n.d.: 17–18; *Southern Ranger* July–August 1997).

But there is also an area of agreement around how the two movements see what is happening to America. One Patriot author, Robert Spear, has described going back to a book he had read some years before, Gary Allen's *None Dare Call It Conspiracy*, in order to make sense of Bush's pronouncements on the New World Order. This and other sources, he notes, all pointed towards a centuries-old conspiracy of wealthy power brokers to bring about one-world government and rule by the Antichrist. In order to understand this conspiracy, he suggested, two books were particularly to be recommended – Gary Kah's *En Route to Global Occupation* and Pat Robertson's *The New World Order*. As we shall see, the relationship between the Christian Right and these three examples of conspiracist writing is of crucial importance (Spear 1992: vii–viii).

In 1991, *The New World Order* was published by a Christian publishing house. As a long-term observer of international events, Robertson wrote, he had come to see a continuity in American policy, a continuity that stretched from Woodrow Wilson to George Bush. The connecting thread was to be found in the concept of a new world order, an idea that was the tool of sinister forces behind the scenes of American politics. Who these forces were, he suggested, was a matter of dispute. Some had linked them to the eighteenth-century group, the Illuminati, some to New Age religion, some to international finance. What was clear, however, was that the desire to unify and control the world did not originate in human hearts, but came from 'the depth of something that is evil' (Robertson 1991: 6–9).

For over two centuries the architects of the new world order had been at work. The Great Seal of the United States, adopted by Congress in 1782 and printed on every dollar bill, showed an unfinished pyramid, underneath which were the words 'Novus Ordo Seclorum', new order of the ages. The incomplete nature of the pyramid implied that as yet the task was incomplete. Was it possible, Robertson wondered, that what was intended was not a land of rights and freedom but a world order of a very different kind? The conspiracy had at that time already come into existence. In 1776, a Bavarian professor, Adam Weishaupt, had created the Order of the Illuminati, a secret society devoted to the destruction of church and private property and the worldwide rule of an elect of illuminated ones. In 1782, it had taken over Continental Freemasonry, from whose lodge in Frankfurt, a city controlled by the Rothschild family, a plan for world revolution was carried forth. Responsible for the French Revolution, Illuminism had passed into Marxism and, as the British author Nesta Webster had shown, the Illuminati themselves had been behind the Bolshevik Revolution (Robertson 1991: 35–6, 67–72, 181).

But the conspiracy was not merely one of confessed radicals. Woodrow Wilson had been brought into office in 1912 to serve the interests of the bankers, and soon after his election had 'helped facilitate the two pillars of the international financial assault on the freedom and integrity of America', the creation 'by the German banker Paul Warburg, the Morgans, and the Rockefellers' of the privately-owned Federal Reserve Board and the introduction of federal income tax. Since his time, presidents had been advised by the elite Council on Foreign Relations (CFR), and since 1940 only one secretary of state had not been a member. It was in this organisation that the notion of a new world order had long been espoused. Other bodies had subsequently come into existence – the United Nations, the Rockefeller-funded Trilateral Commission, with its declared goal of 'managing the world economy', occultist groups with their rejection of divine revelation and their advocacy of the submersion of the individual into some greater whole. Now everything was coming to a head. The UN's authorisation of military action against Iraq was the first occasion since the Tower of Babel that the world's nations had come together, and in the very area that the Tower had been built. God had struck down the first attempt to combine humanity against Him. Now, however, George Bush was 'unwittingly carrying out the mission . . . of a tightly knit cabal whose goal is nothing less than a new order for the human race under the domination of Lucifer and his followers' (Robertson 1991: 64–5, 44, 98, 102, 170, 174, 252, 37).

Initially, with the exception of a stinging attack in the *Wall Street Journal*, the book attracted little attention outside its intended audience. Three years later, however, this was to change. Firstly, it came under fire from the Jewish Anti-Defamation League, which, while it noted that it included 'praise for Israel', saw it as a 'bizarre' example of conspiracy theory rife with anti-Semitic attacks on 'European bankers'. Then, writing in the *Washington Post*, an erstwhile conservative, Michael Lind, also took up the issue, declaring that Robertson's book espoused a conspiracy theory that repeated anti-Semitic libels about the supposed machinations of Jewish bankers. Two years earlier, when still a conservative, he had already attacked the book in an article calling for Republicans to break with the Christian Coalition. Robertson, he now complained, continued to enjoy support from William Buckley and other leading conservatives, despite holding the crackpot theory that 'Satan-worshipping occultists' secretly ruled America. Once, Lind recalled, Buckley had disassociated the respectable right from the extreme theories of the John Birch Society. Now, however, he defended a man whose claims made 'Bircher conspiracy theories look tame' (*Wall Street Journal* 31 December 1991; Cantor 1994: 23–5; *Washington Post* 16 October 1994; *New Republic* 14 December 1992).

It was the beginning of what would become an extended, and increasingly bitter, exchange. In the months that followed, Lind returned to the attack in a cover-article in the prestigious *New York Review*, replies were to appear in a variety of conservative publications, and Lind was to reply in turn. For Lind, a perusal of the bibliography of Robertson's book showed the presence of 'several tracts characterised as anti-Semitic by the Anti-Defamation League'. The book, he argued, had 'little to do with ordinary evangelical Protestant theology' and instead was rooted in 'the underground literature of far-right populism'. As the argument developed, Lind was joined by another former conservative, Jacob Heilbrunn, who argued that in part Robertson's comments on international finance had been drawn from a anti-Semitic book by an 'American conservative writer', Eustace Mullins. His main focus, however, was a comparison of extracts from Nesta Webster with sections of Robertson's book. Not only was the argument the same, he argued, but it was possible to trace which paragraphs of Webster Robertson had used, a process that had involved the deliberate exclusion of those sections with 'the most odious references to Jews'. It was an argument that Lind found wholly compatible with his own. Robertson, he reiterated, held 'far more bizarre and sinister' views than the John Birch Society. But the reason why mainstream conservatives refused to break with Robertson as they had done with the John Birch Society was because the Christian Coalition was too strong (Lind 1995a: 1, 25, 23; Heilbrunn 1995: 68–71; Lind 1995b: 68; Lind 1996: 110, 117).

Lind's argument concerned both conservatives in general and Robertson in particular. How did each respond? *National Review*, for instance, sought to defend Robertson while keeping a distance from what he had actually said. Replying initially in jovial fashion (and ignoring the claim of anti-Semitism), Buckley declared that he and others supported much of Robertson's political stance, but 'if Pat Robertson indeed believes that crazy stuff, I here and now expel him from the conservative movement'. A subsequent reply took a sharper tone towards Lind without moving appreciably closer to Robertson. 'Paranoia about bankers runs deep in the American mind,' it suggested, 'and Robertson has imbibed all of it.' But Lind's attack, it claimed, was that of an ex-conservative, acting on behalf of the liberal establishment. Robertson was not an anti-Semite, and the reasons why conservatives had given 'Robertson's writings . . . a free pass' was because he had never been elected to any office and because they were 'not part of his political pitch'. He had not, the magazine declared, mentioned them 'on the hustings of Iowa', any more than Ralph Reed expounded on them today (*National Review* 21 November 1994, 6 February 1995).

Robertson himself, as we would expect, was far less defensive. The book, he claimed, did not 'embrace a conspiracy theory of history' and was not anti-Semitic. Its central thrust had been to show the danger both to the USA and Israel in a foreign policy controlled by the UN, and only mischief-makers could make the claim that his book contained a concealed anti-Semitism. He did not believe, he declared, that international finance should be seen as Jewish, and he was a supporter of Israel and an opponent of anti-Semitism in America. He had denounced the *Spotlight* on his television programme, just as he had attacked David Duke's candidacy, and his message, like his heart, was 'pro-Jewish' (*Christian American* April, May–June 1995).

Despite such protestations, at first sight the Christian Coalition leader's critics had made an unanswerable case. Heilbrunn had demonstrated the debt Robertson owed to Webster, while Lind had plausibly suggested why Buckley had been more willing to break with the John Birch Society than with Robertson. Nor was *National Review* right, although Lind appears not to have been aware of evidence to the contrary, that Robertson's conspiracy theorising had been absent from either his presidential bid or the Christian Coalition. But, as we shall see, in seeming to uncover the roots of Robertson's conspiracism, Lind's claims of anti-Semitism obscured more than they revealed.

Rather than being excluded from the Christian Coalition, conspiracy theorising was important from its inception. Speaking at a banquet at the Coalition's first convention, Robertson had declared that 'we are hearing noises about a New World Order' whereby the United Nations was 'going to rule the world . . . We're to cede the sovereignty of America to this organization. One world currency. One world army. One world court system, very possibly.' The financial, academic and government elites, he declared, had turned against 'their own society. And into that void steps an organization called the Christian Coalition.' *The New World Order*, indeed, was included with subscriptions to *Christian American* for those who took up membership of the Christian Coalition in the early 1990s, and in recommending the book to its readers, *Christian American* had argued that Robertson had demonstrated that there was a conspiratorial elite agenda, linked both to recent events and to Biblical prophecy (Clarkson and Porteous 1993: 29, 30; *Christian American* January–February 1992).

This notion of a conspiratorial elite agenda was one that *Christian American*, and its then Senior Editor, John Wheeler, would come back to more than once. Even before Robertson's book had appeared, the paper had carried a cover-story on the issue in which Wheeler had noted that for many, President Bush's New World Order was legitimising world government. They believed, he went on, that this was at the heart of the agenda of the CFR and the Trilateral Commission, both organisations to which Bush had belonged, and, as far back as 1959, the former group had produced a study calling for a new international order that had been followed two years later by a State Department document calling for world disarmament and a UN military. Many American patriots, he declared, now feared for America's future, while the Bible, in talking of the coming of the Antichrist, was seen by many as foretelling 'a globally-controlled socialist economy' (*Christian American* May–June 1991).

The argument was to surface again in two interviews published in the paper. In the first, Wheeler initially asked Alan Keyes, an African-American former Assistant Secretary of State, his ideas on black politics and the future of black conservatism. The bulk of the interview, however, was devoted to a very different question – the drive to one-world government. Keyes defended the Republican record, arguing that during the Reagan years, those who sought to strengthen the UN and weaken America had been held at bay. But the New World Order had been promoted by Bush, Wheeler declared, and American foreign policy since Kennedy had sought to bring about the creation of a UN army. With Keyes still resisting Wheeler's argument (neither Nixon nor Reagan, he declared, had followed such a policy) the interviewer retreated to the suggestion that some people, perhaps career State Department figures, were pursuing such an agenda. Keyes was more willing to accept this, though only in the sense of the Reagan administration's differences with a foreign policy bureaucracy that did not share its assumptions. A conspiracy theory had been put forward, but not by the interviewee. This was not, however, how an editorial comment interpreted the interview. Alan Keyes, it reported, had confirmed 'that those with a globalist agenda have dominated United States' foreign policy for much of the 20th Century' and that the Clinton administration's disarming of America and steps towards a UN army had their roots in a plan hatched in the Kennedy years (*Christian American* January 1994).

It was to be a theme that Wheeler would return to when interviewing another former Reagan era Assistant Secretary of State, Elliot Abrams. Ever since the Council for Foreign Relations document on the issue, and the resultant Kennedy era proposals for world disarmament, Wheeler suggested, 'our foreign policy', under both Republicans and Democrats, had been moving in the direction of a UN army. Abrams, unsurprisingly, did not concur. Bush, he thought, had pursued multilateralism without believing in it. Clinton did believe in it. But 'I don't believe that you can say that happened under the Reagan years' (*Christian American* March 1994).

That such material should appear in the pages of *Christian American* should not be surprising. Robertson had long believed in the existence of an elite conspiracy. When first entering politics, at the end of the 1970s, he had declared in his newsletter, 'Unless Christians desire a nation and a world reordered to the humanistic/atheis-tic/hedonistic model, it is absolutely vital that we take control of the United States government from the Trilateral Commission and the Council on Foreign Relations.' During his bid for the presidency, he was the subject of several biographies, one of which argued that such notions had almost disappeared, and had been replaced by 'prag-matic' and 'rational' statements in line with other conservatives. Yet, the year after it appeared, the journal of the Libertarian Republican

Organizing Committee was to note that his campaign speeches in Michigan and Iowa contained numerous references to the power of the CFR and the Trilateral Commission. Similarly, in a book published the year before the one Lind had attacked, Robertson had already raised some of its themes, attacking the CFR, the Trilateral Commission and Bush administration talk of a New World Order (*U.S. News and World Report* 24 September 1979; Harrell 1987: 190–91; *Libertarian Agenda* February 1988; Robertson 1990: 104, 265–6).

Nor was this a concern unique to the Christian Coalition. We noted earlier a Patriot author's recommendation of books by Pat Robertson and Gary Kah. Kah too attributed a secret meaning to the Great Seal of the United States, and referred to the 1959 CFR study on international order and a wide range of other material to argue that a 'plot to establish a New World Order', having twice used war to extend supranational organisation, could now be increasing the powers of the United Nations as a preliminary to precipitating another 'major global conflict . . . to take humanity the rest of the way in to an all-out occult based world government'. When this occurred, the Antichrist would be revealed. This work, which has been sold by such groups as the Militia of Montana, has also attracted interest on the Christian Right (Kah 1992: 33–4, 141–2; Militia of Montana 1994: 7).

In 1993, Kah was interviewed on *Beverly LaHaye Live*, a radio programme chaired by the leader of Concerned Women for America. During the programme, the CWA magazine reported, he discussed the existence of a 'well organized movement' to bring about a new world order and the role of Clinton, a member of the CFR, in its plans. Nor was this his only involvement with LaHaye's organisation. His book, along with an audiotape of the interview, was offered to *Family Voice* readers for a donation of $20, and shortly after he spoke at the CWA 1993 Convention, arguing that the Federal Reserve, the CFR and the Trilateral Commission were linked in a drive towards one-world government (*Family Voice* June, November–December 1993).

As Paul Boyer has shown in great detail, evangelicals have long expected the emergence of a tyrannical world ruler in the final days before the return of the Lord. In the 1930s, for instance, Mussolini and Hitler were both seen as candidates for the Antichrist, while more recent suggestions have ranged from J. F. Kennedy to King Juan Carlos of Spain. Efforts to extend political organisation beyond the purely national, he argues, were inevitably associated with the forces of evil. Thus in 1983, for instance, the religious broadcaster Jack Van Impe warned that such organisations as the CFR were part of the preparations for 'a new world order', while two years earlier, in *The 1980s: Countdown to Armageddon*, the top-selling apocalyptic writer Hal Lindsey (whose 1970 book *The Late Great Planet Earth* had been printed in 28 million copies by 1990) declared that the Trilateral Commission and the CFR were linked to 'the political-economic one-world system the Bible predicts for the last days' (Boyer 1992: 108, 275, 148, 264, 418, 416, 419, 266, 5).

In perhaps the most interesting instance of all, one can turn to a 1983 edition of a conservative Christian paper, the *Christian Inquirer*, a publication whose editorial board included Tim and Beverly LaHaye, another leading Christian Right figure, Bill Billings, and the anti-abortion leader, Judie Brown. The cover declared 'The Sell-out To World Bankers Seems Complete And The Stage Set To Force World Government'. For twelve years, it reminded readers, the *Christian Inquirer* had been warning that 'an antichrist, dictatorial world government can likely be anticipated shortly'. The theme of such a government, to be brought into being by 'the international bankers', was repeated again later in the issue. Readers, the paper urged, should write in to order a *New World Order Special Report* (*Christian Inquirer* February 1983; Moen 1992: 17–18).

When President Bush called for a new world order, Berlet has noted, his use of this term 'surged through' sections of the right 'like an electric shock'. Lind is certainly right to argue that conspiracy the-orising is rife on the anti-Semitic right. But it is not the only source of such thinking. As Tim LaHaye recalled in the early 1990s, for twenty years he and his wife 'worked tirelessly' against 'the satanically-inspired, centuries old conspiracy to . . . establish a new world order'. Having read at least fifty books on the Illuminati, he was convinced of their existence and their power. Not only the fear of one-world government but the very term 'new world order' was common cur-rency among conservative Christians, and where Lind had portrayed Robertson's argument as distinct from 'ordinary' evangelicalism, it in fact is but one expression of a long evangelical tradition. And, if we examine Robertson's book more closely, we shall find that a third source needs to be considered (Berlet 1998: 19; LaHaye 1992: 136).

At one point, for instance, he praises the 'excellent work *The Naked Capitalist*' by 'my friend Cleon Skousen'. Skousen, a former FBI agent and veteran Mormon political activist, had already argued some twenty years earlier that there was increasing evidence that 'the highest centers of political and economic power have been forcing the entire human race towards a global, socialist, dictatorial-oriented society'. While his book dates back to 1970, another work drawn on by Robertson, William Still's *New World Order: The Ancient Plan of Secret Societies*, appeared the year before Robertson's own. Still and Robertson both use some of the same writers, but there are important differences, one of which is that the former's account draws on a writer we have already encountered, Gary Allen. Allen's 1971 book, *None Dare Call It Conspiracy*, was concerned with the Insiders, a group of 'power-seeking billionaires' intent on the creation of a world state. It was an argument he was to develop in later work. In one book that appeared in 1976, in addition to discussing the 1961 State Department document later cited in the *Christian American*, he was to argue that the Insiders were cloaking their drive for world power under the term New World Order. In another book the same year, he argued that the term was 'a CFR code phrase for a one-world government' (Robertson 1991: 111, 274; Skousen 1970: back cover, 24; Aho 1990: 118–19; Still 1990: 200; Allen 1971: 33, 35; Allen 1976a: 91–2, 61–2, 1976b: 72).

If Allen was absent from Robertson's book, he was not only cited by Still but by Gary Kah too. Robertson's use of Still, like the Concerned Women for America's utilisation of Kah, was to draw on Allen's work at one remove, and takes us back to a crucial aspect of Lind's argument. He had claimed that Robertson's theory was far more extreme than that of the John Birch Society thirty years earlier. In fact, the two are far more closely related, since Gary Allen was a highly visible figure in the Society, and his arguments about the Insiders, the Council on Foreign Relations and the drive for world government were a distillation of Birchite doctrine once the Society had moved beyond its initial anti-Communism and come to see Communism as merely part of an all-encompassing plot, a plot that included the engineering of the French and Bolshevik Revolutions by the Illuminati. It is not surprising, then, that when the paperback edition of *The New World Order* appeared, it should carry on its cover an extract of a favourable review from the magazine of the John Birch Society (Kah 1992: 33, 216; Mintz 1985: 142–8; Lipset and Raab 1971: 250–53; Boston 1996: 131).

The denunciation of the John Birch Society by Buckley and others in the 1960s had drawn a dividing line between mainstream conservatism and the radical right, and, as we have noted, the Society was subsequently to experience a substantial decline. Nonetheless, its ideas were carried far beyond its immediate supporters through the widespread circulation of some of its publications. To take perhaps the most important example, Allen's *None Dare Call It Conspiracy* reportedly sold over 3 million copies. A wide array of the right have imbibed Birchite material, and some in turn have drawn on it for their own writings. It is through such convoluted routes, then, that the arguments presented by Allen have exerted an influence among evangelicals and among conservatives (and, of course, among those who are both) (Allen 1976b: 70).

This is not to deny that some of the sources for Christian Right conspiracism have a rather different provenance. This is particularly the case for Nesta Webster, but also for Eustace Mullins, whose political career extends from his involvement in the minuscule pro-Nazi National Renaissance Party in the early 1950s to his influence on the modern Patriot movement in the 1990s. But here we are faced with an important problem. As Berlet has recently noted, 'Mullins writes in two styles.' While his writings on such topics as 'Jews and Ritual Murder' are unashamedly anti-Semitic, his better-known book on the Federal Reserve is not so easily pigeon-holed. It is one of the weaker parts of Heilbrunn's case, then, that, as well as strangely describing Mullins as a 'conservative', he does not show that the book Robertson draws on is as incontrovertibly anti-Semitic as Mullins has been on other occasions (George and Wilcox 1992: 353–4; Z *Magazine* March 1992; Berlet 1998: 10; Baron 1995: 31–2).

Replying to his critics, Robertson obscured what his book had actually argued. He had indeed warned that the New World Order was a danger to both Christians and Jews and that the war against Iraq would be followed by a Satanic onslaught against Israel. But he had, of course, also argued much more. Yet one need not agree with his peculiar account of the book's focus or his denial (in contrast, one might note, to *Christian American*'s own review of his book) that his work espoused a conspiracy theory of history, to find his denial of deliberate anti-Semitism persuasive. In one of his most interesting comments on the subject, Lind noted that, when interviewed on the subject in late 1995, the Christian Coalition leader rejected the accusation of anti-Semitism and blamed a research assistant for misleading him into reliance on Nesta Webster. Allen, over twenty years earlier, had sought to promote a conspiracy theory in which he gave prominence to the role of Jewish bankers while rejecting the claim that 'the entire conspiracy' was Jewish, only to find his disavowal of anti-Semitism disbelieved. Now the same had happened to Robertson (Robertson 1991: 256–8; Lind 1996: 115–16; Mintz 1985: 147–9; Aho 1990: 255–7).

Robertson's arguments had been portrayed as both idiosyncratic and classically anti-Semitic. Instead, however, the most important source of his claims, as for much modern conspiracism, is not the extreme right but the radical right, above all the society whose reprint of a eighteenth-century attack on the Illuminati is to be found in Robertson's bibliography (and, we might add, whose training seminars Tim LaHaye has described himself as often addressing). With Cleon Skousen a member of its Speakers' Bureau and, despite its frequently expressed opposition to anti-Semitism, with Nesta Webster's books prominently featured on its bookshop list, the John Birch Society comes into sight at almost every turn. As Frank Mintz has shown, the Society was not the first to express concern about the Council on Foreign Relations, nor to see the Illuminati as a dangerous presence in twentieth-century America. What it did, however, was to construct an elaborate theory that reached far beyond its boundaries. The Christian Right, as we have seen, has become a vital part of both the Republican Party and the conservative movement. But it is linked too to the radical right, and provided a crucial new constituency for a tradition that once linked Eisenhower with the Kremlin and in recent times links both Bush and Clinton with the forces of Hell (Robertson 1991: 273; Lipset and Raab 1971: 252–3, 283, 318; LaHaye 1992: 145–6; Epstein and Forster 1966: 26–8, 31; Gilman, 1982: photograph facing 49; Mintz 1985: 82–3, 20, 59–63).

7

The Patriot movement

If the Christian Right has been strongly inclined to conspiracism, that is even more true of the Patriot movement. We shall shortly discuss to what degree the two movements concur on the nature of the threat to America. We shall, however, also be examining the different strategies that have emerged among Patriots and the different issues that have concerned them, and we shall begin this chapter by turning our attention to the issue that brought the movement into existence, taxation. Conservatives, as we might expect, have frequently given attention to this question. Patriots, however, are considerably more radical in their views. Recruiting from among those who have come into conflict with the Internal Revenue Service (IRS), the movement's anger is fuelled by the fear of the confiscation of possessions, the loss of liberty and, unless drawn together by adversity, even the collapse of marriages. Rather than tax reduction, Patriots preach tax resistance, disputing the very constitutionality of the fiscal apparatus that has arisen in twentieth-century America.

Tax protest, according to one of the most prominent Patriots, 'Red' Beckman, was central in the formation of a free nation and is equally vital today. Writing in the early 1980s, he argued that income tax was an unacceptable confiscation of the wealth of productive citizens. Indeed, under the Constitution, taxation was intended to be voluntary, and the very idea of a progressive tax on incomes was to be found not in American experience but in the second plank of *The Communist Manifesto*, intended as a mechanism for the destruction of the middle class. Nor was its introduction into the Constitution by means of the Sixteenth Amendment legitimate. Congress, he declared, had failed to pass a bill in regard to the Amendment, and so had most of the states that had supposedly ratified it (Beckman 1981: 6–7, 97–102).

Beckman's argument was subsequently to be taken yet further, by the claim that none of the states had properly ratified the Amendment. Instead, it had been simply declared in effect in 1913. Such arguments have been much used within the movement; but others also enjoy a popularity. The Internal Revenue Code, tax resisters have argued, does not include wages or salaries within its listing of items contributing to gross income. Instead, they hold, these should be seen as an 'equitable-value barter exchange' of time and talent that cannot be legitimately defined as income. Another argument with even more far-reaching implications centres on the notion of a distinction between a natural person and a citizen of the federal United States. The former, it is held, is outside the government's jurisdiction; only by voluntarily acknowledging US citizenship does a natural person shift from extra-governmental status to one created by government (Beckman 1981: 182; Kershaw 1994: 16, 22–4; Konicov 1995: 46–8).

Such propositions, as we might expect, are likely to bring Patriots into conflict with the IRS and the forces of law enforcement. They are also linked to other contentions. Two areas of concern are already evident: the role of government and the basis of citizenship. But there are connections too, for instance, to disputes about the legal system and the monetary system. And, of course, many of those links are constructed through a resort to the conspiracy theories that so frequently frame understanding among Patriots.

In each case, we need to be mindful of the diversity within Patriot ranks and of the points of continuity and discontinuity between the movement and the conservatism with which it is often equated. We might be deceived, for instance, by the emphasis on the original meaning of the Constitution. Conservatives too have been very concerned with this, arguing, for instance, that many Supreme Court decisions represent a deliberate breach with what the Founding Fathers actually intended. But, as our discussion has already indicated, what the Constitution actually permits and forbids can be construed by Patriots in very distinctive ways. We have noted the contention that people are independent of the federal authorities and thus cannot be eligible for tax unless they acknowledge US citizenship. This occurs, it is argued, when an individual ticks the relevant box when obtaining a Social Security card. It is reasoning along such lines that underpins the efforts of a number of Patriots to extricate themselves from any entanglement with official documentation, efforts which, in turn, make such entanglement all the more likely.

Thus, to take one of many examples, a motorist in Nevada refused to have either a driver's licence or vehicle registration because he believed that he was exercising an individual freedom that the state had no right to deny; in another, an Alabama man whose children had been taken away was subsequently to argue that to register children on a birth certificate terminates parental rights and turns them into 'Federal children' (Bork 1990; *National Review* 14 August 1995; Konicov 1995: 46–8; *American's Bulletin* October 1996, October 1997).

These are not arguments that most conservatives would accept. Such views, it also needs to be emphasised, are a matter of dispute amongst Patriots. As one of their proponents observes, 'There are many Americans who simply want to stop paying taxes or join a militia.' But, he contends, if they do not regain their sovereignty, then they will remain as subjects. This sovereignty began to be lost after the Civil War, and, after a 130-year assault on the Constitution, republican government can only be restored by individual sovereigns reclaiming their rights and then voluntarily coming together in self-governed townships, counties, states and a Union of sovereign states. The first stage, then, is to withdraw from the jurisdiction of the federal government by revoking all 'adhesion contracts', from social security documents to marriage licences. In its place can be chosen either American nationality, state citizenship or the status of a freeman or woman, free of all legal disability (*Preparedness Journal* January–February 1996).

Considering the frequent claims of the movement's racism, the suggestion that the decline of the republic began in the aftermath of the Civil War might well set off warning bells, and any study of Patriot writings would very quickly encounter the argument that the Fourteenth Amendment, which granted citizenship to former slaves after the defeat of the Confederacy, represents a fundamental revision of what had previously been considered as citizenship. Thus, according to one Patriot document, a state or *de jure* Citizen has 'inalienable natural rights . . . protected by his/her state Constitution against State actions and against federal intrusion'. A federal or Fourteenth Amendment citizen, however, is a subject of Congress, their rights granted by and thus able to be taken away by that body. Where this distinction makes no reference to race, another, put forward by one of the leading figures in the movement, Richard McDonald, describes the latter grouping as those in receipt of statutory civil rights, the former as 'White Common Law State Citizens' (Collins 1994; Anon. 1990; Abanes 1996: 33–4; for McDonald's claim that he only uses the term 'White' because it was in the original laws, see Abanes 1996: 34).

Yet how we are to read the claim that the Fourteenth Amendment diminishes rights rather than extending them is not as obvious as it might first seem. Those persuaded by Patriot arguments are frequently urged to abandon their federal citizenship without any suggestion that only those of a certain colour are eligible to do so; and some advocates of sovereign citizenship have indignantly denied suggestions of racism. Indeed, one writer has explicitly argued that her objection to the Fourteenth Amendment is that it created 'the category of Federal subject', not that it gave rights to former slaves. Blacks, she argues, 'should never have been slaves in the first place, had the Southern states respected everyone's god-given sovereignty'. Others, in contrast, clearly do intend to make a racist demarcation into first- and second-class citizens. Thus, in one discussion of 'the Dismantling of a Christian Nation', published, not insignificantly, in the journal of the racist organisation, Aryan Nations, two authors associated with a Patriot group, Republic vs. Democracy Redress, have argued that the Fourteenth Amendment had created a new status that had subsequently encompassed the original sovereign citizens by bringing them into the Social Security scheme and a subordinate relationship with the federal government. Before this usurpation, they argued, states had been sovereign and white males had rightly monopolised the franchise (*Flatlands* 11, 1994; *Calling Our Nation* 51, n.d.).

But this argument was put forward as part of a dispute within the movement. As the Aryan Nations publication made clear, the organisation with which the two writers were associated held that the 'facts about the United States Constitution' that it was seeking to bring to light had not been 'covered by Patriots before', and a later exchange between one of the authors, Robert Wangrud, and the prominent Patriot, Jack McLamb, was to make the differences between them brutally obvious. In claiming that the Patriot movement drew from different ethnic groups, Wangrud declared, McLamb had failed to understand the difference between white posterity and non-whites and between citizens under organic law and those under the Fourteenth Amendment. Whites had inalienable rights, non-whites only statutory rights, and for McLamb to obscure this was wilfully to avoid the issue of race: 'You and your breed of constitutionalists continually avoid the original intent of the Constitution and always feed your adulterated version to an unknowledgeable public' (*Calling Our Nation* 51, n.d.; *Aid & Abet* 11, n.d.; *BEHOLD!* May 1989; for McLamb's belief, however, that 'working with a black brother or sister to try to save America' does not mean that Patriots should go against 'God's plan' and promote interracial marriage, see Crawford *et al.* 1994: 2.24).

If there is dispute about the nature of citizenship, even using the term 'Constitutionalist' to encompass all the Patriot movement can be misleading. Certainly, it is true that most within the movement look to the original US Constitution and the Bill of Rights. But, just as some within the original Patriots of the 1770s opposed the eventual creation of a federal government, so some latter-day Patriots regard the Constitution as betraying the Revolution, not consummating it. This is particularly evident in the recent appearance of a book which claims to prove that 'Under the Constitution, Americans and their states have *no* legally enforceable avenue to counter federal hege- mony' and that this was intended by those who created it. In this argu- ment, the Fourteenth Amendment and the filling out of paperwork describing oneself as a US citizen remain crucial in marking the end of citizen sovereignty; but the basis for this dispossession is to be found in the decision of the 1787 Constitutional Convention to define Americans as citizens 'of the United States'. The decision of the Militia of Montana, one of the main distributors of Patriot material, to recom- mend this book led to one correspondent's claiming that it repre- sented an attack on 'our cherished American Institutions' and 'our history' that walked 'hand in hand with the goals outlined' in the *Communist Manifesto* and the *Protocols of the Elders of Zion*. But the work in question, and the Montana group's decision to distribute it, did not represent an isolated aberration. Simultaneously, one of the main Patriot publications, *Media Bypass*, was promoting another work, *The Constitution That Never Was*, which it described as indicting 'our founding fathers' for creating a Constitution that had allowed power to be wrenched from the people in the two years that followed its inception (Royce 1997: Preface/2–3, 2/10, 6/6–8; *Taking Aim* August, December 1997; *Media Bypass* September 1997).

While some Patriots have doubts about the original US Constitution, this is more to be understood as evidence of the move- ment's diversity (and radicalism) than a necessary consequence of its belief-system. But if most Patriots would reject such a pessimistic reading of the creation of the republic, many do see hostile forces at work from at least soon after its inception and, in doing so, have turned to one of the longest traditions in American history, that of opposition to what in the nineteenth century was described as the Money Power (Davis 1971: 153, 192).

Where, in some Patriot narratives, the origin of the American Revolution lay in protest against unjust taxation, in others the more important factor lay in Britain's efforts to stop the American colonies from issuing their own currencies. This, it is argued, was in order to serve the interests of the Bank of England and 'the European money changers', and, in the years that followed, international financiers increasingly sought to abrogate the Constitutional provision granting Congress the power to 'coin Money' and 'regulate the Value thereof'. Ultimately, the bankers were able to engineer a financial crisis in the first decade of the twentieth century and thus achieve the passing of the 1913 Federal Reserve Act, whereby they gained 'the privilege of creating money out of nothing and loaning it to the U.S. government at interest. The way had now been prepared for the looting of the American nation by the International vultures' (Griffin 1989: 168–70, 84–5).

As with the critique of taxation, so with this onslaught against 'the International Banksters' Patriots can both refer to a body of argument and appeal to a constituency of those who have directly come into conflict around the issue. One Patriot writer, Byron Dale, for instance, describes how his experience as a rancher had led him to question the nature of the debt burden that was strangling agriculture. In his case, interestingly, he had already encountered Patriot writings on money, but it was his position in an endangered sector of the economy that was to lead him to find its answers so persuasive. These answers, as we have noted, have occurred more than once in American history, manifestations of a highly potent populism that portrays a healthy political system and a productive people under attack by malignant and alien forces. We have already encountered some of its facets in our discussion of Pat Robertson. Patriot conspiracism, however, both converges with and diverges from the arguments that circulate on the Christian Right (Griffin 1989: 172; Dale 1993: 5–12).

Both are not only concerned with the power of international finance but tend in turn to place this in the context of secret societies. Thus, if we were to examine Patriot writings for references to Adam Weishaupt and the Illuminati, we would find them in abundance. Des Griffin, for instance, attributes the French Revolution to the machinations of 'the Money Barons – the Illuminati', sees them as the force behind the publication in 1841 of a political text written by Clinton Roosevelt, an ancestor of Franklin Roosevelt, and accuses Marx of plagiarising Weishaupt and Roosevelt in the service of his Illuminati employers. In the twentieth century the Russian Revolution is portrayed as funded by an American banker, Jacob Schiff, and the New Deal as an attempt 'to inflict on the nation every last phase of Clinton Roosevelt's Illuminist blueprint for destroying our Constitution and government' (Griffin 1989: 45, 62, 65, 91, 95).

Above all, Griffin argues, the greatest danger to America in recent decades has been the attempt by internationalists to destroy its national sovereignty and merge it into a one-world government. At the forefront of this attack have been a number of international bodies with which we are already familiar, most notably the CFR and the Trilateral Commission, and a number of prominent figures, above all that of David Rockefeller. Ultimately, all these machinations are intended to culminate in the consummation of the Illuminati's scheme to bring about a New World Order. Having failed with the League of Nations, it is argued, the plotters have now turned to the United Nations to enslave America (Griffin 1989: 113, 136–7, 150).

First published in the mid-1970s and then issued in a revised edition in 1989, Griffin's book usefully represents how many Patriots saw the progress of their conspiratorial foes before George Bush's celebrated speech to Congress in September 1990. This speech, which brought the New World Order image out of foreign policy elite discussion (and conspiracist agitation over that discussion) into the foreground of political debate, was at first sight to radicalise Patriot thinking yet further. Thus, according to a pamphlet published by Jack McLamb's Police Against the New World Order, what the term really represented was a plan 'for an oligarchy of the world's richest families to place 1/2 the masses of the earth in servitude under their complete control, administered from behind the false front of the United Nations'. As for the other half, they would be eliminated 'through war, disease, abortion and famine by the year 2000' (Griffin 1989: ii; Stern 1996: 156–7; Anon. 1992: 9, 3).

In such writings, the UN has moved to the centre of the conspiracy. Indeed, according to a number of accounts, combat-ready UN troops are already on American soil. According to one book, for instance, more than 40,000 of these soldiers are stationed in and near San Diego, nearly as many near Sacramento and a further 22,000 are to be found in the Cleveland National Forest, south of Los Angeles.

Thousands more are to be found in Kansas, at Fort Drum in New York, in Michigan and, in total, 'at least 500,000 rabid anti-American UN troops' are now within the USA. Thousands of UN vehicles have been sighted on American military bases, on railroad cars and in convoys on highways from Iowa and Michigan to Arkansas and Arizona. Vast numbers of black helicopters have also been seen, unmarked but under UN command. Why all this manpower and equipment is here is beyond doubt. When the conspirators deliberately bring about race riots or economic collapse and the President declares martial law, they will be used 'to brutally police our towns and cities', conduct house-to-house searches to confiscate firearms and food stores and arrest people in the middle of the night, dispatching them to 'one of many concentration camps' already set up for those who are seen as a threat to the New World Order (Jefferson 1994: 13, 15–16, 23–43, 64, 48).

This apparent escalation in conspiracist thinking, however, is better understood as the increased visibility of an already existing body of argument. As early as 1951, the anti-Semitic paper, *Common Sense*, attributed the most sinister motives to training exercises in California in which American troops fighting an imaginary enemy had issued proclamations in the name of the United Nations. Little noticed at the time, such fears revived in the early 1960s, when the announcement of planned military manoeuvres in Georgia involving officers from other countries led to much-publicised claims that foreign paratroops would descend on the state in concert with a UN invasion from Canada and Mexico and an amphibious landing of Chinese troops (*Common Sense* 1 August 1951; McCann 1966: 20–28, 51–2).

If the danger of UN invasion has long agitated the far right, it has been equally concerned that plans exist for the mass incarceration of resisters. In the 1950s, there was considerable anxiety over the Alaska Mental Hospital Act, in which the grant of a substantial expanse of land to fund the state's mental health programme was envisaged as intended instead for mass imprisonment. In 1976, a Patriot in Houston, William R. Pabst, unsuccessfully filed suit in US District Court against what he described as 'the concentration camp program of the Department of Defense'. The Army, he declared, was holding records on millions of American citizens, and detailed plans were in existence for the declaration of a national emergency and the dispatching of masses of prisoners to camps designated under the 1950 Detention Act. The later creation of the Federal Emergency

Management Agency (FEMA) convinced Patriots that here was to be found a new stage in plans to introduce martial law in the United States (*Dixon Line–Reason* December 1966–January 1967; Pabst 1979; *Z Magazine* January 1992; Diamond 1996: 194).

Patriot fear of the UN is far from new and echoes claims made for decades on the far right. Indeed, modern publications even cite earlier reports. Thus, in 1994, the Militia of Montana reprinted part of a 1951 report on the California troop manoeuvres of that year, while in the preceding year one of the key movement publications, *Patriot Report*, had noted that 'Through the past 50 years, patriots have collected documents showing the strategy of the international bankers to control the nations with a U.N. army.' But exactly how many foreign troops were already concealed has been a matter of dispute within the movement. Where one leading figure, Mark Koernke, had portrayed a combined force of 'a little over 300,000' personnel ready to 'be deployed against the American people', M. W. Jefferson, as we have seen, has estimated nearly twice as many. Even more were claimed in a leaflet produced by a Michigan Patriot group, which declared that 'Over a million foreign troops are already here to back up a tyrannical dictatorship being imposed on us by the New World Order.' In part, it was precisely such allegations that distinguished major sections of the Patriot movement from the John Birch Society, which, in an extended article in its magazine, has cast doubt on such claims. Foreign troops, it declared, had been trained in the USA for service as UN peacekeepers, something which the Society opposed. But there was no credible evidence of UN troops massed on American soil, and to propagate such 'fables' would only give fuel to claims that the so-called radical right were 'paranoid misfits'. In differentiating itself from what it sees as conspiracism run riot, the John Birch Society is not rejecting conspiracy theory in general or its application to the New World Order in particular. Indeed, just as we have seen when discussing conspiracism on the Christian Right, Patriots not only explicitly draw on Birchite writings but, where they cite earlier sources, these are often the very writers, from John Robison in the aftermath of the French Revolution to Nesta Webster in the aftermath of the Russian, whose arguments underpin the interpretative apparatus of the Society. But there are important differences, the most important of which concerns anti-Semitism (*Taking Aim* Special Edition 1994; *Patriot Report* October 1993; *Nexus* February–March 1994; American Freedom Network, n.d.; *New American* 31 October 1994).

Where the John Birch Society rejects anti-Semitism, this is not true of the Patriot movement. In part, this is connected with its antagonism towards the banking system. Thus, in discussing the Federal Reserve system, the leading Patriot 'Bo' Gritz remarks that 'Eight Jewish families virtually control the entire FED – only three are American jews.' In this, as in many other accounts, the figures of the Rothschild family loom large. Another Patriot author, James Wardner, portrays Baron Alfred Rothschild as the 'mastermind' behind the Federal Reserve Act, while both he and Police Against the New World Order attribute to another member of the family the claim that if one were given control of a nation's money, it would not matter who made the laws (Gritz 1991: 609; Wardner 1994: 27–9; Anon. 1992: 16).

If one factor in the Patriot propensity for anti-Semitism is hostility to banking, another is the influence of the Christian Identity belief-system. 'God's true Israelites', *Patriot Report* argues, are 'the white Europeans that founded this nation . . . The conspirators for a New World Order are trying to destroy our identity and enslave us as a race.' Another influential publication, the *Jubilee,* similarly champions the true Israelite identity of the 'Celto-Saxon peoples' (and describes the banking system as 'Jewish'), while one of the most popular Patriot exposés of 'money-control over America', which presents Nazi Germany as brought down by 'the Bankers' and attributes Lincoln's death to the machinations of 'the Rothschild Bank', is by Christian Identity Pastor Sheldon Emry (*Patriot Report* January 1996; *Jubilee* November–December 1996, January–February 1992; Emry 1986; on Emry, see Zeskind n.d. (*c*.1987): 39–40, 49).

Adherents of the Christian Identity world-view are to be found in a range of Patriot groupings. In the militias, for instance, one of the leading figures, the Militia of Montana's John Trochmann, is an Identity believer, while the Michigan Militia has suffered a split in which the influence of Christian Identity among the breakaway group was a factor. We have argued earlier why Identity leader Pete Peters's 1992 Estes Park gathering was not so important for the origins of the militias as some have suggested. As early as 1994, however, another leading Identity figure, Dave Barley, was calling for militias to be organised. But, as the reference to the Michigan split should remind us, only some Patriots are Identity believers. A more important factor is to be found in the enthusiasm for conspiracism itself. It has often been argued by critics of the movement that to believe in an all-encompassing plot, let alone a bankers' plot, is necessarily anti-

Semitic. Thus Richard Abanes sees the origins of 'today's patriot/ militia movement' as lying in a decision by white supremacists to hide their bigotry and emphasise instead their hostility to the federal government and internationalist conspirators. There are, he acknowledges, non-racist Patriots, but the claims about the New World Order they believe in 'come directly from anti-Semitic conspiracy theories'. Similarly, Loretta Ross holds that the militia movement 'serves the interests of the white supremacist movement'. Many of its ideas and conspiracy theories, she continues, are 'directly copied' from that movement. Even Kenneth Stern, who rejects the argument that anti-Semitism and white supremacism are the basis of the militia movement, believes that they are certainly crucial to its rise, not only because of the leading role played by such figures as Trochmann and Gritz and the circulation of material by anti-Semitic groups at militia meetings, but because 'the conspiracy theories that underlie the movement' are rooted in anti-Semitism. When militia leaders denounce international bankers or the Trilateral Commission, he argues, they are speaking in code, drawing people into a movement that is covertly anti-Semitic (*Esquire* July 1995; Stern 1996: 68–70, 245–7; Mariani 1998: 133–4; Crawford *et al.* 1994: 3.14, 3.33; Abanes 1996: 172–5; Ross 1995: 1).

This argument has already been disputed both within our earlier discussion of the rise of the militias and in our examination of the role of conspiracy thinking in the Christian Right. But this is not to deny that in searching for evidence that can substantiate or a theory that can explicate their belief in a conspiratorial force threatening America, Patriots are very likely to encounter, and may be persuaded by, the highly developed body of anti-Semitic writing. In particular, it is important to take note of the popularity among Patriots of the most famous conspiracist text of all, *The Protocols of the Learned Elders of Zion*. Thus one can find extended excerpts from the *Protocols* in Griffin's *Fourth Reich of the Rich*. 'This document,' he argues, 'is indisputably . . . the "Long Range Master Plan"' by which a 'small group of immensely wealthy, diabolically clever and extremely influential men' plan to destroy all governments and create 'a One-World totalitarian dictatorship'. Similarly, a Patriot monthly, the *Free American*, has not only described the *Protocols* as 'The blueprint used for the New World Order', urging its readers to buy copies to send to people who were disbelievers in conspiracies; it has also published the lyric of Patriot singer Carl Klang on the subject:

It's the cause to the chaos that's occurring in the land
It's the source of communism, it's the global master plan
You'll never read about it in a book of history
'Cause it's been hidden from the masses to control our destiny

It's the news behind the news and the methods that they use
It's the blueprint and the plan they all rely on
And it's written in the Protocols of the Learned Elders of Zion
(Griffin 1989: 194–222; *Free American* January 1994, December 1997).

As Norman Cohn has shown in considerable detail, while the Protocols claim to set out the details of a Jewish bid for world domination, they originated as a Tsarist forgery at the end of the nineteenth century. But even a belief in the *Protocols* may not be what it seems. Remarkably, Griffin, while emphasising the prominent role in the conspiracy of Marx, the Rothschilds and others of Jewish background, claims that the actual text of the *Protocols* has been deliberately reworked to conceal the true nature of the plot, the work not of a racial group but of the Satanic Illuminati. This claim also turns up elsewhere. One prominent Patriot activist, William Cooper, has reproduced the entire text, arguing that 'Every aspect' of it has come to pass, 'validating the authenticity of conspiracy', while also claiming that it was 'written intentionally to deceive', with every reference to Jews actually referring to the Illuminati. Another activist, Jeff Baker, involved in both the Patriot movement and the US Taxpayers Party, claims that the *Protocols* have existed in more than one version, and while the one published in the early twentieth century presents the plot as Jewish in nature, this is an 'erroneous' interpretation that is 'most probably part of the coverup of the true intent' (Cohn 1996; Griffin 1989: 194–7; Cooper 1991: 267–332; Baker 1993: 47; Planned Parenthood 1995).

Many Patriots believe in a UN or bankers' conspiracy without necessarily holding an anti-Semitic notion of its composition or purpose. Others, indeed, may not believe in an all-encompassing theory at all, and may even only be concerned with a particular issue. But, distinguishing it again from anti-Semitism, the movement also contains conspiracy theories that look in very different directions than to the Elders of Zion to explain the threat to America. Issues of one Patriot publication, the *American's Bulletin*, are particularly interesting in this regard. Thus, in one version, the American Revolution was not victorious at all, and the British monarchy continued to subject America financially. Many of the familiar aspects of the Patriot argument are to be found here, from the central role of the Fourteenth Amendment to the pernicious nature of the Federal Reserve, but, as the author notes, 'I know a lot of patriots won't like this. Your (our) argument has been that the government . . . is operating outside . . . the . . . United States Constitution.' Yet in reality, he claims, the country has always been ruled by Britain. In a second version, the British throne is itself under the control of a foreign master, and it is that force, the Papacy, that really controls America. In yet another version, constitutional government has been ended and the separation of powers has been undermined by the legal profession, a group with 'virtually unlimited political power' that has become 'an elitist class similar to the European aristocracy of the eighteenth century' (*American's Bulletin* September, October 1996, November, February 1997).

It is clearly not the case, then, that Patriot conspiracy theory is always undisguised or even disguised anti-Semitism. Instead, it is composed of a wide-ranging array of attempts to understand the Patriot predicament, only some of which derive from the racist right. But if the movement is not defined by anti-Semitism or white supremacism, what are we to make of one of the other suppositions often made about it, that its extremist beliefs and confrontational behaviour necessarily lead it on a collision course with American democracy?

In understanding the potential for such a conflict, it is important to examine the considerable range of organisational strategies that have emerged among Patriots in recent years. Some of these may well be more conducive to confrontation than others, and the degree to which they are adopted is likely to have a major impact on how government and movement react to each other.

The strategy with which we are undoubtedly most familiar is the building of militias. As we have seen, these groups, from their inception, have argued that America was threatened by an out-of-control government. For the Michigan Militia, the militia was the only force that could stop a repetition of what had occurred at Waco. As with the revolutionary events of two centuries before, it held, citizens had physically to resist an attack on their liberties. For the Militia of Montana, too, the fate of the United States now hung in the balance. 'Just as our Founding Fathers of this Country shook off their shackles of bondage', it declared, 'so must we' (Northern Michigan Regional Militia n.d. (1994); Mariani 1998: 144; Militia of Montana n.d.: 6, 11).

Yet, for both organisations, as for others, there was an ambiguity in their stance towards the government. Soon after its creation, one of the Michigan Militia's founders, Norman Olson, declared that 'The tyrants are trying to destroy our America.' He did not believe, however, that that meant armed action was inevitable. Sixty per cent of all warfare, he suggested, was 'psychological – if you rattle your sword loudly enough, people will go away.' But while Olson empha-sised that over-mighty government could be controlled by the threat of rebellion, his co-founder, Ray Southwell, appeared more pessimis-tic, predicting that 'within the next two years' the Constitution would be suspended and 'Christian fundamentalists' would be the first victims of the new regime. Such ambiguity continued after the Oklahoma bombing. Testifying before the Senate Sub-committee on Terrorism, the Militia of Montana characterised the movement as 'a giant neighbourhood watch' made up of 'a cross section' of Americans 'from all walks of life'. But it also cited the Declaration of Independence, with all its revolutionary implications, arguing that Americans were rightly outraged at the level of taxation, the use of millions of dollars 'to bail out the banking elite', the training of foreign forces on American soil and the use of murderous force at Waco and Ruby Ridge. The militia movement, it declared, had mobilised against 'the flagrant injustices' of 'oppressive public servants'. Like Southwell, it too believed confrontation was imminent, and the previous year had declared that a global UN dictatorship was intended by March 1995. Militia supporters, it urged, should fight politically 'like we have never fought before' but they also needed to store the '**THREE B's** (Boots, Beans and Bullets)' should they be unable to avert 'the coming storm over America' (*MetroTimes* 26 April–2 May 1995; *Northern Express* 22 August 1994; *Taking Aim* June 1995, Special Edition 1994).

As such language so graphically reminds us, militias did not come into existence simply to call for the defence of the Second Amendment or even just as propaganda vehicles for the Patriot message. Unlike the Order, or more recently the Aryan Republican Army, militias are not terrorist bands, but the belief-systems that underpin them do make violent clashes with authority a constant possibility. Nor have the mili-tias been the only recent development among Patriots that has involved a potential or actual resort to arms. One area of particular tension, for instance, is the argument that the United States has illicitly incorporated territory that deserves and, if necessary will fight for, its independence. Three rival groups, for instance, each describing itself as the Republic of Texas, have claimed that the state was illegitimately annexed in 1845 and is legally still independent. In December 1995 delegates met and elected a Provisional Government, which subsequently called upon George W. Bush to step down as governor and instructed 175 banks to pass all the state's assets to the Republic. In 1997 armed supporters of one of the factions held two hostages briefly before eventually surrendering to the authorities. One man who escaped was later killed in a gunfight with law enforcement officers (Anon. 1997: 13–15; *Jubilee* November–December 1996; Bushart *et al.* 1998: 183–4).

The use of violence has also been mooted when Patriots have sought to challenge the legal system. In the same period that modern militias have emerged, movement activists have also sought to popularise another idea – that 'common law rights' had been retained after the break with Britain and stood superior to statute law. Once again, we can trace earlier roots to this development, most obviously in the Posse Comitatus and the Committee of the States, but also in lesser-known efforts later in the 1980s to create Christian Common Law Courts in Arizona. In 1992 a common law court emerged in Florida; but it was those that were created first in Montana and then in Oklahoma at the end of 1993 that have proved of most importance in leading to similar initiatives by Patriots in other localities. They have emerged in a considerable number of states, sometimes in concert with militia groups, sometimes independently. In 1994, for instance, the Florida-based Constitutional Court of the People issued arrest warrants for a number of local judges, while the following year indictments were issued against judges in Ohio. While most of these incidents involve what has been termed 'paper terrorism', this has sometimes threatened to take more physical forms. Thus in 1996, for instance, three activists in another Florida group, the Constitutional Common Law Court, were jailed for filing indictments threatening judges with capital punishment. That this sounds strangely familiar should be no surprise. Opponents have noted that one leading group, the United Sovereigns of America, continues to sell the Posse Comitatus Blue Book, with its instruction publicly to hang officials convicted by a citizens' jury (Burghart and Crawford 1996; *American Mercury* Fall 1976; *National Educator* December 1989; Anon. 1997: 17).

If the arguments behind the common law courts are radical, an even more fundamental challenge both to government and to the monetary system, that of the grouping known as the Freemen, resulted in a much-publicised siege in Montana in early 1996. The potential attraction of the Freemen's arguments is well illustrated by the cover article in the January 1995 issue of the Militia of Montana newsletter, in which an anonymous writer described how after years spent in study, 'rescinding my contracts with the State and Federal Governments', arguing in courts and serving time in prison, he had at last found a solution. The Freemen, he reported, had established a township in Montana with its own Notary, Clerk, Justices of the Peace and Constables and, in four-day training sessions, they were showing others how to establish local self-government. Furthermore, they had also found how to achieve restitution for all the harm the supposed government had done to the real governors, the people. They were sending signed confessions of guilt to figures such as IRS agents, and if they were not returned or replied to within ten days, this was being interpreted as an admission of guilt. They were then sending the accused a lien form, specifying how much the person was held to owe them, and if a reply was not received in fifteen days, were filing both the document and a foreclosure form in the relevant county office, publishing a default notice in the county newspaper and then taking certified copies of the documents to a bank where an account had been established, and instructing the bank to deposit the liens as an asset from which a line of credit is to be received. Billions of dollars, the article declared, had been deposited, cheques had been written on the accounts to credit card companies, computer equipment had been purchased and IRS liens and hundreds of thousands of dollars in farm mortgages had been paid off (*Taking Aim* January 1995).

Both the militia and the common law court strategies involve at least the threat of force. The Freemen's challenge to the monetary system, not itself violent, went hand in hand with the threat 'to use our Lawful force by whatever means necessary', and ended in the protracted siege at Justus Township. Other approaches, however, while still radical, are less confrontational. One that has attained considerable attention in recent years is that of jury nullification. According to its pioneer, 'Red' Beckman, Americans have not one vote but three. One is exercised on election day, but the other two are rarely rightly used. The first is the Grand Jury, which the government must convince if a prosecution is to be allowed to progress. The other is the Jury, which will decide a case that has been allowed to go forward. In both cases, he holds, jurors should not merely judge the facts of the case in the light of the law. Instead, they must examine the law itself to decide if it is just. If it is not, then jurors, or even just one juror, can nullify the law. This argument is not espoused only by Patriots. Both during the mass arrests of Operation Rescue activists and since, this notion has been drawn on by direct action anti-abortion militants. In 1989, for instance, an Idaho-based group, Friends of Operation Rescue, publicised the argument under the title 'keep the just from going to jail', while in the early part of the following year Operation Rescue itself published an advertisement enjoining jury nullification in a California newspaper. More recently, during the trial of Shelley Shannon for the attempted murder of a doctor, advertisements appeared calling for jury nullification, while during the murder trial of another militant, Michael Griffin, the direct action magazine, *Life Advocate*, published an article on the subject. Jury nullification has also appealed to Reconstructionists; but, most importantly, it has additionally resulted in the creation of an organization, the Fully Informed Jury Association (FIJA), that has brought Patriots together with activists in the Libertarian Party. This is a development, however, that may not necessarily strengthen the Patriot movement, or at least not its most militant elements. Indeed, in the issue of the FIJA paper that appeared in the aftermath of the Oklahoma bombing, while its leading figure, Larry Dodge, defended militia involvement within its ranks, emphasising the desirability of retaining the organisation's nature as a broad coalition, another writer suggested that jury nullification could function as an alternative to militias, dampening down the 'explosive anger' of their supporters and averting armed confrontation with government (Burghart and Crawford 1996: 20–21; Beckman 1981: 46–50; *Wanderer* 12 October 1989, 22 February 1990; *Life Advocate* May, April 1994; Clarkson 1997: 158–9; *Libertarian Party News* March 1994; *FIJActivist* Summer 1995).

Other approaches have also been put forward, calculated to minimise the danger of clashes between government and Patriots. Some take the form of retreat from any contact with authority. Thus one group, the House of Common Law, has argued against what it sees as the potentially confrontational approach espoused by others in the movement. Rather than advocating the demise of the federal government or being immobilised by fear of an impending New World Order take-over, it suggested, Patriots should set about 'taking back responsibility for our lives' by peacefully attaining sovereign status and creating what it termed jural societies or townships. In Austin, Texas, it reported, every adult member of the township donated time every month to a school and day care centre for the children of the members, while in the San Francisco area serious consideration was being given to the Mondragon worker co-operative in the Basque region of Spain as a possible blueprint for providing employment for members and producing goods and services for the sovereign community nationally. Trade and exchange between different townships, it argued, would be crucial in supporting those 'who have chosen to take back conscious stewardship of their lives and of the planet'. But at the same time, it was vital to understand that as well as a 'Creator endowed right of self-government and self-determination', there was also a right not to exercise it (*American's Bulletin* April 1996).

Others, meanwhile, have moved more into the political arena. One theory that both enjoys a significant following within Patriot circles and has proved conducive to working within conventional political channels is that of Eugene Schroder. In his argument, the crucial year in the downfall of the republic is 1933. The election of Franklin Roosevelt, he argues, resulted in the use of war and emergency powers to compel people to turn over their gold coin, gold bullion and gold certificates to the government, establish 'a banking system based on the debts of the people' and bring about government control of a wide range of economic activity. The powers that Roosevelt relied on have never been repealed, Schroder declares, and America has lived under dictatorship ever since. Despite first appearances, that this approach focuses its attention on emergency powers has tended to take Patriots in the direction of lobbying legislators. In August 1995, for instance, a Patriot gathering declared itself the First Assembly of Colorado People's Common law Grand Jury. Having heard Schroder's testimony, it then sent a packet of documentation on the issue to every state legislator and demanded they show cause within thirty days why they were continuing with the emergency government begun in 1933 (Schroder with Nellis 1995: 25, 27, 110–11; *American's Bulletin* January 1997).

In reply to this approach, the state legislature's Legal Services Committee argued that common law had ceased to pertain in Colorado and that emergency government no longer existed. Lobbying legislators is an approach that can, at one and the same time, draw some into mainstream politics and turn others in more radical directions as a result of disappointment with the response of decision-makers. It also poses other questions, about whether Patriots should themselves enter the electoral arena and what stance they should take towards both the Republican Party and the conservative movement (*American's Bulletin* January 1997).

How they have resolved those questions has varied considerably. As we saw earlier, one of the most important Patriot initiatives of the 1980s took the form of a third party, the Populist Party. More recently, as we discuss in the next chapter, there has been interest both in the Buchanan insurgency within the Republican Party and the US Taxpayers Party outside it. Whether a third party or the GOP (if either) is the way forward continues to be a matter of dispute, and even the Populist Party argued in the run-up to the 1988 elections for what it called a 'tri-partisan approach', in which its programme could be carried forward not only through the party itself but also through the main two parties. While the Populist Party enjoyed the support of the *Spotlight*, in the same period another Patriot publication, the *Justice Times*, suggested that while Patriots should not abandon the electoral process they should not resort to a third party that would be doomed to failure. Instead, they should try to take over a major party. Despite this argument, however, the paper remained sympathetic to third party activity, in the form of the Presidential candidacy of former Texas Congressman Ron Paul, who had recently abandoned the Republican Party for the Libertarian Party (*Monitor* August 1987, November 1988).

As we have seen with the Fully Informed Jury Association, Patriot links with Libertarians have continued since Paul's 1988 campaign. They have taken a number of forms. One of the state citizenship documents cited earlier, for instance, is to be found on a Libertarian Party website, while, more dramatically, when, in 1996, a number of members of a militia-type group in Arizona were charged with conspiracy involving explosives, four were registered Libertarians, one of whom had stood for the state legislature. Party candidates have also included the leader of the New Jersey Militia, while in the run-up to the 1996 election the *Free American* praised the Libertarian Party's platform, and in the following year urged readers to join the party. But just as it continued to promote other avenues, so too have other Patriots (Collins 1994; *Liberty* September 1996; Militia Watchdog 1996; *Free American* September 1996, June 1997).

This has sometimes involved working with sympathetic Republicans, usually at state level. In Colorado, a state senator, Charles Duke, was particularly active, not only in support of Schroder's argument about emergency powers but also, for instance, in promoting a resolution intended to revitalise the Tenth Amendment, which had reserved for the states any powers not expressly delegated to the federal government by the Constitution. In California, another state senator, Don Rogers, was similarly involved. Even at national level, some support has been found within the Republican Party, whether in the form of Texas Congressman Steve Stockman's taking up of Patriot concerns that the federal government might be planning to launch a national attack on the militia movement or in Idaho, where Samuel Sherwood, the leader of the United States Militia Association, claimed to have mobilised a thousand volunteers for the successful campaign for Congress by Helen Chenoweth (*American's Bulletin* January 1997; Anon. 1997: 30–31; Stern 1996: 174–5, 212; *New Yorker* 10 July 1995).

But if Patriots can find common ground with some in the Republican Party, this is against a background of profound mistrust of the mainstream right. This was already evident in the 1980s. In a collection of essays first published in 1982, for instance, the *Spotlight* argued that what it called populism was a fundamental alternative to what passed for conservatism. Conservatives, it declared, pursued foreign entanglements, were committed to free trade that denied the nation's interests and advocated integration rather than 'racial integrity'. They were aligned with international finance, while populism supported free enterprise and the middle class. The *Spotlight*, as we have emphasised, represents only one strand of the movement. But others too saw the mainstream right as representing different concerns and different interests than their own. This was most evident among those attracted to armed struggle. (As is too often forgotten, groups like the Christian-Patriots Defense League and the Committee of the States came into conflict with law enforcement under a Republican Administration, not a Democrat one.) But non-violent Patriots were also estranged from right-wing orthodoxy. Thus, in 1985, for instance, in an open letter to President Reagan, a columnist for the *Justice Times* called on him to abandon plans to reform 'the Marxist income tax' and turn instead to its abolition, along with that of the Federal Reserve system. Just as the people had risen in the 1770s, so they had risen in the 1970s for the same goal, 'freedom from oppressive taxation and an inflationary monetary system'. He spoke of terrorism, she observed, while ignoring the terrorism of the IRS, and, if he was the American he claimed to be, he would sign a pardon for every person in federal prison for income tax offences (Carto 1983: ix–xiv; *Justice Times* July 1985).

Surprisingly as it may appear, the Patriot critique of Reaganism deepened yet further with the furore in the mid-1980s over the Reagan Administration's covert funding of the Nicaraguan Contras. The shredding of documents by a key figure in the saga, Oliver North, and allegations of links between the provision of weapons to the Contras and the smuggling of drugs fitted well with Patriots' conspiratorial reading of American politics. Given their anti-Communism, we might expect Patriots to support North, who would later turn his popularity on the Republican right into a bid for the Senate. Instead, however, after they had already accused the Reagan government of planning to intern tens of thousands of dissidents, the publication in mid-1987 of details of an alleged contingency plan prepared by North for the suspension of the Constitution and a take-over of government by FEMA and the military seemed to confirm Patriots' worst fears. Nor has the rise of figures such as Newt Gingrich brought Patriots and Republicans closer. Gingrich, Patriots warned, was a member of the CFR, a supporter of the accretion of power by the World Trade Organization and a proponent of the ideas of the futurists Alvin and Heidi Toffler, who, they observed, had declared that nationalism was an outdated philosophy and globalisation the force of the future (Rozell and Wilcox 1996; *Minnesota Patriot* June 1988; *Upright Ostrich* August 1987; *Christian Crusade For Truth Intelligence Newsletter* July 1987; Gurudas 1996: 185–6, 290; *Taking Aim* August 1996, June 1995; *Patriot Report* March 1995).

As a movement, Patriots are likely neither to immerse themselves in the Republican Party nor to forge a closer relationship to libertarians. Their preferred strategies and the issues they prioritise significantly differ from both; yet how the movement will grapple with the problems it faces remains far from clear. In its white supremacist form, the political system Patriots champion envisages second-class citizenship for minorities or even their wholesale exclusion – or worse. Even if not racist, what Michael Barkun has called radical localism easily takes the form of a communitarianism that believes in the primacy of shared values and the use of strict laws against those who do not share them. The commitment to the sovereign individual, to the township, the county, the state and, finally, to America, all have different implications, and Patriots vary drastically over which has the greatest call on their loyalty. But if the movement is divided in strategy and exhibits both authoritarian and libertarian impulses, aspects of each have the potential to bring its adherents into conflict, sometimes bloodily, with a federal government that they see as a threat to their rights and a servant of their enemies (Barkun 1997: 217–22).

8

Pat Buchanan
and the post-Reagan right

As we have noted, the 1992 Republican Convention was particularly marked by the controversy over the speech by Bush's challenger in the party primaries, Pat Buchanan. There was a religious war taking place for the soul of America, he proclaimed, and where Bill and Hilary Clinton stood for abortion on demand, homosexual rights and women in combat, such change could not be tolerated in a land that could still be called 'God's country' (Buchanan 1992).

This was not the only memorable image in Buchanan's peroration. He called too for the Republican Party to 'reconnect' with those who were facing unemployment. 'They don't read Adam Smith or Edmund Burke, but they come from the same schoolyards and playgrounds and towns as we did.' Republicans, he declared, had to show that 'we care', and they needed to reach out to other groups too. They needed to stand, for instance, by 'the brave people of Koreatown who took the worst of the LA riots', yet who still believed in the American Dream. But it was in those riots, he claimed, that one could see hope. The mob had looted and burned, terrifying the old and the weak. But, eventually, it had been stopped, driven back by the courage of American soldiers. 'And as they took back the streets of LA, block by block, so we must take back our cities, and take back our culture, and take back our country' (Buchanan 1992).

As Gary Wills noted, it had been little noticed that this speech was a reworking of the commencement address he had given to graduates of the evangelical Liberty University three months earlier. Where, Buchanan had asked, had the mob come from? His answer had been a sweeping indictment: 'It came out of public schools from which God and the Ten Commandments and the Bible were long ago expelled. It came out of corner drugstores where pornography is everywhere on the magazine racks. It came out of movie theaters and away from TV sets where macho violence is romanticized. It came out of rock concerts where rap music celebrates raw lust and cop-killing. It came out of churches that long ago gave themselves up to social action, and it came out of families that never existed' (Wills 1992: 9).

There were other themes too, undiscussed by Wills, that we can find in this lesser-known speech. As we might expect, we find the notions of a religious war, and the symbolic equation between the restoration of authority in the streets of Los Angeles and the battle to regain America. But the full tenor of his argument was spelt out particularly dramatically in the claim that 'When we conservatives and traditionalists were fighting and winning the Cold War against communism', the war for America was being lost. For thirty years, religion and morality had been under attack, from 'the public classroom to the TV screen, from the movie theater to the museum'. 'Will America', he asked, 'one day become like the poor old man with Alzheimer's abandoned in the stadium, who did not even know where he came from, or to what family he belonged?' (*Human Events* 23 May 1992).

In Buchanan's imagery, the America that was under threat faced an army of foes. If it no longer faced the Soviet Union, it faced attacks on its moral values, its economic prosperity and even its very identity. We have already discussed some of the views that place him in the pro-life and pro-family camps in American politics. But if these are views that are also espoused by large and decades-old movements, his economic and cultural nationalism define a much more distinctive politics. In this chapter, we will discuss his economics, his understanding of America as a nation and his crucial notion of the need to move beyond the existing boundaries of American conservatism. We will examine these in the context both of the arguments made by his paleoconservative and paleolibertarian allies and his conflict with other groupings in the conservative movement. Finally, we will turn to his relationship with three sections of the right, none of which, despite assumptions to the contrary, has wholeheartedly embraced him: the Christian Right, the Patriot movement and the extreme right.

Buchanan's decision to enter the 1992 contest, as we saw in Chapter 1, was framed by a number of grievances among both economic and social conservatives. Buchanan challenged George Bush as both soft on moral issues and weak on taxes. But, rather than unite the conservative movement, he has continued to divide it. His earlier opposition to the Gulf War saw him attacked as an isolationist whose politics were to be equated with those of the anti-war – and unpatriotic – left. Buchanan's reply was to emphasise the breadth of the divisions in conservative ranks. The Gulf War's conservative critics, he declared, were 'Old Church and Old Right . . . disbelievers in a Pax Americana. We love the Old Republic, and when we hear phrases like "New World Order," we release the safety catches on our revolvers' (*Wanderer* 29 November 1990).

Such fighting talk had already been sounded the previous year as tension rose between neoconservatives and their paleoconservative rivals. A recent article by Paul Gottfried, Buchanan declared, had shown in considerable detail how neoconservatives had gained control of conservative foundations, ensuring that only those of whom they approved received any funding. Those they opposed, Buchanan claimed, were smeared as racists and anti-Semites, a situation that left 'many conservatives wondering if we hadn't made a terrible mistake when we brought these ideological vagrants in off the streets and gave them a warm place by the fire'. With 'the unifying issue of anti-communism fading', he declared, the conflict between neoconservatives and 'traditional conservatives' was coming to the fore. 'Before true conservatives can ever take back the country, they are first going to have to take back their movement' (*Washington Times* 1 May 1991).

In this struggle to redefine conservatism, Buchanan, as we will see, attracted to his standard a wide range of different groupings on the right. He attracted, too, considerable criticism. For both his supporters and his critics, one key question was a political economy that moved increasingly away from that dominant on the right during the Reaganite 1980s. Thus, as early as 1990, one conservative critic complained, he was to be found attacking 'the vulture capitalists of the leveraged buyout' and by early the following year, he was arguing that if free trade gave work to Mexico's unskilled while leaving American workers unemployed, then it could not be supported. 'A foreign policy that looks out for America First', he declared, 'should be married to an economic policy that considers first the well-being of our own workers' (*American Spectator* July 1991).

Buchanan's opposition to the Gulf War, allied to his vitriolic attack on neoconservatism and accusations that he was engaging in anti-Semitism, all combined to make him a highly divisive figure. But it was his arguments on trade, as John Judis predicted in early 1992, that had the potential to cause the most conflict within the conservative camp. As early as the first term of the Reagan administration,

Judis noted, arguments had broken out within the conservative movement over the effects of imports upon the country's industrial base. Failing to persuade the Heritage Foundation to modify its stance on free trade, a reluctance that cost the Foundation a number of financial contributions, those who advocated restrictions turned for support instead not only to such publications as *Chronicles* but outside the conservative movement altogether. Arguing that the real struggle was now between nationalists and internationalists, leading protectionists on the right sought to forge links with the unions. Buchanan, originally resistant to their arguments, came to be persuaded by them, and by 1991 he was writing the foreword to a book advocating economic protectionism (Judis 1992: 23–5).

If, during his 1992 campaign, Buchanan had attacked Bush's policies on trade, then the need to endorse the President in the name of party unity made it impossible for him to spell out his alternative from the podium at Houston. Unable to call openly for tariffs, he was reduced to suggesting that Republicans display compassion. After Bush's defeat, however, he was under no such constraint, and the decision of Clinton to press through, first with the North American Free Trade Agreement (NAFTA), and then with the General Agreement on Trade and Tariffs (GATT), brought both Buchanan and others into action against them.

Just as Maastricht was the surrender of European nations' sovereignty, he declared in 1993, so NAFTA was 'the legal instrument of piecemeal surrender of American sovereignty'. Transnational bureaucrats would be empowered to supervise US industries and impose trade sanctions, American jobs would be lost to Mexico, and under the pretence of free trade the country risked succumbing to 'the virus of globalism'. The subsequent fight against NAFTA was to generate some surprising alliances, and Buchanan was particularly pleased by a *Wall Street Journal* account of a rally in California, where one unemployed Perot supporter was described passing out a NAFTA special issue of the *Spotlight*, while another, a non-union employer, carried a trade union 'Don't Send My Job to Mexico' sign. To the *Journal*, Buchanan declared, NAFTA was Bush's 'boldest legacy', where 'the interests of corporate elites come before those of citizens'. In such a vision, 'fellow Americans' were 'no longer seen as members of the family, for whom we look out first, but as obsolete body parts, over-the-hill ballplayers who can't hack it and have to be cut from the team'. But if Americans would join together, whether left, right, or centre, they could defeat NAFTA and stop this giant 'step toward a New World Order' (*Conservative Chronicle* 1, 8 September 1993).

The struggle against NAFTA, he was to declare shortly after, had laid the grounds for a new alliance drawing on forces from within the Republicans, the Democrats and the Perot movement. But it had not succeeded, and he was no more successful in calling for 'a second war of American independence' against the globalist bureaucracy he saw emerging if the GATT treaty were not defeated. By his 1996 campaign for the presidential nomination, his protectionism had moved from being one of several concerns to the most prominent feature of his argument. Congress's passing of GATT, he emphasised, had been 'with the collaboration of Republican leaders', and within his argument free trade was indicted as an attack on national sovereignty, on jobs and on communities. What was good for General Motors, he declared, was not good for America if the company deserted America for low-wage economies, and new measures were called for. 'The policies I would put in place', he declared, 'would attract Democrats and working people by the millions. Let me tell you, the group that would be alienated would be some of the financial community and some of the folks heading up the big corporations. They're the people that would be to the back of our bus' (*Conservative Chronicle* 15 December 1993, 18 May 1994; Buchanan 1996b; *International Herald Tribune* 2 January 1996).

It was a view he would continue to develop after the 1996 election in his book, *The Great Betrayal*. Setting out to show 'How American Sovereignty and Social Justice' was being 'Sacrificed to the Gods of the Global Economy', Buchanan argued in considerable detail that protectionism had long been the American way until such figures as Woodrow Wilson and Franklin Roosevelt had pushed the nation in the direction of a liberal free trade utopia. The Republican Party, historically the party of tariffs, had been misled by the pressures of the Cold War to subordinate the American economy to the securing of foreign alliances, but now, at last, a 'humane economy', in which the market would serve the nation, could be constructed, and traitorous elites and the globalism they represented could be swept from the scene (Buchanan 1998: cover, 114, 21, 253, 258, 26–30, 288–9, 97–108).

In making such arguments, Buchanan was seeking to stake out out a distinctive stance in what he saw as a crucial argument 'over what it means to be a conservative . . . in the post-Reagan era'. Unlike 'some of our brethren of the Right', he declared, he recognised that there were 'higher things in life than the bottom line on a balance sheet . . . Community and country are two of those things.' As Judis pointed out during the 1996 campaign, Buchanan saw his position as rooted in Catholic social theory. But there were other factors at play too. One was his conviction that world trade agreements were to be seen as part of the New World Order's 'skeletal structure for world government'. Another, evident in both his comments on General Motors and his Houston speech, was his attempt to win over those who were experiencing not new opportunities but falling living standards and downsizing. This linked, in turn, with an argument that he had long espoused, that conservatism could not afford to lose issues – or voters – to its right. In a memo to Nixon in 1970, Buchanan had urged the President to take up the 'social issues' Wallace had raised, and after Nixon's fall, he had drawn attention to the continuing significance of Wallace's appeal to those who shared his 'indignation at high taxes . . . forced busing' and 'an arrogant distant bureaucracy'. He was to resurrect this argument in the late 1980s. 'The way to deal' with David Duke, he declared, was 'the way the GOP dealt with the far more formidable challenge of George Wallace. Take a hard look at Duke's portfolio of winning issues; and expropriate those not in conflict with GOP principles.' But if such political dexterity explained for him some of the electoral success of the Republican Party in the past, its absence also explained the problems of the GOP in the 1990s. *Chronicles* columnist Sam Francis was right, he declared at the beginning of 1998, to argue that the reason why the Republicans had been defeated in the 1990s was because they had lost what he described as Middle American Radicals. It was these people, mainly white and middle-class, who had supported Wallace, who had been won over by Nixon and by Reagan and who had deserted Bush for Perot. To win them again, the Republican Party would have to take up the issues that concerned them, from opposition to affirmative action and the surrender of national sovereignty to support for immigration restriction and prayer in schools (Buchanan 1993; Judis 1996: 19; Carter 1995: 396, 512; Buchanan 1975: 12, 24–5; *Wanderer* 9 March 1989; *Middle American News* March 1998).

As our earlier references to the Houston and Liberty University speeches suggested, Buchanan's notion of a country in danger gave a particular meaning to his social conservatism. America was not only threatened by sexual immorality or a disregard for 'the unborn', it was endangered by enemies of the nation itself. Thus, in the speech announcing his candidacy in early 1995, his calls for a nationalist economic and foreign policy were joined to an argument about immigration and American identity. The country, he declared, had to be defended not only against foreign powers but against the millions that illegally crossed its borders and demanded its social benefits. And it had to be defended too against those who indoctrinated children with 'moral relativism' and 'an anti-Western ideology', and who, in attacking southern war memorials, or the celebration of Columbus Day, or the singing of Christmas carols in public schools, were seeking to undermine the symbols of America's past (Buchanan 1995).

But if the nation was under attack, who exactly was to be included within it and who to be defined as the attacker was far from clear. In articles written before the 1992 campaign, he had given an ethnic coloration to his argument against immigration. Thus, in 1991, he had praised anti-immigration campaigners for raising the question of America's right to protect its character as a predominantly white society, while in the preceding year, having quoted writers in *Chronicles* and the similarly hard-line *Conservative Review*, he had proclaimed that America would become 'a Third World country' if it did not 'build a sea wall against the waves of immigration rolling over our shores'. In the face of both high rates of non-European immigration and black militancy, who, he asked, would speak for 'the Euro-Americans' who had founded the country? At other points, however, as with his invocation of Korean Americans in his Houston speech, he had drawn the boundaries of the nation very differently. During the bitter dispute over the Gulf War, for instance, one of the accusations of his anti-Semitism had derived from his claim that if Israel and its supporters took the country into war, the fighting would be done by 'kids with names like McAllister, Murphy, Gonzales, and Leroy Brown', while during the 1996 campaign, he was even to claim that 'we've got to provide a voice for the working men and women of this country, Hispanic-American, Asian, White, Black-Americans . . . whose jobs are being sold out in trade deals for the benefit of multinational corporations without any loyalty to their country or any allegiance to their workers' (*From the Right* August 1991; *Washington Inquirer* 6 July 1990; Buckley 1992: 28; Buchanan 1996a; for another Buchanan invocation of the need to defend the interests of 'those who work with their hands, tools and machines, many of whom are black and Hispanic and rural white', see Diamond 1998b: 105).

In constructing an argument that combined a populist economics with a social conservatism that shifted uneasily in and out of ethnic politics, Buchanan attracted considerable criticism on the right. Thus in 1992 he was opposed by both neoconservatives and others within the conservative camp. For the neoconservative Bill Bennett, Buchanan represented 'the dark side, conservatism in retreat, not the city on the hill but the fortress with a moat'. For another leading conservative, the former Congressman Vin Weber, Buchanan had to be opposed because, where the Republican Party stood for internationalism and free enterprise, Buchanan advocated protectionism and attacked capitalism. Furthermore, he argued, mainstream conservatism had successfully forged an alliance with neoconservatives and with conservatives within black and other minority communities. Buchanan's stance would enable conservatism to be identified with bigotry and destroy this coalition (*New Republic* 30 March 1992).

If in 1992 Buchanan's conservative critics primarily attacked him as an quasi-fascist, his 1996 campaign saw a major shift in their argument. Buchanan's economic nationalism had become increasingly hostile to much of big business, a development that now led to his being attacked as a quasi-socialist. Thus, for the director of domestic policy studies at the Heritage Foundation, Buchanan was 'far to the left of most of the people in the Democratic Party', while Reagan's former domestic policy adviser, Martin Anderson, described him as 'taking the left-wing position'. It was a note of attack that was most sharply sounded in the recently established neoconservative periodical, the *Weekly Standard*. 'Buchanan', it declared, had 'turned his back on the fundamental convictions that have defined American conservatism for 40 years.' He was, it jibed, 'America's last leftist' (*Washington Post National Weekly Edition* 4–10 March 1996; Grant 1996: 80).

Attacked in such different ways, Buchanan's politics were clearly difficult firmly to locate. One article during the 1996 campaign made a particularly interesting attempt to do so. Beneath the Buchanan campaign's enthusiastic populism, it suggested, lay an intellectual tradition – paleoconservatism. It was figures such as Samuel Francis and the *Chronicles* editor Thomas Fleming who shaped 'the centrality of culture in the politics of Buchananism', a politics that rejected the economics-centred conservatism of such figures as Kemp and Gingrich and harked back instead to the rural communities of the Old South and the virtues of an agrarian middle class. It still fondly recalled the Confederate cause and was unashamed in calling for the defence of an endangered white race. 'Blood and soil are central to their creed', the author concluded, and, that being so, Buchananism was 'at war' with modern American conservatism (Brooks 1996: 17–21).

That this article should appear in the *Weekly Standard*, just as capable of accusing Buchanan of a left deviation as a right-wing one, is somewhat ironic. There were problems with the argument, too. Paleoconservatism has, indeed, significant roots in the south, and Buchanan has eulogised those who died in the war with the Union. But, as Ashbee has shown, to see paleoconservatism as a southern tradition is to mistake its championship of the local and the small-scale for the defence of a particular region. As we shall see when we discuss Samuel Francis further, the central figure in his conservatism is not the southern white but the Middle American, as much at home in urban New York or small town Oregon as in the rural fastnesses of Alabama. There is another difficulty with the *Weekly Standard*'s argument – that Francis has denied that he is a paleoconservative. But, while not wholly convincing, the article is right in at least two regards: firstly, in arguing that paleoconservatism represents an important influence on Buchanan's thinking; and, secondly, in drawing our attention to the crucial role of Samuel Francis (Grant 1996: 98; Ashbee 1999b).

In 1991 Buchanan joined the John Randolph Club, an organisation set up to bring together paleoconservatives with their paleolibertarian allies. He has been described by a leading representative of the former grouping, Paul Gottfried, as its 'self-declared spokesman', and has signed a letter endorsing the work of its main organisation, the Rockford Institute. We could also note the prominence of paleoconservatives among his supporters. In 1995, for instance, it was Gottfried who was to explain why conservatives should support his candidacy to the readers of the Heritage Foundation's journal, *Policy Review*, while Thomas Fleming had argued in his support in *USA Today*, praising his opposition to NAFTA and a 'transnational elite class that owes loyalty to no nation and no people'. But it is the work of his 'old friend', Samuel Francis, that is of most importance in understanding how Buchanan's campaigns relate to paleoconservative concerns (Ashbee 1999b; *Policy Review* Summer 1995; *USA Today* 21 February 1996; *Conservative Chronicle* 15 December 1993).

Francis's arguments particularly involve two propositions. The first is the need for a new American Revolution, instigated by a stratum he terms 'Middle Americans'; the second a strategy for that Revolution taken from, somewhat surprisingly, the Italian Marxist theorist Antonio Gramsci. Gramsci, he told the assembled conservatives at the 1993 conference of Buchanan's American Cause Foundation, argued that overthrowing or capturing the state was of little use unless the ideological hegemony of the ruling class had first been undermined. If 'the cultural right' was to be victorious in America, he argued, they would need to understand, as Gramsci had done, that people obeyed their rulers because they accepted many of their assumptions and values, and that only the construction of an alternative to the dominant cultural apparatus in America would enable 'the federal leviathan' to be broken and give its opponents the opportunity to 'take back our country and our culture' (Francis 1997: 174–87; Diamond 1995: 298).

During the speech, Francis alluded to an exploited 'Middle American core' and 'a politically subordinated and culturally dispossessed majority of Americans'. Elsewhere, he developed his concept of revolutionary agency more fully. In the early 1990s he had already raised a number of key themes in a first collection of essays, a collection that had been described by Buchanan as 'brilliant'. But it is his second volume, a series of columns originally published in *Chronicles* and then brought together by a newly established monthly, *Middle American News*, that enables us to understand his argument more clearly. Drawing on the Italian elite theorists of the late nineteenth and early twentieth centuries and the formerly Trotskyist and subsequently conservative thinker, James Burnham, it represents, as we by now might imagine, a strikingly radical approach to the situation the American right faces in the post-Reagan period (Francis 1997: 186, 176, 7; *Christian American* April 1994).

The bourgeois elite of the late nineteenth and early twentieth century, he argues, has long since ceased to rule America. It had been displaced by a managerial elite that was taking the country into a transnational order. Increasingly crushed between the new elite and the underclass, the middle class that had survived the passing of the bourgeois order lacked the material independence of the middle class of the past, and was increasingly taking on the attributes of a proletariat. If it wished to avoid extinction, he held, then it had to develop an identity and consciousness of itself independent of 'the techno-bureaucracy of the global managerial order' and capable of forming 'the core of a new political and cultural order in which it can assert its hegemony' (Francis 1997: 52–7).

Exactly who made up Middle America in this argument is far

from clear. In one account, it is described as a 'broad social and political spectrum . . . mainly distinguished by its location on the receiving
end of the fused political, economic, and cultural apparatus of the
dominant elites in the United States' and 'not necessarily identical to
the middle class'. At another point, it is portrayed as a diverse grouping made up of small businessmen, small farmers, 'white ethnic blue-
collar workers' and 'similar groups', its unity provided by a
resentment of the state on which they depend. At times, as with
Buchanan, what appeared to be an economic issue becomes a racial
one. Powerful forces, Francis argues at one point, seek to 'dispossess
white Americans economically, politically, and culturally and gain the
loyalty of their non-white following in the black underclass and the
government-created middle class'. In turn, such forces are supported
by bureaucratic elites in the state, the corporations, the unions and the
media, 'who use them to expand their own power'. Not only in this
account has ethnicity edged out economics, but the middle class is
now seen as fractured, with a major segment outside the Middle
American identity (Francis 1997: 231, 92, 60).

But if it is not always clear who makes up the newly insurgent
group, it is clear that its material situation distinguishes the programme that can mobilise it from that of traditional conservatism.
Francis, as one would expect, is fiercely hostile to a mainstream conservatism he sees as compromising or worse. Opposed to free trade,
to immigration and to multiracialism, he is an opponent of the
Republican leadership and of neoconservatism. But he overtly dis-
agrees too with paleoconservative support for small government and
its belief in the restoration of the old republic. Middle Americans,
Francis argues, are dependent upon the state and would expect health
insurance, unemployment benefits, pensions and economic policies
to protect their jobs, farms and businesses (Francis 1997: 136–7, 13, 90,
92–3).

If, in this argument, paleoconservatism was irrelevant to Middle
America, what of the religious right? This, Francis holds, is 'the
current incarnation of the on-going Middle American Revolution',
but a highly inadequate one. Under cultural attack since the 1960s,
Middle Americans had summoned up a religious movement to
defend their moral code and resist the loss of their dominance. But
religion was not 'the most effective political and ideological vehicle'
for Middle Americans. The religious right's ideology strengthened its
militancy, its ability to resist at the local level and its alienation from

the ruling elite. What it did not do was mobilise its members to 'prevent inundation of the country by anti-Western immigrants, stop the cultural and racial dispossession of the historic American people, or resist the absorption of the American nation into a multicultural and multiracial globalist regime'. It either did not understand or took the wrong side on such issues, and burdened with what Marxists called false consciousness, its political action did not undermine the existing order but ultimately worked to sustain it (Francis 1997: 208–12).

Seeking a revolutionary movement, Francis found it in Buchanan's campaigns. It was Buchanan, he argued, who articulated 'the concepts of America as a nation with discrete national political and economic interests and of the Middle American stratum as the political, economic, and cultural core of the nation'. The state, he understood, was not simply to be opposed as too big, but because it was the instrument of a hostile social group. Controlled by a different force, it could support Middle American interests and values. Thus he had unsettled free market conservatives by supporting higher unemployment benefits and criticising Republican proposals on Medicare. In this, as in his opposition to free trade, Francis argued, he had demonstrated that his candidacy should not be seen as the expression of an orthodox conservatism, but the championing of a social force whose political identity transcends 'the division of the political spectrum' into left and right (Francis 1997: 136, 240–41, 237–8, 235).

For Francis, Buchanan was the standard-bearer of a new movement, emerging out of the crisis of a conservatism that, from its inception in the mid-1950s, had never come to understand the need not to preserve but to overthrow the existing order. In this, Francis differs markedly from another element in the Buchanan coalition, paleolibertarians. For them, the right is not to be identified with the movement that initially grew up around *National Review*, nor is Buchananism a new movement for new times. Instead, the authentic right had been destroyed by the machinations of Buckley and his colleagues, and Buchanan's movement is to be understood as the return of the repressed. In a book published in 1993 and with a foreword by Buchanan, the paleolibertarian Justin Raimondo argues that the Old Right that had emerged to do battle with Roosevelt's New Deal had been displaced by, first, the *National Review* Right, and then the neoconservatives, both of which rejected isolationism and a rootedness in America in order to pursue a global crusade against Communism.

Coming from the left themselves, key figures around Buckley's journal and within neoconservatism brought alien values into a movement that by the late 1980s, in the shape of such Republican politicians as Jack Kemp, claimed there were such things as rights to housing or jobs rather than remaining true to a conservative commitment to 'untrammeled free enterprise' and limited government. Now, with the passing of communism, the global messianism of the supposed conservative movement was not coming to an end, but was being reinvigorated in calls for a new crusade to promote democracy throughout the world. Paleoconservatism, conversely, had emerged as the descendant of 'the America First wing of the conservative movement', and its rise, in turn, had shown another dissident grouping of the right, paleolibertarianism, that the Old Right coalition of conservatives and libertarians could be revived. *National Review* had purged conservatism of both libertarianism and the John Birch Society in its bid to create a homogeneous and globalist movement. Now, with the rise of Buchanan's challenge for the Republican presidential nomination, there was a chance to create a movement and an ideology that could restore authentic conservatism (Francis 1993; 225: Raimondo 1993: 2–7, 9, 217–18, 187–93, 220–21).

But the movement, Raimondo argued, had, as yet, not fully thought through what it stood for. In particular, in reviving 'the Old Right with all its virtues', Buchanan had 'also resurrected its major flaw'. In arguing for an economic policy that prioritised the needs of 'our own workers', Raimondo held, he was allowing his 'ardent nationalism' to overwhelm his burgeoning libertarianism. But if his protectionism could not be accepted, his foreign policy and his stance on the domestic economy were both 'indistinguishable from the Old Right libertarian opposition to big government and empire-building', while in his cultural conservatism he understood, as had his political predecessors, that 'the free society is only possible if nurtured by a healthy culture' (Raimondo 1993: 221, 229–32).

Raimondo's book was published by the Center for Libertarian Studies, through which he and other paleolibertarians waged a battle with their former colleagues. Its journal, the *Rothbard-Rockwell Report*, vigorously championed Buchanan's candidacy. Over time, however, the intensity of its support would diminish. It was quite right, Murray Rothbard argued during the 1992 campaign, for a libertarian to back a candidate who did not defend free trade or immigration. As with the original Old Right, disputes over such issues as free trade were permissible within a shared ideology of property rights and minimal government. Indeed, Rothbard continued, in choosing the libertarian Ron Paul as his chief economic adviser, Buchanan demonstrated a greater affinity to free trade than did those establishment conservatives who favoured massive subsidies, foreign aid and international financial agreements. (*Rothbard–Rockwell Report* February 1992).

By 1996, however, the balance was to shift. Buchanan's protectionism, Llewellyn Rockwell argued, had evolved from seeking to save certain industries to 'a full-blown theory of political economy' which was both economically destructive and encouraged big government rather than small. Similarly, when Buchanan denounced companies for laying off workers, this was to deny that only employers could know what was in the company's interest in the competitive marketplace. As his campaign progressed, Rockwell argued, Buchanan 'redirected his ire away from government and toward business'. His 'mercantilism' was 'plain wrong', and so too was his position on abortion. (Instead of banning abortion by a constitutional amendment, paleolibertarians held that abortion decisions should be returned to the states.) Hopefully, Rockwell declared, Buchanan would come to 'embrace the entire paleo program', from economic freedom and no tariffs to an America First foreign policy and cultural conservatism. But in 1996, he had 'turned what was supposed to be a right-wing populist campaign into what sounded, on occasion, like a left-wing one' (*Rothbard-Rockwell Report* March, April 1996).

Buchanan's campaign was supported by both paleoconservatives and, amidst some criticism, by paleolibertarians. He was opposed by neoconservatives and others in the mainstream of American conservatism. But what of the Christian Right? Here, as we have already noted, we need to be aware of both points of contact and divergence. In language very similar to Buchanan's, for instance, Pat Robertson has attacked a 'fifth column' within the media and education working to undermine America's culture. Buchanan's fervent nationalism is also to be found among Christian Right activists, as was particularly strikingly demonstrated when their victory in elections to a Florida school board in the early 1990s led to an attempt to replace multiculturalism with the teaching of America's superiority 'to all other cultures, past and present'. But there are also important strains between the Christian Right and Buchanan or, more precisely, within the Christian Right in relation to issues championed by Buchanan. One such divide concerns the all-important issue of foreign trade. In late

1993 the *Wall Street Journal* reported that, as part of the broadening of its agenda, Ralph Reed planned that the organisation would campaign in support of NAFTA. Buchanan, however, predicted that this would meet with resistance from Coalition supporters, and within weeks the same paper was to report that, 'amid private grumbling about Trilateral Commissions and other global conspiracies', Reed's plan had been abandoned. Tensions between the two camps were also evident in 1996 when, to the fury of Samuel Francis, the Coalition sought to influence Congress by producing a letter opposing proposed restrictions on immigration on the basis that it was 'anti-family' to limit the number of relatives an immigrant could bring to America (Robertson 1993: 136; Martin 1997: 334–8; *Wall Street Journal* 7 September 1993; *Reason* January 1994; *Samuel Francis Letter* April 1996).

What stance did the Christian Right take towards Buchanan's campaign for the Presidency? While the leadership of the Christian Right supported Bush in 1992, the first issue of the *Christian American* for the year declared that many in the movement were disillusioned with Bush and wanted Buchanan to challenge him for the presidential nomination. A poll of viewers of Pat Robertson's television programme, *The 700 Club*, showed them supporting Buchanan by more than 2 to 1, while Gary Bauer was reported to be 'privately cheering' Buchanan's attacks on the president. The subsequent tensions between sections of the movement and the Republican hierarchy substantially increased Christian Right support for Buchanan's second challenge. Many grass-roots activists backed him, while, at leadership level, Bauer declared in 1995 that: 'There is a growing desire for the entire pro-family movement to endorse one candidate . . . and certainly many people believe that candidate should be Buchanan.' For the Christian Coalition, however, supporting Buchanan was out of the question. In part, this was due to a judgement that he would not win. Ralph Reed, Grover Norquist declared, had 'always assumed that Dole was inevitable'. It was also, one Dole adviser suggested, because Dole was seen as someone who needed the Coalition's support and would thus be amenable to its demands. The problem with Buchanan, in this account, was that he already had a base amongst Christian Right activists and had the potential to threaten the Christian Coalition's position as the dominant force for social conservatism (*Christian American* January–February 1992; *New Republic* 30 March 1992; *Human Events* 21 April 1995; *New Yorker* 25 March 1996).

Writing in the immediate aftermath of the campaign, Reed argued that while there were 'significant overlaps' between Buchanan and the 'pro-family movement's agenda', there were also 'substantive differences'. While some had 'climbed aboard the Buchanan express as a means to hold the party's feet to the fire on the social issues', others were distrustful both of his attitude to Israel and his protectionism. Buchanan was innocent of anti-Semitism, Reed argued (although not of insensitivity towards Jewish suffering), while religious conservatives did not speak with one voice on foreign trade. 'Privately', he concluded, 'we did not expect Buchanan to win the Republican nomination, but we also knew that it was important for us to remain allies.' If 'relatively minor tactical differences' were allowed to undermine such co-operation, then those who wanted the party to 'abandon cultural issues' would be all the stronger (Reed 1996b: 144–5, 248–9, 155).

As Buchanan supporters such as Samuel Francis and Phyllis Schlafly made clear, they had no hope of winning over the Christian Coalition leadership, but did believe there was significant support at the movement's grass roots. But while Buchanan could hope for some support, it was not to be enough to win over the Christian Right as a whole. Indeed, more than one account has claimed that it was the Christian Coalition that ultimately deprived him of victory. The momentum of his campaign, it has been argued, was stopped by the manoeuvring of the South Carolina political establishment to ensure victory in the state primary for Bob Dole. While Dole's campaign manager was highly favourable about the role of Roberta Combs, the Christian Coalition's South Carolina director, the Buchanan campaign saw things rather differently. Combs, one Buchanan supporter declared, had been particularly pernicious in arranging for the Governor of the state, a Dole supporter, to address the Coalition's leading activists in the state after Buchanan had won in Louisiana. Both of them, the complaint continued, had then called upon 'conservative and evangelical pastors' to support Dole at a meeting at the Governor's Mansion (*New Yorker* 25 March 1996; *New York Times Magazine* 14 July 1996; *Christian News* 18 March 1996).

If in 1996 Buchanan was opposed by a significant section of the Christian Right, by the time of his next candidature the situation had complicated yet further, with the entry into the race of Gary Bauer, who, as Oldfield has noted, sought to 'steer a middle course' between those who embraced the New World Order and those who called for America First. Meanwhile, the Christian Coalition, as we have seen, has avoided supporting either Bauer or Buchanan. But if the Christian Right is not to be identified with support for Buchanan, what of the Patriot movement? Michigan Militia members enthusiastically supported his 1996 campaign, while the Militia of Montana announced that it supported him for his opposition to 'GATT, NAFTA, Gun Control, the U.N., Abortion, and everything else that has left America in shambles'. But for both militia activists and others in the Patriot movement, there were problems with the candidacy. Thus, in the very statement that expressed support for the campaign, the Montana group noted 'suspicions' that Buchanan was really 'an insider', while Clayton Douglas, the editor of the *Free American*, argued that while the US Taxpayers Party was 'the best choice out there for conservative Americans', Howard Phillips's 'open wooing of Buchanan' cast doubt on his judgement. Buchanan had failed to campaign against the Federal Reserve, and if he were elected, then, like Reagan before him, he would do nothing to stop the 'slide into the abyss of One World Government' (Oldfield 1999: 11; Mariani 1998: 147; *Taking Aim* February 1996; *Free American* October 1996).

While Douglas subsequently declared that he had argued at the time that Buchanan's intention was 'to try to capture and neutralise the Patriot vote', others in the movement took longer to become disenchanted with his candidacy. 'Many of us thought highly of Pat Buchanan', one Patriot paper commented, but in endorsing the 'conservative impersonator', Bob Dole, he had 'sold out to the NWO/ Establishment Republicans'. It was this view that appears to have been more common, perhaps best demonstrated by the changing views of the leading Patriot publication, the *Spotlight* (*Free American* March 1997; *Wake-Up Call America* September–October 1996).

Despite concerns over Buchanan's continued involvement in the GOP, the *Spotlight* indicated its sympathy for his campaign during 1995 and was particularly pleased when it was described by a journalist as the 'newspaper of choice among grass-roots Buchanan supporters'. At the beginning of 1996, Liberty Lobby's Board of Policy overwhelmingly voted to endorse Buchanan's candidacy, a decision the paper was to describe as 'no surprise considering the fact that Buchanan's presidential campaign platform reads like . . . a statement of Liberty Lobby's positions on the issues'. But it was a romance that would sharply cool. Following Buchanan's decision to endorse Dole, the *Spotlight* attacked his 'surrender . . . to the plutocracy' and claimed that it now fell upon 'the shoulders of Liberty Lobby . . . to take command of his scattered flock'. When once again he announced his candidature for the Republican nomination the paper refused to support him. His defection to the Reform Party, however, introduced a new dynamic, and the Lobby was soon to be found alongside others on the far right in support of his bid. (Dobratz and Shanks-Meile 1997: 250–51, 306; *New Yorker* 22 April 1996; *Spotlight* 2 September 1996, 15 March 1999; *Searchlight* May 1999; *Washington Post* 23 July 2000).

As we have seen, both Buchanan and Francis have made pronouncements calling for a specifically white politics. The 1996 campaign proved particularly controversial in this regard, with critics not only attacking one of Buchanan's key supporters, Larry Pratt, but also denouncing others in his campaign for their previous involvement with David Duke. Buchanan, who defended Pratt, removed former Duke activists and declared that anyone who belonged to a racist group would be excluded from his campaign. This was not the only link between the campaign and the racist right, however, and an article in *USA Today* argued that a number of substantial contributors had what it described as 'radical' links. Nearly $12,000, it stated, had come from 18 people who had helped finance David Duke, while Sam Dickson, a lawyer 'active in racist and anti-Semitic causes', had donated $250. A closer reading of the article made it clear, however, that the situation was complex. Where Dickson was quoted suggesting that Buchanan was 'much less committed on the race issue than I am', one of the most militant figures on the extreme right, the White Aryan Resistance leader Tom Metzger, characterised Buchanan as 'tickling the ears of many white racists, but only with economic and racist code words designed to keep as many shekels coming in as possible'. It alluded to another dynamic, too, when it quoted another prominent extreme right activist, Richard Barrett, declaring that many people who had never given money to candidates before were contributing to Buchanan. 'The interesting thing', he suggested, 'is many of these people had given up on the system, and he's bringing them back' (*USA Today* 8 March 1996).

If Metzger saw Buchanan as deliberately misleading racists, Barrett was making a different argument: that the candidacy was deradicalising if not their racism, at least their strategy for pursuing it. Buchanan was not the subject of extreme right unanimity but a subject of debate, as was particularly well illustrated by a six-month-long exchange of views on a racist computer mailing-list controlled by David Duke's one-time successor as leader of the Knights of the Ku

Klux Klan, Don Black. Some of those who had taken part in the discussion, Black noted, enthusiastically supported Buchanan, while
others saw him as 'just another Establishment shill'. But, regardless of
his motives, Black argued, Buchanan had long criticised affirmative
action, immigration and a foreign policy that failed to put America
First. In 1992, he had played a pernicious role in undermining David
Duke's bid for the presidential nomination in the Republican primaries. Today, however, he was the only candidate taking the side of
white working people against the exporting of jobs to Mexico, the
subsidising of the welfare underclass and 'anti-White racism'. This
did not make him a White Nationalist. His politics were rooted in traditional Catholicism, and he did not realise the central role of race. But
he did deserve racialist support as a trailblazer who would 'make
White Americans more aware of the real issues and of their real
enemies' and would open the way for 'other, more racially oriented,
candidates' in the future (Black 1996).

It was a view which attracted others on the extreme right. One
racist journal, *Instauration*, argued that the Republican establishment's attack on Buchanan had brought nearer the time when 'the
beachhead' Buchanan had established could be used by others more
willing than he to expose fully 'Jewish control' of America. This was
an argument, too, that appealed to one of the most hard-line of
American racists, National Alliance leader William Pierce. At the
beginning of 1992, his magazine declared that conservative accusations of Buchanan's hostility to Jews demonstrated that whether he
was an anti-Semite or merely a traditional Catholic, he was clearly
someone outside Jewish control. In a radio broadcast in 1996, Pierce
returned to the subject. Buchanan, he contended, was not 'a revolutionary' but a Christian conservative. But he was 'an outsider', and
the attacks on him could lead his supporters 'to understand who their
real enemy is' (*NAAWP News* 92, n.d., *c*.1996; *National Vanguard*
January–February 1992; *Free Speech* March 1996).

The text of Pierce's broadcast was subsequently made available
to the organisation's supporters in its monthly publication, *Free
Speech*. A later broadcast, however, offered a more jaundiced view.
Under the title 'Betting on Both Horses' another National Alliance
speaker suggested that only 'a few' paleoconservatives were 'forthright in their ideas on racial matters'. But while 'courageous' on race,
even they were wary of 'the Jewish question'. It was significant, then,
the broadcast remarked, that the July issue of *Chronicles* should

include a defence of Buchanan in which 'the Jewish author' Paul Gottfried had noted that around half of Buchanan's 'inner circle' was Jewish. Buchanan was 'not a racial patriot' and the high percentage of Jews among his advisers suggested that, just as they were active in the Patriot movement, so too they had moved in on a supposedly pro-white conservative campaign in order to stop it from recognising the role of 'organized Jewry' (*Free Speech* August 1996).

As both Metzger and, more tortuously, this broadcast had recognised, the Buchanan campaign was both attractive to the extreme right and disruptive of its priorities. The ambiguities in Buchanan's ethnic politics meant that the America he invoked fell significantly short of the racial separatism that extreme rightists sought, while the dispute about his earlier pronouncements on Israel was largely absent from the 1996 campaign. For Buchanan, the championing of issues associated with such figures such as George Wallace or Duke was intended to weaken rival movements. One effect of such a strategy was to draw activists from more militant strands of the right into his campaign. This could only work, however, if they left what distinguished them from him either behind or, at least, out of sight, and the problems that Buchanan experienced in this regard drew sharp comment from Samuel Francis.

Buchanan had been right, Francis declared, to defend Larry Pratt, despite his addressing 'some rather bizarre groups on the right'. But he had been wrong to remove campaign workers who had previously worked for David Duke. There could be 'no serious national campaign of the Populist Right', he declared, 'without former Duke supporters, militia members, and other inhabitants of the margins of national politics', and to exclude them allowed those in power to define 'political boundaries'. But if Francis wanted to bring 'inhabitants of the margins of national politics' into the movement that he saw as forming, it was because of what they might become, not what they already were. Writing in 1994 on the rise of 'populist' campaigns against immigration, NAFTA and homosexuality, he had suggested that, unlike previous movements, they had mercifully attracted very few of those obsessed by 'the Elders of Zion and Satanic conspiracies'. The following year, in the aftermath of the Oklahoma bombing, he had discussed a report that had appeared in the *Washington Post* of interviews of some of the inhabitants of a Pennsylvania town. One of those quoted, he noted, had declared that while he 'didn't want anything to do' with militias, he understood 'their attitude. If you ran a small business, you'd understand too.' Another had found it naive to think that bloodshed could be avoided, while a third believed that 'you've got to have radicals like militias'. Such views, Francis suggested, expressed a revolutionary consciousness 'bred by the economic and cultural annihilation they and their communities are facing' and the very fact that many were drawn to 'bizarre conspiracy theories and fantasies of armed resistance' was because they lacked any other explanation for their situation or strategy for its reversal (Francis 1997: 247–9; *Chronicles* January 1994, August 1995).

Once again, as with his evaluation of the Christian Right, Francis's peculiar appropriation of Marxism had resulted not only in the claim that Middle Americans were an oppressed social group but that they suffered from false consciousness. Nor was such a view unique to him. In a review of Buchanan's book, *The Great Betrayal*, the editor of *Middle American News* (and, it should be noted, the author of the preface to Francis's second collection of essays) praised it both for its attack on free trade and its exposure of 'the new transnational elite'. Right-wing activists, he declared, needed the kind of knowledge Buchanan provided 'to lead them to a more realistic understanding of their political predicament. Militia groups, for example, need to learn that their real enemies are more likely to be found riding in black limousines than in black helicopters' (*Middle American News* May 1998).

Neither a spokesman for the Christian Right nor a conventional conservative, Buchanan has posed considerable problems for those trying to locate his politics. If his denunciations of big business sometimes made him sound like a socialist (although hardly America's last one), his willingness, at least on occasion, to espouse a militantly ethnic politics and his undoubted appeal to Patriots and racist rightists made him the standard-bearer of a politics that stretched and threatened to break the boundaries between conservatism and other forms of right-wing politics. He was engaged in a battle not only to define America, but to define conservatism; not only to argue who or what could enter a nation, but who or what belonged inside a movement. It is the nature of those boundaries, and how we can best understand the movements that are divided by them, or united across them, to which we shall now turn.

9

The dispossessed

In a recent discussion of Pat Buchanan's third bid for the Republican Party's presidential nomination, Justin Raimondo returned once again to the subject of the candidate's role in the contemporary right. He was, Raimondo declared, the descendant of the isolationism that had heroically sought to avert US involvement in the Second World War and the heir of the Old Right that had succeeded it. He had brought about a fundamental realignment, separating 'American conservatism at its best' from 'the political hacks, neoconservative ex-Trotskyites, and professional Cold Warriors' who made up the official conservative movement. Above all, Raimondo argued, Buchanan was 'skeptical of all foreign entanglements' and thus, speaking in Iowa in August 1999, he had attacked the presence of American troops 'all over the world . . . defending borders in Korea, in Kuwait, in Kosovo' when, instead, they should be home 'defending the southern border of the United States of America' (Raimondo 1999).

Buchanan, indeed, was defending two kinds of border. He was defending, as he had done in previous elections, a particular vision of America against immigration. But he was also seeking to defend a particular construction of the right – the authentic right, in his eyes – from an equally unwelcome invasion. In part, he was continuing with the metaphor of over a decade earlier when, in a 1986 symposium on 'The State of Conservatism', the paleoconservative Clyde Wilson had declared 'we have simply been crowded out by overwhelming numbers. The offensives of radicalism have driven vast herds of liberals across the border into our territories.' But, despite his clashes with the neoconservatives of whose rising influence Wilson complained, Buchanan was not solely concerned with them. The whole thrust of conservatism, he was arguing, had gone astray before their arrival, and an economic – and cultural – nationalist movement would be significantly different from the politics of William Buckley or Newt Gingrich (Diamond 1995: 282).

It is not, however, the only attempt to remake the American right. With some shared concerns with Buchanan and, equally importantly, some crucial divisions amongst themselves, the Christian Right are also seeking to reshape conservatism, while, to their right, the Patriot movement, again amidst both overlap with other forces and internal tensions, is attempting to articulate a form of politics distinct from either the Christian Right, with its evangelical underpinning, or the Old Right whose passing Raimondo and Buchanan mourn. Each is engaged in defining both the right and the nation in particular ways; each is seeking to include some within borders that will exclude others. If the metaphor of borders, both disputed and needing to be defended, is crucial here, so are two other interconnected images. One is the dominant image of the book – taking America back. The other, evident not only in Samuel Francis's writings but in crucial studies of the 'radical right' some thirty years earlier, is that most suggestive picture of the right's constituency – as the dispossessed.

The idea that America must be regained can be found in each of the movements with which we are concerned. In the late 1980s, preaching at a California Identity church, a member of the militia attached to the Committee of the States compared Patriots to the original American revolutionaries. The congregation, he urged, should arm themselves in readiness. 'Just like your ancestors were at Concord Bridge. A moment's notice . . . and we'll take this nation back . . . And we won't lose it this time.' The later militia movement, so transfixed with such comparisons, is equally devoted to the notion of regaining America. Thus, in an early leaflet, the Militia of Montana warned of federal government plans to bring the country under UN control. Over 25 million American veterans, it declared, had taken an oath to defend the Constitution. 'Let's Take America Back!' In like vein, Mark Koernke was 'a featured speaker' at a Taking Our Country Back Conference in Florida in the spring of 1995. The sheer ubiquity of the notion can perhaps best be demonstrated by the appearance of a cartoon in a number of Patriot periodicals and on the cover of a Patriot book, showing Uncle Sam pointing a finger, with the caption accusing an unidentified 'They' of 'Stealing Our country' and calling on the readers to 'Take It Back!' (Seymour 1991: 20, 26; Militia of Montana, n.d. (c.1995); Bennett 1995: 458; *Patriot Report* November 1993; *Spotlight* 17 January 1994; *American's Bulletin* September 1996; Jefferson 1995: cover).

The image has appeared amongst the Christian Right, too. Thus, an early Christian Voice leaflet declared, 'WE WANT OUR COUNTRY BACK! – The way it was <u>before</u> God was banned from the classroom – <u>before</u> the vilest pornography was allowed to be put on the magazine shelf in every corner drugstore – and . . . before the liberals made our streets safe for rapists and muggers, but not for God-fearing people.' Later, the notion has even appeared in the anti-gay movement, with groups opposed to local gay rights measures adopting the names Take Back Tampa and Take Back Cincinnati. One can detect it, too, in the more ambitious of the goals that Christian Coalition leaders have set for their movement. Thus Ralph Reed declared soon after the inception of the organisation that 'We think the Lord is going to give us this nation back one precinct at a time, one neighbourhood at a time, and one state at a time', just as Pat Robertson was to declare in 1992 that 'If Christian people work together, they can succeed during this decade in winning back control of the institutions that have been taken from them over the past 70 years' (Christian Voice, n.d. (c.1982); Gallagher and Bull 1996: 166–7; *Christianity Today* 23 April 1990; Clarkson and Porteous 1993: 80).

But, as we have already seen, the regaining of America is most associated with Pat Buchanan. In 1993, addressing a conference organised by his American Cause Foundation, he declared that the goal of conservatism should be to 'Recapture the culture.' One of 'the heroines' of this struggle, he went on, was the woman who had been the leading figure in the fight against the introduction of a pro-gay curriculum in New York schools. 'With the spirit of Mary Cummins, we can win the war for the soul of our country. We can take back America.' Five years later, discussing his economic policy, he argued that in 'building a Global Economy and a new world order', America's elites had betrayed 'everything the Founding Fathers stood for . . . If we are to take back our country, we must understand where and how it was taken from us' (*Conservative Chronicle* 2 June 1993; Buchanan 1998: 114).

Taking America back, as these last two examples suggest, is a phrase with more than one possible meaning. This is a point, indeed, that has been made by one of Buchanan's most controversial supporters. Writing in early 1996, Joseph Sobran argued that 'Taking our country back' spoke 'resonantly to different groups of people. It grabs workers who worry about their jobs when the government signs 2,000–page trade treaties; it grabs churchgoing people who are flabbergasted and enraged when the Supreme Court tells them their long-standing laws against killing unborn children show that they don't know how to govern themselves constitutionally.' Buchanan, he declared, was 'reshaping the Republican Party. Using a base of social conservatives, he is bringing in those who feel they have been ignored and betrayed by the nation's elites and are being dispossessed of everything from their jobs to their culture' (*Wanderer* 29 February 1996).

It was an argument he was to repeat elsewhere. Thus, in an excerpt from his own newsletter which appeared in the 'anti-Zionist' periodical, *Capitol Hill Voice*, the following month, he commented again on 'Buchanan's war on the elites' and the different meanings of 'taking back our country' to 'ordinary Americans . . . Pro-lifers, devout Christians, laborers, taxpayers, small businessmen, distressed patriots – all feel deeply that their country has been taken *from* them' (*Christian News* 13 May 1996).

With all the categories Sobran had mentioned, one – that of race – was missing. In some ways, this is surprising – in the mid-1980s, before his removal from *National Review*, he had already come under fire for his description of the racist magazine *Instauration* as 'often brilliant'. As we have seen, however, a neglect of race was not something that could be alleged about the use of the term by another of Buchanan's supporters. White men, Samuel Francis complained in 1993, were increasingly accepting 'their continuing demotion as the masters of American culture'. Instead of 'weeping over their impending dispossession', he declared, they should remember that in the past, in both America and 'their European homelands', they had broken 'whatever got in their way and set up a nation and a civilization that centered around them and things they liked.' When they understood they still had 'the economic and political muscle to keep doing that' they would be able 'to take their country and their culture back' (Diamond 1995: 283, 399; *Populist Observer* May 1993).

It was an argument that was integral to his attempt to appropriate Gramsci for the right. But he did not only look to a long-dead Italian Marxist for inspiration. The Republican Party, he argued later in the decade, was failing to take up such issues as immigration restriction, opposition to affirmative action or defence of national sovereignty, and in order to learn how to do so, 'the Populist Right' would be well advised to learn from France's National Front. It had set up its own professional associations, tenants' organisation and other groups, and was 'undertaking the long march through the institutions of French society, constructing its own counter-culture as an alternative to the institutions controlled by the elites and laying the groundwork for grassroots political mobilization'. This, he declared, was 'how you get your country back – not by swaggering around in the woods' but by slowly and patiently organising (*Middle American News* April 1997).

As we have seen, for both Francis and Sobran, taking America back is integrally connected with the notion of dispossession. It was an image that has been drawn on by others on the right. Shortly after his defection to the Reform Party, Pat Buchanan came under fire for an article in which he had argued that non-Jewish whites were being discriminated against in admissions to Harvard and that the only way to stop this 'dispossession' was to introduce quotas in their favour. The White Aryan Resistance leader Tom Metzger used the term when commenting on the Oklahoma bombing, just as twenty years earlier it was to appear in the National Alliance's vocabulary. But the most important use of the term predates all of them. Writing in the early 1960s, Daniel Bell sought to explain 'the radical right' as the 'rearguard action' of a group, or, more precisely, a series of groups, threatened by social change and declining status. Economically, he suggested, they were most associated with the old middle class of small businessmen, independent physicians and farm owners. Geographically, they were concentrated in the South, the Southwest and California. And in terms of religion, they were most identified with Protestant fundamentalism. As we discussed earlier, we should be careful not to assume that only one social group is drawn to the right, and careful too in recognising distinctions in its appeal in different periods. But however reluctant we should be to transpose Bell's portrayal to other periods, in the title of his essay, 'The Dispossessed', he had captured evocatively the acute sense of loss that another early writer on the subject, Richard Hofstadter, encapsulated even more aptly. Bell, he wrote, had examined a movement that felt that 'America has been largely taken away from them and their kind, though they are determined to try to repossess it and to prevent the final destructive act of subversion.' It was, to return to our motif, seeking to take America back, and we will not be able to understand the right of either then or since if we assume that it has only one answer to who America's enemies, and who its rightful possessors, might be (*Washington Post* 27 September 1999; *New York Times* 23 April

1995; *Attack!* January 1975; Bell 1962: 1–2, 28–32, 24, 26; Hofstadter 1967: 23).

Who it has been taken by can vary quite significantly. Where, as we have seen, many on the far right see a globalist conspiracy, they differ as to whether it is a Zionist one. If no such hesitation characterises the overtly anti-Semitic sections of the extreme right (thus, in the early 1970s, the cover of a special issue of the National Alliance paper declared 'Let's Take America Back! Time to End Zionist Domination is Now') we have seen that even the credence given by some Patriots to the *Protocols of the Learned Elders of Zion* may not be proof of anti-Semitism. Conversely, as with Eustace Mullins's writings on banking, the most important Patriot periodical, the *Spotlight*, thrives in part because, like the taking America back image itself, it can be read in more than one way (*Attack!* Special Issue, n.d. (1972)).

If we are to be careful in arguing whether or not a conspiracist understanding of 'the banksters' is anti-Semitic, other claims to reveal who really controls America are even further from a belief in what some on the extreme right describe as ZOG, the Zionist Occupation Government. This is often true of concerns with the Trilateral Commission or the Illuminati, and it is particularly the case with the more widespread conviction that America has fallen under the sway of secular humanism. But there are other accounts too. In one recent example, for instance, 'the arrival of lesbians and gays . . . into the power structures of media, government' and elsewhere was seen as leading to the aggressive suppression of masculinity. The 'new gay–feminist managerial elite', it declared, oppressed and deformed 'the ordinary and natural man-child' in an assault whose ultimate target was 'the father, both God in Heaven and the male parent'. This article, which appeared in a traditionalist Catholic weekly, drew on a number of interviews, the most vivid of which was with the editor of *Chronicles*, Thomas Fleming. Boys, he declared, knew they would be discriminated against. 'The straight, white male knows that homosexuals and feminists control all the institutions' (Dobratz and Shanks-Meile 1997: 88, 195, 280; *Wanderer* 6 May 1999).

In this account, in which the beleaguered male becomes assimilated into a single ethnic category, it was homosexuals and feminists who had seized control of both home and homeland. In other narratives, it is not so much who rules America but who threatens to dismember it. We have referred earlier to fears of a *reconquista*, a reconquest of parts of the USA by Mexican immigration. When, for instance, an anti-immigration campaigner in California declares 'We've got to take back our country', yet another interpretation of who the land must be wrested from comes into view (Chavez 1997: 68).

If the right has different answers about who America is to be taken from, it diverges too over where it is to be taken to. Writing in the mid-1980s, the neoconservatives Brigitte and Peter Berger suggested that in order to understand the different strands of American conservatism, it is 'useful to bear in mind' that most believe that the present marks a downfall from the past. 'It is in where they locate the relevant catastrophe that contemporary American conservatisms define and distinguish themselves.' For Catholic conservatives, they proposed, society had been in decline ever since the Middle Ages; for Southern traditionalists, the Civil War marked the divide; for neoconservatives, the late 1960s; and for the New Right, 'especially in its evangelical embodiment', the small-town America of the nineteenth century represented the world that had been lost. It is an illuminating approach to the question of differences on the right. As we shall see, however, exactly how far back the Christian Right wants to travel may be somewhat different from what they suggest (Berger and Berger 1986: 62–3).

In picturing the America they seek, prominent figures in the Christian Right have evoked a number of themes. Ralph Reed, for instance, speaking in 1996, asked: 'What kind of America do religious conservatives believe in? It is an America in which we would all like to live, a nation of safe streets, strong families, schools that work, marriages that stay together, with a smaller government, lower taxes, and civil rights for all.' The following year, the then-President of the Christian Coalition, Donald Hodel, told the organisation's annual conference that 'We want an America where women have a real choice between a career and staying at home . . . A nation where men and women and children of every race are reconciled to one another . . . where abortion is abolished and adoption is in its place.' Gary Bauer too has contrasted America as it is with America as it should be. In his vision, he declared, women would no longer be looked down upon for wanting to stay at home with their children, and people would be judged by their character and not by their colour. But his account had other emphases too: 'I want to see an America where I don't have to worry about date rape when my daughter goes out for the first time at college . . . where families no longer have to hide behind barred windows . . . where children can play in public parks again without fear . . .' (*Imprimis* April 1996; *Christian American* November–December 1997; *Focus on the Family* March 1996).

A number of points could be made about such portrayals. In describing women as choosing whether or not to work outside the home, both Bauer and Hodel bring new evidence to the argument by Moen and others that the Christian Right has learned over the years to speak in the language of rights rather than Scripture. Bauer's emphasis on the danger of crime suggests that Reed's argument that the movement must broaden its agenda may not have been without influence even among those who criticised his pragmatism. But one question that particularly deserves addressing is what point in America's past is being evoked by such declarations. The answer is somewhat surprising. 'What most religious conservatives really want', Reed argued earlier in the decade, 'is to reclaim some of the strengths of the America that most of us grew up in, the post-World War II America that was proud, militarily strong' and 'morally sound'. Such a view is by no means unique to him. Falwell, at the beginning of the 1980s, had advocated 'a return to where America was fifty years ago, morally'. Writing in the late 1990s, Tim LaHaye defended 'the good old days of 40 or 50 years ago', when the divorce rate was low, 'single-parent families were rare' and the streets were safe. It was an argument, however, that Reed found it particularly important not to have misunderstood. Many of the changes of the last thirty years, he insisted, had been good. It was right that women had achieved equality in the workplace and that the civil rights movement had brought full equality closer. 'I want to make it perfectly clear', he declared, 'that I do not want to go back to the 1950s' (Reed 1994: 3–4; Hunter 1981: 133, 138; LaHaye 1998: 247; Cromartie 1994: 41; for another argument, this time by the Vice President of the American Family Association, that while most things have changed for the worst, 'civil rights for blacks' was among the improvements, see *AFA Journal* April 1993).

Gary Bauer, too, has harked back to this period, but has been no less cautious than Reed in claiming that the goal is not a restoration of the 1950s as such: 'We are not talking about an America in which police break down the bedroom door. Adults will always be free to do what they please behind closed doors . . . But the America we envision is one in which deviant behaviour receives no special recognition . . . Homosexuality would be seen, once again, for what it is – aberrant and unhealthy'. 'These goals', he declared, 'may seem impossible, but they're not that far from what America was like only 30 or 40 years ago' (*Focus on the Family Citizen* January 1990).

If we might doubt the Bergers' suggestion that the Christian Right wants to take America back to the small towns of the last century, we should be sceptical too of the *Weekly Standard*'s portrayal of Buchanan's politics as a championship of the antebellum South. Writing in *Human Events* in late 1991, he asked if 'Our Old America' was 'Passing away?' Much of the article was devoted to a discussion of the claim by Larry Auster, a leading anti-immigration campaigner, that mass non-white immigration and multiculturalism were pushing America towards 'national suicide'. It was preceded, however, by extended extracts from another author's account of the film *Back to the Future*, in which the small town of the 1980s, 'littered with dirty streets, run-down stores' and a movie theatre that 'showed only "X" rated films', is contrasted with that of thirty years earlier, 'clean . . . well kept . . . well-behaved' (and showing a Ronald Reagan movie) (*Human Events* 14 September 1991).

We have discussed at length Buchanan's ambiguous relationship to the far right; and it is an intriguing example of this that the account he should draw on was authored not by a conservative but by a supporter of the extreme right Populist Party. Yet, only the year before, Buchanan published his own invocation of a lost world, this time of the Catholicism of his youth, in which he had argued that 'Segregation in the '50s was truly the biggest thing wrong with a country about which so very, very much was right' (*Human Events* 14 September 1991; *Populist Observer* September 1991; Buchanan 1990: 58–79, 306).

If such a strong force-field seems to pull much of the right towards the 1950s, it is not, of course, the only period for whose certainties its adherents yearn. Patriots, as we have seen, identify with the American Revolution, but diverge as to when America's subsequent fall from grace occurred. For some, indeed, even the foundation of the United States is not beyond suspicion; for many others, the passing of the Fourteenth Amendment marks the republic's demise. For tax resisters and many of those who prioritise the fight against bankers, the key moment is later; and in that they have a parallel among religious conservatives. It was untrue, its leading figure announced in 1992, that the Coalition on Revival's agenda included the death penalty for abortion, adultery and homosexuality. On abortion, he declared, he advocated a restoration of the legal situation that

pertained in the 1950s; but 'I really would like to go back to the founding fathers . . . That's quite a ways back from the '50s. I mainly want
to get back before 1913, when the IRS and the Federal Reserve were
started' (Clarkson and Porteous 1993: 41).

Other groups, too, hark back to the more distant past. The whole
dispute between paleos, whether of the conservative or libertarian
persuasion, and neoconservatives revolves around a wish to restore a
movement and a polity that predates not only the moment from
which neoconservatives trace America's decay but the creation of
modern conservatism itself. And this, of course, is one of the most
important features of the widespread nostalgia for the Eisenhower
years. It is not just that paleoconservatism's leading champion, Pat
Buchanan, should, despite our expectations, be drawn to the period.
What is even more worthy of note is that, when once modern conservatism was created in reaction to the 1950s, now it is this very decade
that much of the right wishes to regain.

This is not to argue that the modern American right has abandoned its war against liberalism. If much of it has lowered its sights,
its arguments about what the state can do and how it should spend
still represent a wide-ranging alternative to the politics that prevailed
in the 1960s and 1970s. If the Reagan administration marked the first
foray against those assumptions, the *Contract With America* was to represent another offensive, and Clinton's celebrated triangulation, in
which he outmanoeuvred conservative Republicans in part by separating himself from liberal Democrats, is a measure not only of conservative failure, but of conservative success. In signing the 1996 welfare
legislation, for instance, Clinton could argue that he had resisted the
more unacceptable measures. But it is true, too, that what he had
agreed to represented an important gain for the right (Joffe 1998: 290).

In other areas too conservatives have continued to oppose liberalism. If they are wary of frontally attacking affirmative action, then,
as Bauer's reference to judging by character rather than colour attests,
and the success of the California Civil Rights Initiative confirms,
many on the right believe that they can find ways to oppose it while
averting accusations of racism. And if some on the Christian Right
have wanted to move away from a focus on homosexuality, and
others have argued that they do not intend to enforce legal prohibition, it remains the case that laws are on the statute books of many
states by which sodomy is a crime, and that the movement wishes
their retention. To seek to restore the 1950s, if not what the right once

wanted, is a highly conservative objective. It will not, however, satisfy all of the right; and here we need to visit again the notion of groupings that lie beyond the mainstream right and how they might best be defined (Focus on the Family n.d. (1991): 15–20; *Reason* October 1998).

Here we enter a dense linguistic thicket in which it is easy to become completely lost. 'Libertarianism', the term that has been used for one of the component strands of modern conservatism, is applied at one and the same time to those who champion the free market and those who want the minimum possible restrictions in sexuality, drug use and other areas where they see the law as impinging on natural rights. The former, economic conservatives, are very much part of the mainstream right. The latter, full-fledged libertarians, are not, although, as Jean Hardisty as noted, through such groups as the Cato Institute they have undoubtedly exerted an influence on mainstream right thinking and, we would argue, partly breached the boundaries that lie between the two groupings. Other terms too have been the object of dispute, not least, of course, 'radical right' and 'extreme right' (Hardisty 1998b: 123–6).

The first of these terms, we suggested in the Introduction, should be retained for those groupings that see the world through a conspiratorial lens but not a racist one. The latter grouping, we proposed, is the extreme right, and the two together, along with those who could be described as inhabiting the contested boundaries between them, can be usefully described as the far right. The John Birch Society is the most important example of the radical right, and the influence of some of its ideas is a good measure of the extent to which the Christian Right, in particular, can be said to have adopted a radical right framework. But the arguments of figures such as Ralph Reed, and the attraction of many in the movement towards such candidates as Forbes or Bush, are a gauge of the extent to which the Christian Right has not become part of the radical right as such, but is instead contested territory between the movement that drove the John Birch Society out and those it excluded. Indeed, the situation is complicated still further by the partial rehabilitation of the Society after the events of the 1960s, in which it both forged links with the New Right and, through a rightwing co-ordinating group, the Council for National Policy, can be found alongside leading Christian Rightists and other prominent conservatives (Mintz 1985: 162, 227; Bellant 1991: 36–46).

The Buchanan campaign represents, as we have already suggested, not the chosen vehicle of the Christian Right but an alternative to it. Its sounding of both anti-capitalist and anti-immigration themes has led it to be characterised as both leftist and extreme rightist, and its association with the Perot movement makes clear definition yet harder still. It draws on paleoconservatives, yet has also been supported by some libertarians, and the extreme right has seen it as both an opportunity and a potential rival. It is, in general, to the right of the 'pro-family' movement and certainly of the mainstream right, but giving it a settled definition remains problematic not least because, unlike the Christian Right, it is not a movement with a clear core constituency and deep roots in society. Writing on the 1992 Perot insurgency, Diamond has argued that to be a social movement involves 'independently generated resources, a well-conceived ideology and set of policy objectives, and dense networks of individuals and organisations' with a long-term commitment to each other and the goals they share. We have already argued that the Christian Right, despite such characteristics, is not best understood as occupying one defined position within the rightist spectrum. This has been even more the case with a figure who has drawn on diverse forces and utilised variant appeals during his periodic electoral forays, and to what extent we can regard him as presenting a clearly defined alternative form of rightism to the politics of Gingrich and Buckley (or Robertson and Dobson) is still somewhat unclear (Diamond 1995: 295–6).

The Patriots, at least at first sight, match our notion of the far right perfectly. Influenced by both Birchism and anti-Semitism, they include both radical rightists and extreme rightists, as well as those between the two. Even here, however, there are pulls towards mainstream conservatism and, surprising as it may seem, it may well be that many in the militias are the least radical. We have emphasised the importance of conspiracism for Patriots, and its appeal is certainly evident in the militias. But just as we have not been persuaded that it is racist conspiracism that militia activists necessarily espouse, others will be resistant to an overarching plot narrative altogether. In this, they are already strangers to the world-view that gives the term radical right its meaning. Instead, it may be gun control or environmental regulation that has drawn them into the movement, and forces on the Republican right could be well placed to win them back. Here, too, it is worth considering the question of multiple membership among political activists. For two months in 1995, for instance, Kaplan attended meetings of the Granada Forum, a Patriot grouping in greater Los Angeles. She was able to survey 77 of the members and found that exactly the same percentage (46.8 per cent) described themselves as either Republicans or third-party supporters (nearly half the latter identifying with the Libertarian Party) and that 18.8 per cent also belonged to militias, 37.5 per cent to the John Birch Society and 15.6 per cent to the Liberty Lobby. In such plural affiliations, libertarian and mainstream conservative identifications can both rival and influence self-definition as a Patriot, and for both militias and the Patriots more broadly, the ways in which politics are seen, and activists are to be politically located, will be divergent rather than uniform (Kaplan 1998: 3, Tables 2 and 3, n.p., 25).

An openness to the mutual interaction between different currents on the right is a vital part of their comprehension. So too is an awareness of their fluidity. In the 1970s, for instance, the incipient New Right considered the possibilities of a Reagan–Wallace ticket in the 1976 election and attempted to take over Wallace's former party, the American Independent Party. One of the latter's leading figures, William Shearer, was ten years later to be found in Willis Carto's Populist Party, and ten years after that in the former New Right leader Howard Phillips's US Taxpayers Party, in each case taking his California American Independent Party with him. If libertarianism exerts an influence on Patriots (and vice versa), then Patriots exert an influence on the Taxpayers Party (and, again, the reverse is true) (Diamond 1995: 130, 351; *Monitor* November 1988; *Free American* October 1996).

We should not overstate the degree of overlap. One campaign in Mississippi in the mid-1990s, aimed at placing limits on the length of time elected officials could remain in office, was directed by a field organiser for the Christian Coalition who was also in the NRA. 'The links are all there', he declared. 'All of these grassroots organizations . . . amount to taking back our country for the people.' But, as a study of Oliver North's unsuccessful bid for a Virginia Senate seat in the same period also demonstrated, even though Christian Right and gun lobby activists could support a common candidate, this did not mean that they agreed on why. Christian Right supporters were, as we would expect, socially conservative. NRA supporters, in contrast, were more likely to be libertarian (Balz and Brownstein 1996: 163; Rozell and Wilcox 1996: 155–7).

As Raimondo has complained, modern conservatism was constructed by the exclusion of dissident groupings. In the 1960s the Birchites and then the libertarians were pushed out. But, as we have also seen, it has not been a wholly successful defining of boundaries, and both groupings can be found not only on the borders but within. Nor have the disputes of recent years been settled in the same way. Denunciations of *Chronicles* as nativist or Buchanan as anti-Semitic have not led to their removal from a common movement, and even the Council of Conservative Citizens, despite a decision before the Trent Lott–Bob Barr furore to exclude it from the 1998 Conservative Political Action Conference, has not received the treatment once doled out to Welch and Rothbard. Modern conservatism, however some of its adherents might dislike the term, is a big tent, and it is far from certain that many in the Patriot movement could not be brought within its folds. We noted earlier the *Free American*'s belief that for Patriots to support Buchanan was to succumb to a candidate of the Insiders. But Patriots' admiration for such figures as the leading Republican Congressman Dick Armey or, even more, for Ron Paul, the former Libertarian Presidential candidate, now once again a Republican, is an indicator of the mainstream's potential for neutralising right-wing dissidence. So too, we might add, is the propensity of Patriot publications to draw on syndicated conservative columnists, an inclination that on occasion has begun to pull some publications away from the Patriot movement altogether (Militia Watchdog 1999; *Reason* May 1999; *Free American* September 1998; *Wake-Up Call America* September–October 1998; for examples of Patriot publications using conservative columnists, see *Media Bypass* April, August 1999; *Midnight Messenger* November–December 1998; for Patriot publications moving towards conservatism, see *Justice Times* October 1989; *National Educator* December 1996 (and the comment on the latter publication in *Spotlight* 8 March 1999)).

In many accounts, the far right is presented as already or potentially dominating the right. In Lind's account, for instance, the Christian Right, Buchanan and the militias are not only seen as all part of the far right but as the only substantial forces on the right. Not only have we disputed such a categorisation, but it may be that the mainstream will prove even more successful than it has already been in drawing more militantly right-wing activists into its orbit. This, however, would have highly unpredictable consequences. Firstly, as with Francis's comments on Buchanan's need to recruit from the militias and 'former' Duke supporters, this can easily mean not that those who are recruited abandon what distinguished them, but that the movement they join is radicalised, that it is the mainstream or, in

Buchanan's case, a force between it and the extreme right that is pushed further rightwards. Secondly, it will intensify the tensions within the conservative camp that have already been commented on by a number of commentators. Where many have presented what has been termed a conservative crack-up thesis, contending that a unified conservative movement cannot survive the incompatibility of the Christian Right and libertarians, isolationists and interventionists, Nigel Ashford has argued that the forces of dissolution are either minor, in the case of the paleoconservatives, or amenable to compromise, in the case of the Christian Right. While concurring that 'the Old Right' is unlikely to eclipse what Raimondo has presented as the official conservative movement, this account has been less convinced that the pro-family movement will be satisfied by compromises on such issues as abortion. Yet even if that were the case, it would seem realistic both to expect defection on the part of some in the Christian Right and considerable difficulties for a political project that seeks to gain the votes of many who failed to support the Republican Party in 1996 and 1998 at the same time as it must ensure that neither Buchanan nor any other figure to its right becomes a strong enough force to disrupt its strategy (Lind 1996: 7; Ashford 1995: 117, 132, 135).

This book has tried to do a number of things. Three particularly need emphasising. One has been to argue for caution in describing forces as on the extreme right. Other writers, of course, hold quite a different view, and have to sought to characterise such figures as Pat Robertson or Pat Buchanan in such a way. This book, however, has argued that more complex distinctions are worth making, and where such figures have breached the boundaries that distinguish conservatism from forces to its right, it remains important to understand that contrary pressures have kept them from leaving conservative territory altogether. (For some recent attempts to over-extend the notion of right-wing extremism, see Scheinberg 1997: 67–76; De Armond 1999: 154–9; Hilliard and Keith 1999: 70, 153–4.)

If it is disturbingly common to use such terms as 'extreme right', other writers have eschewed such terms as 'radical' or 'extreme' altogether. The effect of talking in such terms, it is argued, is to celebrate what passes for consensus and make the supposedly mainstream or moderate appear admirable or beyond dispute. Hopefully, however, a case has been made for bringing such terms back into our vocabulary, and applying them with care to the phenomena that they can usefully demarcate (Diamond 1996: 88–9; Berlet 1996: 61–71).

Finally, in arguing the usefulness of such terms as 'the dispossessed', we have suggested that, like the image that gives this book its title, this can enable us to avoid the trap of the 'angry white male' explanation and acknowledge instead that there are a plurality of sources of discontent in America. Writing in the early 1980s, Allen Hunter argued that the images and symbols that the right has used allow people 'in different classes, subcultures, regions, and religions' to 'fill in the details' in their own way. Sobran said much the same in discussing the effectivity of such a slogan as 'taking America back'. Nor is this just a matter of emphasising the variety of grievances that the right can address or articulate. It is important too to recognise that different forms of the right can tap into them and be shaped by them in different ways (Hunter 1981: 133).

If the American right has been remarkably successful in defining the bounds of the possible, it has proved unable permanently to displace either the Democratic Party or liberalism. In the twenty-first century it will continue its pursuit of just those goals, and those outside mainstream conservatism will seek to go yet further still. The right's divisions and differences and dilemmas will not be the same as those we have examined. But one of the most important preconditions for coming to grips with the right of the future is to look again at it today, and come to a better understanding of the role of abortion, the nature of the militias, the character of the Christian Right and much else that has made the American right so vital to comprehend but so easy to misunderstand.

References

Abanes, R. (1996), *American Militias: Rebellion, Racism and Religion*, Downers Grove, IL, InterVarsity Press.

Abraham, K. (1997), *Who Are The Promise Keepers? Understanding the Christian Men's Movement*, New York, Doubleday.

ADL (1998), *The Council of Conservative Citizens*, New York, ADL.

Aho, J.A. (1990), *The Politics of Righteousness. Idaho Christian Patriotism*, Seattle, WA, University of Washington Press.

Allen, G. (1971), *None Dare Call It Conspiracy*, Seal Beach, CA, Concord Press.

Allen, G. (1976a), *The Rockefeller File*, Seal Beach, CA, '76 Press.

Allen, G. (1976b), *Jimmy Carter Jimmy Carter*, Seal Beach, CA, '76 Press.

American Freedom Network (n.d.), 'You May Not Have A Country After 1995!', leaflet.

American Renaissance (n.d., c.1992), 'Dear Concerned American', leaflet.

Andrew, J.A., III (1997), *The Other Side of the Sixties. Young Americans for Freedom and the Rise of Conservative Politics*, New Brunswick, NJ, Rutgers University Press.

Andrusko, D. (1983), *To Rescue The Future. The Pro-Life Movement in the 1980s*, Toronto, Life Cycle Books.

Anon. (1990) 'Which Constitution?', *The Patriot*, January, reproduced in Anon. (1994), *A Season of Discontent. Militias, Constitutionalists, and the Far Right in Montana* (1994), Montana Human Rights Network.

Anon. (1992), *Operation Vampire Killer 2000*, Phoenix, AZ, PATNWO.

Anon. (1995a), *Racist to the Roots. John Trochmann and the Militia of Montana*, Portland, OR, Coalition for Human Dignity.

Anon. (1995b), *The Unauthorized Militia Movement in the United States: Current Status, Historical Context*, Washington DC, Congressional Research Service.

Anon. (1997) *Vigilante Justice. Militias and "Common Law Courts" Wage War Against the Government*, New York, Anti-Defamation League.

Ansell, A.E. (1998), 'The Color of America's Culture Wars' in A.E. Ansell (ed.), *Unravelling the Right: The New Conservatism in American Thought and Politics*, Boulder, CO, Westview Press.

Ashbee, E. (1996), 'The Politics of Black Conservatism', paper presented at the Annual Conference of the American Politics Group.

Ashbee, E. (1997a), 'The Republican Party And The Black Vote: 1964 And After', paper presented at the Annual Conference of the American Politics Group.

Ashbee, E. (1997b), 'The Politics of Contemporary Black Conservatism in the United States', *Politics*, 17(3): 153–9.

Ashbee, E. (1998), 'Immigration, National Identity and Conservatism in the United States', *Politics*, 18(2): 73–80.

Ashbee, E. (1999a), 'The Republican Party and the African-American Vote Since 1964' in P. Eisenstadt (ed.), *Black Conservatism: Essays in Intellectual and Political History*, New York, Garland.

Ashbee, E. (1999b), 'The Politics Of Paleoconservatism', paper presented at the Annual Conference of the American Politics Group.

Ashford, N. (1995), 'The Right After Reagan: Crack-Up or Comeback?' in A. Grant (ed.), *Contemporary American Politics*, Aldershot, Dartmouth.

Ashford, N. (1998), 'The Republican Policy Agenda and the Conservative Movement' in D. McSweeney and J.E. Owens (eds), *The Republican Takeover of Congress*, Houndmills, Macmillan.

Baker, J.A. (1993) *Cheque Mate: The Game of Princes*, Springdale, PA, Whitaker House.

Balz, D. and Brownstein, R. (1996), *Storming The Gates. Protest Politics and the Republican Revival*, Boston, Little, Brown and Co.

Barkun, M. (1997), *Religion and the Racist Right: The Origins of the Christian Identity Movement*, revised edn, Chapel Hill, NC, University of North Carolina Press.

Baron, A. (1995), *Eustace Clarence Mullins. Anti-Semitic Propagandist or Iconoclast?*, 2nd edn, London, InfoText Manuscripts.

Barron, B. (1992), *Heaven On Earth? The Social & Political Agendas of Dominion Theology*, Grand Rapids, MI, Zondervan Publishing House.

Bauer, G.L. (n.d. (1993)), 'Dear Friend', Family Research Council direct mail letter.

Beckman, M.J. (1981), *Born Again Republic*, Billings, MT, Freedom Church.

Bell, D. (1962), 'The Dispossessed' in D. Bell (ed.) (1964), *The Radical Right*, Garden City, NY, Anchor Books.

Bellant, R. (1991), *The Coors Connection. How Coors Family Philanthropy Undermines Democratic Pluralism*, Boston, South End Press.

Bellant, R. (1995), 'Promise Keepers Christian Soldiers for Theocracy' in C. Berlet (ed.), *Eyes Right! Challenging the Right Wing Backlash*, Boston, South End Press.

Bennett, D.H. (1995), *The Party of Fear. From Nativist Movements To The New Right In American History*, 2nd edn, New York, Vintage Books.

Berger, B. and Berger, P.L. (1986), 'Our Conservatism and Theirs', *Commentary*, October: 62–7.

Berlet, C. (1993), 'Marketing the Religious Right's Anti-Gay Agenda', *Covert Action Quarterly*, 44: 46–7.

Berlet, C. (1996), 'Three Models for Analyzing Conspiracist Mass Movements of the Right' in E. Ward (ed.), *Conspiracies: Real Grievances, Paranoia, and Mass Movements*, Seattle, WA, Peanut Butter Publishing.

Berlet, C. (1998), 'Dances with Devils. How Apocalyptic and Millennialist Themes Influence Right-Wing Scapegoating and Conspiracism', *Public Eye*, Fall: 1–22.

Bijlefeld, M. (1997) (ed.), *The Gun Control Debate. A Documentary History*, Westport, CT, Greenwood Press.

Black, D. (1996), http://www.stormfront.org/stormfront/buchanan.htm.

Bork, R.H. (1990), *The Tempting of America. The Political Seduction of the Law*, New York, Free Press.

Boston, R. (1996), *The Most Dangerous Man in America?: Pat Robertson and the Rise of the Christian Coalition*, Amherst, NY, Prometheus Books.

Boyer, P. (1992), *When Time Shall Be No More. Prophecy Belief in Modern American Culture*, Cambridge, MA, Bellknap Press.

Breasted, M. (1970), *Oh! Sex Education!*, London, Pall Mall Press.

Brooks, D. (1996), 'Buchananism: An Intellectual Cause', *Weekly Standard*, 11 March, 17–21.

Bruce, J.M. and Wilcox, C. (1998), 'Introduction' in J.M. Bruce and C. Wilcox (eds), *The Changing Politics of Gun Control*, Lanham, MD, Rowman & Littlefield.

Brudnoy, D. (1982), 'The Missionary's Position on Sex', *Reason*, December, reprinted in R.W. Poole Jr. and V.I. Postrel (eds) (1993), *Free Minds & Free Markets*, San Francisco, Pacific Research Institute for Public Policy.

Bryant, A. (1977), *The Anita Bryant Story. The Survival of Our Nation's Families and the Threat of Militant Homosexuality*, Old Tappan, NJ, Fleming H. Revell.

Buchanan, P.J. (1975), *Conservative Votes, Liberal Victories*, New York, Quadrangle.

Buchanan, P.J. (1990), *Right from the Beginning*, Washington, DC, Regnery Gateway.

Buchanan, P.J. (1992), 'Text of Patrick J. Buchanan's Speech Republican National Convention in Houston, Texas', http://www.buchanan.org/speechtx.html.

Buchanan, P.J. (1993), 'America First, NAFTA Never', http://www.buchanan.org/never.html.

Buchanan, P. J. (n.d., 1995), 'Dear Fellow Pro-Lifer', direct mail letter.

Buchanan, P.J. (1995), 'Announcement Speech by Patrick J. Buchanan', http://www.buchanan.org/announce.html.

Buchanan, P. J. (1996a), 'Speech at Texas GOP Convention', http://www.buchanan.org/txsp0796.html.

Buchanan, P.J. (1996b), 'Pat Buchanan – Rally Speech in Santa Barbara, CA', http://www.buchanan.org/casp396.html.

Buchanan, P.J. (1998), *The Great Betrayal: How American Sovereignty and Social Justice Are Being Sacrificed to the Gods of the Global Economy*, Boston, Little, Brown and Co.

Buckley, W.F., Jr. (1992), *In Search Of Anti-Semitism*, New York, Continuum.

Burghart, D. and Crawford, R. (1996), *Guns & Gavels. Common Law Courts, Militias and White Supremacy*, Portland, OR, Coalition for Human Dignity.

Burkett, E. (1998), *The Right Women. A Journey Through the Heart of Conservative America*, New York, Scribner.

Burtoft, L. (1995), *Setting The Record Straight. What Research Really Says About the Social Consequences of Homosexuality*, n.a., Focus on the Family.

Bushart, H.L., Craig, J.R., and Barnes, M. (1998), *Soldiers of God. White Supremacists And Their Holy War For America*, New York, Kensington Books.

Butler, R. *et al.* (1982), *Nehemiah Township Charter and Common Law Contract*, State of Idaho, County of Kootenai, 12 July.

Calhoun-Brown, A. (1997), 'Still Seeing in Black and White: Racial Challenges for the Christian Right' in C.E. Smidt and J.M. Penning (eds), *Sojourners in the Wilderness. The Christian Right in Comparative Perspective*, Lanham, MD, Rowman & Littlefield.

Campbell, M.C., Jr. (n.d. (1991)), *Kingdoms At War. The Second American Revolution*, Ashland, KY, Maynard C. Campbell.

Cantor, D. (1994), *The Religious Right: The Assault On Tolerance And Pluralism In America*, New York, Anti-Defamation League.

Carter, D.T. (1995), *The Politics of Rage. George Wallace, the Origins of the New Conservatism, and the Transformation of American Politics*, Baton Rouge, LA, Louisiana State University Press.

Carter, D.T. (1996), *From George Wallace to Newt Gingrich. Race in the Conservative Counterrevolution, 1963–1994*, Baton Rouge, LA, Louisiana State University Press.

Carto, W. (ed.) (1983), *Profiles in Populism*, 2nd edn, Old Greenwich, CT, Flag Press.

Chavez, L.R. (1997), 'Immigration Reform and Nativism: The Nationalist Response to the Transnationalist Challenge' in J.F. Perea (ed.), *Immigrants Out! The New Nativism and the Anti-Immigrant Impulse in the United States*, New York, New York University Press.

Christian Voice (n.d. (*c*.1982)), 'Dear Friend', direct mail letter.

Christian Voice (n.d. (1984)), 'Dear Concerned Friend', direct mail letter.

Clarkson, F. (1997), *Eternal Hostility. The Struggle Between Theocracy and Democracy*, Monroe, LA, Common Courage Press.

Clarkson, F. (1998), 'Anti-Abortion Extremism', *Intelligence Report*, 91: 8–12.

Clarkson, F. and Porteous, S. (1993), *Challenging the Christian Right. The Activist's Handbook*, 2nd edn, Great Barrington, MA, Institute for First Amendment Studies.

Cohn, N. (1996), *Warrant for Genocide. The Myth of the Jewish World Conspiracy and the Protocols of the Elders of Zion*, London, Serif.

Collins T.W. (1994), 'White Paper on State Citizenship',
http://www.netaxs.com/~delcolib/whitepaperonstatecitizenship.htm.

Colorado for Family Values (n.d. (*c*.1993)), *The Colorado Model. Colorado for Family Values and the Amendment 2 Campaign*, CO, Colorado Springs, Colorado for Family Values.

Committee on the Judiciary (1983), *Constitutional Amendments Relating to Abortion. Hearings Before the Subcommittee on the Constitution of the Committee on the Judiciary United States Congress Ninety-Seventh Congress First Session, vol. 1*, Washington DC, US Government Printing Office.

Cooper, M.W. (1991), *"Behold a Pale Horse"*, Sedona, AZ, Light Technology Publishing.

Council of Conservative Citizens (n.d. (1990s)), 'Why Are We Unique? Because We're Effective!', leaflet.

Craig, B.H. and O'Brien, D.M. (1993), *Abortion and American Politics*, Chatham, NJ, Chatham House Publishers.

Crawford, A. (1980), *Thunder On The Right. The "New Right" And The Politics Of Resentment*, New York, Pantheon Books.

Crawford, R., Gardner, S.L., Mozzochi, J. and Taylor, R.L. (1994), *The Northwest Imperative. Documenting A Decade of Hate*, Portland, OR, Coalition for Human Dignity.

Crippen II, A. (ed.) (1996), *Reclaiming The Culture. How You Can Protect Your Family's Future*, Colorado Springs, CO, Focus on the Family.

Cromartie, M. (ed.), (1993), *No Longer Exiles. The Religious New Right In American Politics*, Washington DC, Ethics and Public Policy Center.

Cromartie, M. (ed), (1994), *Disciples and Democracy. Religious Conservatism and the Future of American Politics*, Washington DC, Ethics and Public Policy Center.

Dale, B. (1993), *Bashed by the Bankers*, Boring, OR, Christian Patriot Association.

Daniels, D. (1998), 'The Feminist Debate in the Evangelical Community', paper presented at the Annual Meeting of the American Political Science Association.

Danzig, D. (1962), 'The Radical Right and the Rise of the Fundamentalist Minority', *Commentary*, April: 291–8.

Davidson, O.G. (1993), *Under Fire. The NRA And The Battle For Gun Control*, New York, Henry Holt.

Davis, D.B. (1971), *The Fear of Conspiracy. Images of Un-American Subversion from the Revolution to the Present*, Ithaca, NY, Cornell University Press.

De Armond, P. (1999), 'A Time for New Beginnings (or This Singular Epidemic Among the Sheep)', *Studies in Conflict and Terrorism*, 22(2): 153–69.

Dees, M. with Corcoran, J. (1996), *Gathering Storm. America's Militia Threat*, New York, HarperCollins.

Diamond, S. (1989), *Spiritual Warfare. The Politics of the Christian Right*, Boston, South End Press.

Diamond, S. (1995), *Roads To Dominion: Right-Wing Movements and Political Power in the United States*, New York, Guilford Press.

Diamond, S. (1996), *Facing the Wrath. Confronting the Right in Dangerous Times*, Monroe, LA, Common Courage Press.

Diamond, S. (1998a), 'The Personal Is Political: The Role of Cultural Projects in the Mobilization of the Christian Right' in A.E. Ansell (ed.), *Unravelling the Right. The New Conservatism in American Thought and Politics*, Boulder, CO, Westview Press.

Diamond, S. (1998b), *Not by Politics Alone. The Enduring Influence of the Christian Right*, New York, Guilford Press.

Dobratz, B.A. and Shanks-Meile, S.L. (1997), *"White Power, White Pride!" The White Separatist Movement In The United States*, New York, Twayne Publishers.

Dobson, J. (1998), letter to Hon. Tom Coburn, 5 March, Focus on the Family, PRNewswire.

Dobson, J. and Bauer, G.L. (1990), *Children At Risk. The Battle for the Hearts and Minds of Our Kids*, Dallas, Word Publishing.

Dreyfuss, R. (1996), 'Political Snipers' in R. Kuttner (ed.), *Ticking Time Bombs*, New York, New Press.

D'Souza, D. (1995), *The End of Racism. Principles for a Multiracial Society*, New York, Free Press.

DuBowski, S. (1996), 'Storming Wombs and Waco: How the anti-abortion and militia movements converge', *Front Lines Research*, 2(2): 1–11.

Eatwell, R. (1989a), 'The Nature of the Right, 1: Is There An "Essentialist" Philisophical Core?' in R. Eatwell and N. O'Sullivan (eds), *The Nature of the Right. European and American Thought since 1789*, London, Pinter Publishers.

Eatwell, R. (1989b), 'The Nature of the Right, 2: The Right as a Variety of "Styles of Thought"' in R. Eatwell and N. O'Sullivan (eds), *The Nature of the Right. European and American Thought since 1789*, London, Pinter Publishers.

Edsall, T.B. (1997), 'The Cultural Revolution of 1994: Newt Gingrich, the Republican Party, and the Third Great Awakening' in B.E. Shafer *et al.*, *Present Discontents. American Politics in the Very Late Twentieth Century*, Chatham, NJ, Chatham House Publishers.

Edsall, T.B. with Edsall, M.D. (1992), *Chain Reaction. The Impact of Race, Rights, and Taxes on American Politics*, New York, W.W. Norton & Co.

Edwards, L. (1995), *Goldwater. The Man Who Made a Revolution*, Washington, DC, Regnery Publishing.

Ehrenreich, B. (1983), *The Hearts Of Men. American Dreams and the Flight from Commitment*, London, Pluto Press.

Eisenstein, Z.R. (1984), *Feminism and Sexual Equality. Crisis in Liberal America*, New York, Monthly Review Press.

Emry, S. (1986), *Billions for the Bankers Debts for the People*, Washington DC, Spotlight.

Epstein, B.R. and Forster, A. (1966), *Report on the John Birch Society 1966*, New York, Vintage Books.

Faludi, S. (1992), *Backlash. The Undeclared War Against Women*, London, Chatto & Windus.

Falwell, J. (1980), *Listen, America!*, New York, Bantam.

Falwell, J. with Dobson, E. and Hindson, E. (1981), *The Fundamentalist Phenomenon. The Resurgence of Conservative Christianity*, New York, Doubleday-Galilee.

Feagin, J.R. (1997), 'Old Poison in New Bottles: The Deep Roots of Modern Nativism' in J.F. Perea (ed.), *Immigrants Out! The New Nativism and the Anti-Immigrant Impulse in The United States*, New York, New York University Press.

Finch, P. (1983), *God, Guts and Guns*, New York, Seaview/Putnam.

Flynn, K. and Gerhardt, G. (1989), *The Silent Brotherhood. Inside America's Racist Underground*, New York, Signet.

Focus on the Family (n.d. (1991)), *The Homosexual Agenda*, n.p.

Francis, S. (1993), *Beautiful Losers: Essays on the Failure of American Conservatism*, Columbia, MO, University of Missouri Press.

Francis, S. (1997) *Revolution from the Middle*, Raleigh, NC, Middle American Press.

Francome, C. (1984), *Abortion Freedom. A Worldwide Movement*, London, George Allen & Unwin.

Gallagher, J. and Bull, C. (1996), *Perfect Enemies. The Religious Right, the Gay Movement, and the Politics of the 1990s*, New York, Crown Publishers.

George, J. and Wilcox, L. (1992), *Nazis, Communists, Klansmen, and Others on the Fringe. Political Extremism in America*, Buffalo, NY, Prometheus Books.

Georgianna, S.L. (1989), *The Moral Majority And Fundamentalism. Plausibility and Dissonance*, Lewiston, ME, Edwin Mellen Press.

Gilder, G.F. and Chapman, B.K. (1966), *The Party That Lost Its Head*, New York, Alfred A. Knopf.

Gillespie, E. and Schellhas, B. (eds) (1994), *Contract with America. The Bold Plan by Rep. Newt Gingrich, Rep. Dick Armey and the House Republicans to Change the Nation*, New York, Times Books.

Gilman, R. M. (1982), *Behind World Revolution. The Strange Career of Nesta Webster*, Ann Arbor, MI, Insights Books.

Glasow, R.D. (1988), *School-Based Clinics, The Abortion Connection*, Washington, DC, National Right to Life Educational Trust Fund.

Glazer, N. (1987), 'Fundamentalism: A Defensive Offensive' in R.J. Neuhaus and M. Cromartie (eds), *Piety and Politics. Evangelicals and Fundamentalists Confront the World*, Washington, DC, Ethics and Public Policy Center.

Goldberg, R.A. (1995), *Barry Goldwater*, New Haven, CT, Yale University Press.

Gordon, L. and Hunter, A. (1977–78), 'Sex, Family & The New Right: Anti-Feminism as a Political Force', *Radical America*, 12(1): 8–25.

Granberg, D. (1978), 'Pro-Life or reflection of Conservative Ideology? An Analysis of Opposition to Legalized Abortion', *Sociology and Social Research*, 62(3): 414–29.

Granberg, D. (1981), 'The Abortion Activists', *Family Planning Perspectives*, 13(4): 157–63.

Grant, G. (1996), *Buchanan Caught In The Crossfire*, Nashville, TN, Thomas Nelson.

Grant, G. and Horne, M.A. (1993), *Legislating Immorality. The Homosexual Movement Comes Out of the Closet*, Chicago, Moody Press/Legacy Communications.

Griffin, D. (1989), *Fourth Reich of the Rich*, Clackamas, OR, Emissary Publications.

Gritz, J.B. (1991), *Called To Serve*, Sandy Valley, NV, Lazarus Publishing Co.

Gurudas (1996), *Treason. The New World Order*, San Rafael, CA, Cassandra Press.

190 References

Hardisty, J. (1998a), 'Kitchen Table Backlash: The Antifeminist Women's Movement' in A.E. Ansell (ed.), *Unravelling the Right. The New Conservatism in American Thought and Politics*, Boulder, CO, Westview Press.

Hardisty, J. (1998b), 'Libertarianism and Civil Society: The Romance of Free Market Capitalism' in E. Ward (ed.), *American Armageddon: Religion, Revolution and the Right*, Seattle, WA, Peanut Butter Publishing.

Harrell, D.E., Jr. (1987), *Pat Robertson. A Personal, Religious, and Political Portrait*, San Francisco, Harper & Row.

Heilbrunn, J. (1995), 'On Pat Robertson. His Anti-Semitic Sources', *New York Review*, 20 April, 68–71.

Herman, D. (1997), *The Antigay Agenda. Orthodox Vision and the Christian Right*, Chicago, University of Chicago Press.

Herrnstein, R.J. and Murray, C. (1994), *The Bell Curve. Intelligence And Class Structure In American Life*, New York, Free Press.

Hill, S.S. and Owen, D.E. (1982), *The New Religious Political Right in America*, Nashville, TN, Abingdon.

Hilliard, R.L. and Keith, M.C. (1999), *Waves of Rancor. Tuning In The Radical Right*, Armonk, NY, M.E. Sharpe.

Hixson, W.B., Jr (1992), *Search for the American Right Wing. An Analysis of the Social Science Record, 1955–1987*, Princeton, NJ, Princeton University Press.

Hofstadter, R. (1967), *The Paranoid Style in American Politics and Other Essays*, New York, Vintage Books.

Hunter, A. (1981), 'In The Wings: New Right Ideology and Organization', *Radical America*, 15(1–2): 113–38.

Jaffe, F.S., Lindheim, B.L. and Lee, P.R. (1981), *Abortion Politics: Private Morality and Public Policy*, New York, McGraw-Hill.

Jefferson, M.W. (1994), *America Under Siege*, Knoxville, TN, Freedom & Liberty Foundation.

Jefferson, M.W. (1995), *America In Peril. "A Call To Arms"*, Knoxville, TN, Freedom & Liberty Foundation.

Jeffrerys-Renault, T. and Sloan, J. (1993), *Without Justice For All: A Report on the Christian Right in Sacramento and Beyond*, Sacramento, CA, Planned Parenthood of Sacramento Valley.

Joffe, C. (1998), 'Welfare Reform and Reproductive Politics on a Collision Course: Contradictions in the Conservative Agenda' in C.Y.H. Lo and M. Schwartz (eds) *Social Policy and the Conservative Agenda*, Malden, MA, Blackwell Publishers.

Jorstad, E. (1987), *The New Christian Right 1981–1988. Prospects for the Post-Reagan Decade*, Lewiston, ME, Edwin Mellen Press.

Judis, J.B. (1988), *William F. Buckley, Jr., Patron Saint of the Conservatives*, New York, Simon and Schuster.

Judis, J.B. (1992), 'The Tariff Party', *New Republic*, 30 March, 23–5.

Judis, J.B. (1996), 'Taking Buchananomics Seriously', *New Republic*, 18 March, 18–20.

Junas, D. (1995), 'The Rise of the Militias. Angry White Guys With Guns', *Covert Action Quarterly*, 52, 20–25.

Kah, G.H. (1992), *En Route to Global Occupation*, Lafayette, LA, Huntington House Publishers.

Kaplan, D. (1998), 'Republic of Rage. A look inside the patriot movement', paper presented at the Annual Meeting of the American Sociological Association.

Kaplan, J. (1993a), 'The Context of American Millennarian Revolutionary Theology: The Case of the "Identity Christian" Church of Israel', *Terrorism and Political Violence*, 5(1): 30–82.

Kaplan, J. (1993b), 'America's Last Prophetic Witness: The Literature of the Rescue Movement', *Terrorism and Political Violence*, 5(3): 58–77.

Kaplan, J. (1995), 'Absolute Rescue: Absolutism, Defensive Action and the Resort to Force', *Terrorism and Political Violence*, 7(3): 128–63.

Kershaw, P. (1994), *Economic Solutions*, Boulder, CO, Peter Kershaw.

Kintz, L. (1997), *Between Jesus And The Market. The Emotions That Matter in Right-Wing America*, Durham, NC, Duke University Press.

Klatch, R.E. (1987), *Women of the New Right*, Philadelphia, Temple University Press.

Konicov, B. (1995), *The Great Snow Job: The Story of Taxes and Money/Fraud and Slavery*, Alto, TX, E.L.I. Press.

Ladd, E.C. (1995), 'The 1994 Congressional Elections: The Realignment Continues', *Political Science Quarterly*, 110: 1–23.

Lader, L. (1973), *Abortion II: Making The Revolution*, Boston, Beacon Press.

LaHaye, T. (1980a), *What Everyone Should Know About Homosexuality*, Wheaton, IL, Tyndale House Publishers.

LaHaye, T. (1980b), *The Battle for the Mind*, Old Tappan, NJ, Fleming H. Revell Co.

LaHaye, T. (1982), *The Battle for the Family*, Old Tappan, NJ, Fleming H. Revell Co.

LaHaye, T. (1992), *No Fear of the Storm*, Chichester, New Wine Press.

LaHaye, T. (1998), 'America's Perilous Times Have Come' in W.T. James (ed.), *Fore Warning*, Eugene, OR, Harvest House Publishers.

LaPierre, W.R. (1995), *Guns, Crime, And Freedom*, New York, HarperPerennial.

Leahy, P.J., Snow, D.A. and Worden, S.K. (1983), 'The Antiabortion Movement and Symbolic Crusades: Reappraisal of a Popular Theory', *Alternative Lifestyles*, 6(1): 27–47.

Lienesch, M. (1982), 'Right-Wing Religion: Christian Conservatism as a Political Movement', *Political Science Quarterly*, 97(3): 403–25.

Lienesch, M. (1993), *Redeeming America: Piety and Politics in the New Christian Right*, Chapel Hill, NC, University of North Carolina Press.

Lind, M. (1995a), 'Rev. Robertson's Grand International Conspiracy Theory', *New York Review*, 2 February, 1, 22–5.

Lind, M. (1995b), 'On Pat Robertson. His Defenders', *New York Review*, 20 April, 67–8.

Lind, M. (1996), *Up From Conservatism. Why the Right is Wrong for America*, New York, Free Press.

Lippis, J. (1978), *The Challenge To Be "Pro Life"*, Santa Barbara, CA, Santa Barbara Pro Life Education.

Lipset, S.M. and Raab, E. (1971), *The Politics of Unreason. Right-Wing Extremism in America, 1790–1970*, London, Heinemann.

Lively, S. and Abrams, K. (1995), *The Pink Swastika. Homosexuality in the Nazi Party*, Keizer, OR, Founders Publishing Corporation.

Luker, K. (1984), *Abortion And The Politics of Motherhood*, Berkeley, CA, University of California Press.

Macdonald, A. (1980), *The Turner Diaries*, 2nd edn, Hillsboro, WV, National Vanguard Books.

Magnuson, R. (1994), *Informed Answers to Gay Rights Questions*, Sisters, OR, Multnomah.

Mansbridge, J.J. (1986), *Why We Lost the ERA*, Chicago, University of Chicago Press.

Mariani, M. (1998), 'The Michigan Militia: Political Engagement or Political Alienation?', *Terrorism and Political Violence*, 10(4): 122–48.

Martin, C.S. (1968), *The Declaration of the Third Continental Congress*, Christian Coalition Party ephemera, Iowa Right-Wing Collection (microfilm).

Martin, C.S. (1970), *Clarification of the New and Unusual Position of the Original and Official Constitution Parties of the United States*, Christian Coalition Party ephemera, Iowa Right-Wing Collection (microfilm).

Martin, W. (1997), *With God On Our Side: The Rise Of the Religious Right in America*, New York, Broadway Books.

Maxwell, C.J.C. (1995), 'Introduction: Beyond Polemics and Toward Healing' in T.G. Jelen (ed.), *Perspectives on the Politics of Abortion*, Westport, CT, Praeger.

Maxwell, C.J.C. and Jelen, T.G. (1995), 'Commandos for Christ: Narratives of Male Pro-Life Activists', *Review of Religious Research*, 37(2): 117–31.

McCann, I.G. (1966), *Case History Of The Smear By CBS Of Conservatives*, Washington, DC, McCann Press.

McKeegan, M. (1992), *Abortion Politics. Mutiny in the Ranks of the Right*, New York, The Free Press.

McLemee, S. (1994), 'Spotlight on the Liberty Lobby', *Covert Action Quarterly*, 50: 23–32.

Melich, T. (1996), *The Republican War Against Women. An Insider's Report From Behind The Lines*, New York, Bantam Books.

Merton, A.H. (1981), *Enemies of Choice: The Right-to-Life Movement and Its Threat to Abortion*, Boston, Beacon Press.

Meyer, F.S. (1964a), 'Freedom, Tradition, Conservatism' in F.S. Meyer (ed.), *What Is Conservatism?*, New York, Holt, Rinehart and Winston.

Meyer, F.S. (1964b), 'Consensus and Divergence' in F.S. Meyer (ed.), *What Is Conservatism?*, New York, Holt, Rinehart and Winston.

Militia of Montana (n.d.), *Information & Networking Manual*, Noxon, MT, MOM.

Militia of Montana (1994), *Catalog*, Noxon, MT, MOM.

Militia of Montana (n.d. (c.1995)), *Executive Orders for The New World Order*, leaflet.

Militia Watchdog (1996), 'Extremism and the Electorate: Campaign '96 and the "Patriot" Movement', http://www.militia-watchdog.org/elect96.htm.

Militia Watchdog (1999), 'The Council of Conservative Citizens "in the News": A Chronology of Events', http://www.militia-watchdog.org/ccc.htm.

Mintz, F.P. (1985), *The Liberty Lobby and the American Right. Race, Conspiracy, and Culture*, Westport, CT, Greenwood Press.

Mobley, C.B. (1996), 'Black Conservative Magazines and Organizations: Getting Out the Message, But To Whom?', paper presented to the Annual Meeting of the American Political Science Association.

Moen, M.C. (1992), *The Transformation Of The Christian Right*, Tuscaloosa, AL, University of Alabama Press.

Moen, M.C. (1997), 'The Changing Nature of Christian Right Activism: 1970s-1990s' in C.E. Smidt and J.M. Penning (eds), *Sojourners in the Wilderness. The Christian Right in Comparative Perspective*, Lanham, MD, Rowman & Littlefield.

Moore, W.V. (1992), 'David Duke: The White Knight' in D. D. Rose (ed.), *The Emergence of David Duke and the Politics of Race*, Chapel Hill, NC, University of North Carolina Press.

Mulloy, D.J. (1999), *Homegrown Revolutionaries. An American Militia Reader*, Norwich, Arthur Miller Centre for American Studies.

Nash, G.H. (1976), *The Conservative Intellectual Movement in America Since 1945*, New York, Basic Books.

Neitz, M.D. (1981), 'Family, State, and God: Ideologies of the Right-to-Life Movement', *Sociological Analysis*, 42(3): 265–76.

Nishiura, E. (1998), 'Guns, Gender, and Community', paper presented to the Annual Meeting of the American Political Science Association.

Northern Michigan Regional Militia (n.d. (1994)), *The Michigan Minute Men*, Northern Michigan Regional Militia.

Norquist, G.G. (1995), *Rock The House*, Fort Lauderdale, FL, VYTIS Press.

Novick, M. (1995), *White Lies, White Power. The Fight Against White Supremacy and Reactionary Violence*, Monroe, LA, Common Courage Press.

O'Connor, K. (1996), *No Neutral Ground? Abortion Politics in an Age of Absolutes*, Boulder, CO, Westview Press.

Oldfield, D.M. (1996), *The Right and the Righteous: The Christian Right Confronts the Republican Party*, Lanham, MD, Rowman & Littlefield.

Oldfield, D.M. (1999), 'Resisting The New World Order: The Emerging Foreign Policy Agenda of the Christian Right', paper presented to the Annual Meeting of the American Political Science Association.

Overstreet, H. and Overstreet, B. (1964), *The Strange Tactics of Extremism*, New York, W.W. Norton and Co.

Owens, J.E. (1998), 'The Republican Takeover in Context' in D. McSweeney and J.E. Owens (eds), *The Republican Takeover of Congress*, Houndmills, Macmillan.

Pabst, W.R. (1979), 'A National Emergency: Total Takeover', reprinted in M.W. Cooper (1991), *"Behold a Pale Horse"*, Sedona, AZ, Light Technology Publishing.

Paige, C. (1983), *The Right to Lifers*, New York, Summit Books.

Peron, J. (1981), *Khomeini in America: Moral Majority and the Death of Freedom*, Glen Ellyn, IL, Jim Peron.

Persinos, J.F. (1994), 'Has the Christian Right Taken Over the Republican Party?', *Campaigns and Elections*, September, 20–24.

Petchesky, R.P. (1981), 'Antiabortion, Antifeminism, and the rise of the New Right', *Feminist Studies*, 7(2): 206–46.

Petchesky, R.P. (1984), *Abortion and Woman's Choice: The State, Sexuality, and Reproductive Freedom*, New York, Longman.

Peters, P.J. (1992), *Intolerance of, Discrimination against and the Death Penalty for Homosexuals Is Prescribed in the Bible*, LaPorte, CO, Scriptures for America.

Peters, P. (ed.) (n.d. (1992)), *Special Report on The Meeting of Christian Men Held in Estes Park, Colorado October 23, 24, 25, 1992*, LaPorte, CO, Scriptures for America Ministries.

Phillips, H. (n.d.), 'Why did the National Right to Life Committee take $650,000 from the Dole Campaign?', http://www.ustaxpayers.org/nrtl_letter.html.

Phillips, K. (1970), *The Emerging Republican Majority*, Garden City, NY, Anchor Books.

Pines, B.Y. (1982), *Back To Basics. The Traditionalist Movement That Is Sweeping Grass-Roots America*, New York, William Morrow.

Planned Parenthood (1995), *Urgent Memorandum To: Members of Congress*, 16 May.

Pomper, G.M. (1997), 'The Presidential Election' in G.M. Pomper *et al.* (eds), *The Election of 1996. Reports and Interpretations*, Chatham, NJ, Chatham House Publishers.

Powell, L.N. (1992), 'Slouching toward Baton Rouge: The 1989 Legislative Election of David Duke' in D. D. Rose (ed.), *The Emergence of David Duke and the Politics of Race*, Chapel Hill, NC, University of North Carolina Press.

Public Eye, The (n.d.), 'John Birch Society', http://www.publiceye.org/pra/too-close/jbs.html.

Radl, S.R. (1983), *The Invisible Woman. Target of the Religious New Right*, New York, Delacorte Press.

Raimondo, J. (1993), *Reclaiming The American Right. The Lost Legacy Of The Conservative Movement*, Burlingame, CA, Center for Libertarian Studies.

Raimondo, J. (1999), 'Pat Buchanan: Portrait Of An American Nationalist', http://www.antiwar.com/justin/j081699.html.

Reed, R. (1994), 'What Do Religious Conservatives Really Want?' in Cromartie, M. (ed.), *Disciples and Democracy. Religious Conservatism and the Future of American Politics*, Washington DC, Ethics and Public Policy Center.

Reed, R. (1996a), *After The Revolution. How The Christian Coalition Is Impacting America*, Dallas, Word Publishing.

Reed, R. (1996b), *Active Faith. How Christians Are Changing the Soul of American Politics*, New York, The Free Press.

Reimers, D.M. (1996), 'The Emergence of the Immigration Restriction Lobby Since 1979', paper presented at the Annual Meeting of the American Political Science Association.

Rice, C. E. (n.d.), *The Human Life Amendment: No Compromise*, Stafford, VA, American Life League.

Ridgeway, J. (1990), *Blood in the Face. The Ku Klux Klan, Aryan Nations, Nazi Skinheads, and the Rise of a New White Culture*, New York, Thunder's Mouth Press.

Risen, J. and Thomas, J.L. (1998), *Wrath Of Angels. The American Abortion War*, New York, BasicBooks.

Robertson, P. (1990), *The New Millennium. 10 Trends That Will Impact You and Your Family By The Year 2000*, Dallas, Word Incorporated.

Robertson, P. (1991), *The New World Order*, Dallas, Word Incorporated.

Robertson, P. (1993), *The Turning Tide: The Fall of Liberalism and the Rise of Common Sense*, Dallas, Word Publishing.

Rose, D.D. (1992), 'Six Explanations in Search of Support: David Duke's U.S. Senate Campaign' in D. D. Rose (ed.), *The Emergence of David Duke and the Politics of Race*, Chapel Hill, NC, University of North Carolina Press.

Rose, D.D. with Esolen, G. (1992), 'DuKKKe for Governor' in D. D. Rose (ed.), *The Emergence of David Duke and the Politics of Race*, Chapel Hill, NC, University of North Carolina Press.

Ross, L.J. (1995), 'The Militia Movement – In Their Own Words and Deeds' in N. Chandler (ed.) (1996), *Militias: Exploding Into The Mainstream*, Atlanta, GA, Center for Democratic Renewal.

Royce, K.W. (1997), *Hologram of Liberty. The Constitution's Shocking Alliance with Big Government*, Austin, TX, Javelin Press.

Rozell, M.J. and Wilcox, C. (1996), *Second Coming. The New Christian Right in Virginia Politics*, Baltimore, MD, Johns Hopkins University Press.

Rusher, W.A. (1984), *The Rise of the Right*, New York, William Morrow and Co.

Russell, D.A. (1997), *Who Is Heading The Attack On American Liberty?*, Crestview, FL, Citizens for Constitutional Property Rights.

Sargent, L.T. (ed.) (1995), *Extremism in America. A Reader*, New York, New York University Press.

Scheidler, J.M. (1985), *Closed: 99 Ways to Stop Abortion*, Westchester, IL, Crossway Books.

Scheinberg, S. (1997), 'Right-Wing Extremism in the United States' in A. Braun and S. Scheinberg (eds), *The Extreme Right. Freedom and Security At Risk*, Boulder, CO, Westview Press.

Schroder, E. with Nellis, M. (1995), *Constitution: Fact or Fiction*, Cleburne, TX, Buffalo Creek Press.

Seymour, C. (1991), *Committee of the States. Inside the Radical Right*, Mariposa, CA, Camden Place Communications.

Shaiko, R.G. and Wallace, M.A. (1998), ' Going Hunting Where the Ducks Are: The National Rifle Association and the Grass Roots' in J.M. Bruce and C. Wilcox (eds.), *The Changing Politics of Gun Control*, Lanham, MD, Rowman and Littlefield.

Simkin, J., Zelman, A. and Rice, A.M. (1994), *Lethal Laws*, Milwaukee, WI, Jews for the Preservation of Firearms Ownership.

Skousen, W.C. (1970), *The Naked Capitalist. A Review and Commentary on Dr. Carroll Quigley's Book: Tragedy and Hope – A History of the World In Our Time*, Salt Lake City, UT, published as private edition.

Spear, R.K. (1992), *Surviving Global Slavery. Living Under The New World Order*, Leavenworth, KS, Universal Force Dynamics.

Spitzer, R.J. (1995), *The Politics of Gun Control*, Chatham, NJ, Chatham House Publishers.

Steinfels, P. (1979), *The Neoconservatives. The Men Who Are Changing America's Politics*, New York, Simon and Schuster.

Stern, K.S. (1996), *A Force Upon The Plain. The American Militia Movement and the Politics of Hate*, New York, Simon and Schuster.

Still, W.T. (1990), *New World Order. The Ancient Plan of Secret Societies*, Lafayette, LA, Huntington House Publishers.

Strinowski, N. (1993), 'Oregon's Ballot Measure 9: Religious Fundamentalism, Gay Activism, and the Political Center', paper given at the Annual Meeting of the American Political Science Association.

Sugarmann, J. (1992), *National Rifle Association. Money, Firepower and Fear*, Washington DC, National Press Books.

Switzer, J.V. (1997), *Green Backlash. The History and Politics of Environmental Opposition in the U.S.*, Boulder, CO, Lynne Rienner.

Teixeira, R.A. and Rogers, J. (1998), 'Mastering the New Political Arithmetic: Volatile Voters, Declining Living Standards, and Non-College-Educated Whites' in A.E. Ansell (ed.), *Unravelling the Right. The New Conservatism in American Thought and Politics*, Boulder, CO, Westview Press.

Tuccille, J. (1970), *Radical Libertarianism. A Right Wing Alternative*, Indianapolis, IN, The Bobbs-Merrill Co.

Viguerie, R.A. (1981), *The New Right: We're Ready To Lead*, Falls Church, VA, The Viguerie Co.

Wardner, J.W. (1994), *The Planned Destruction of America*, DeBary, FL, Longwood Communications.

Watson, J. (1997), *The Christian Coalition: Dreams of Restoration, Demands for Recognition*, New York, St Martin's Press.

Weyrich, P. (1999), 'A moral minority?', http://www.freecongress.org/fcf/Specials/Weyrichopenltr.htm.

White, F.C. with Gill, W.J. (1967), *Suite 3505. The Story of the Draft Goldwater Movement*, New Rochelle, NY, Arlington House.

Wilcox, C. (1996), *Onward Christian Soldiers? The Religious Right in American Politics*, Boulder, CO, Westview Press.

Wills, G. (1992), 'The Born-Again Republicans', *New York Review*, 24 September, 9–14.

Woodward, B. (1996), *The Choice*, New York, Simon & Schuster.

Xanthopoulou, P. (1996), 'Pat Robertson Angrily and Boldly Forward (On A Limb)', gopher://gopher.igc.apc.org.70/00/orgs/.alternet2/an.watch/137.

Yurman, D. (1995), '9/10/95; High Country Extreme News', gopher://gopher.igc.apc.org:70/11/environment/forests/western.lands.

Zeskind, L. (n.d. (*c*.1987)), *The "Christian Identity" Movement*, Atlanta, GA, Division of Church and Society of the National Council of the Churches of Christ in the USA.

Zeskind, L. (1995), 'Armed and Dangerous. The NRA, Militias and White Supremacists Are Fostering a Network of Right Wing Warriors', *Rolling Stone*, 2 November, 55–8, 60–61, 84, 86–7.

Index